HOT LU

CW00672861

𝓮mayamada.

HOT LUNCH VOLUME 1

CREATED & WRITTEN BY: NIGEL TWUMASI
ILLUSTRATOR: PINALI (A L JONES)
CONCEPT ARTIST: CAREY UKANDU
EDITOR: LARA-LEE GREEN

EMAIL US: HELLO@MAYAMADA.COM
VISIT US ONLINE: WWW.MAYAMADA.COM

PUBLISHED BY MAYAMADA
HOT LUNCH © 2019 MAYAMADA LTD
ALL RIGHTS RESERVED

ISBN: 978-0-9931121-5-7

HOT LUNCH VOLUME 1 IS A STORY ABOUT A TIGER ON A MISSION TO PROTECT HIS FAMILY, AND WHAT CAN HAPPEN WHEN SMALL GROUP WORK TO CHANGE THE STATUS QUO.

HOT LUNCH IS JUST ONE OF THE STORIES WITHIN THE MAYAMADA UNIVERSE, A TELEVISION NETWORK WHERE EACH GRAPHIC NOVEL TELLS THE STORY OF EACH SHOW ON THE NETWORK. THEY'RE NOT ANIMATED SHOWS...YET

MAYAMADA IS A MANGA BRAND INSPIRED BY THE JAPANESE STORYTELLING MEDIUM, FOUNDED IN LONDON BY NIGEL TWUMASI AND LAO K.

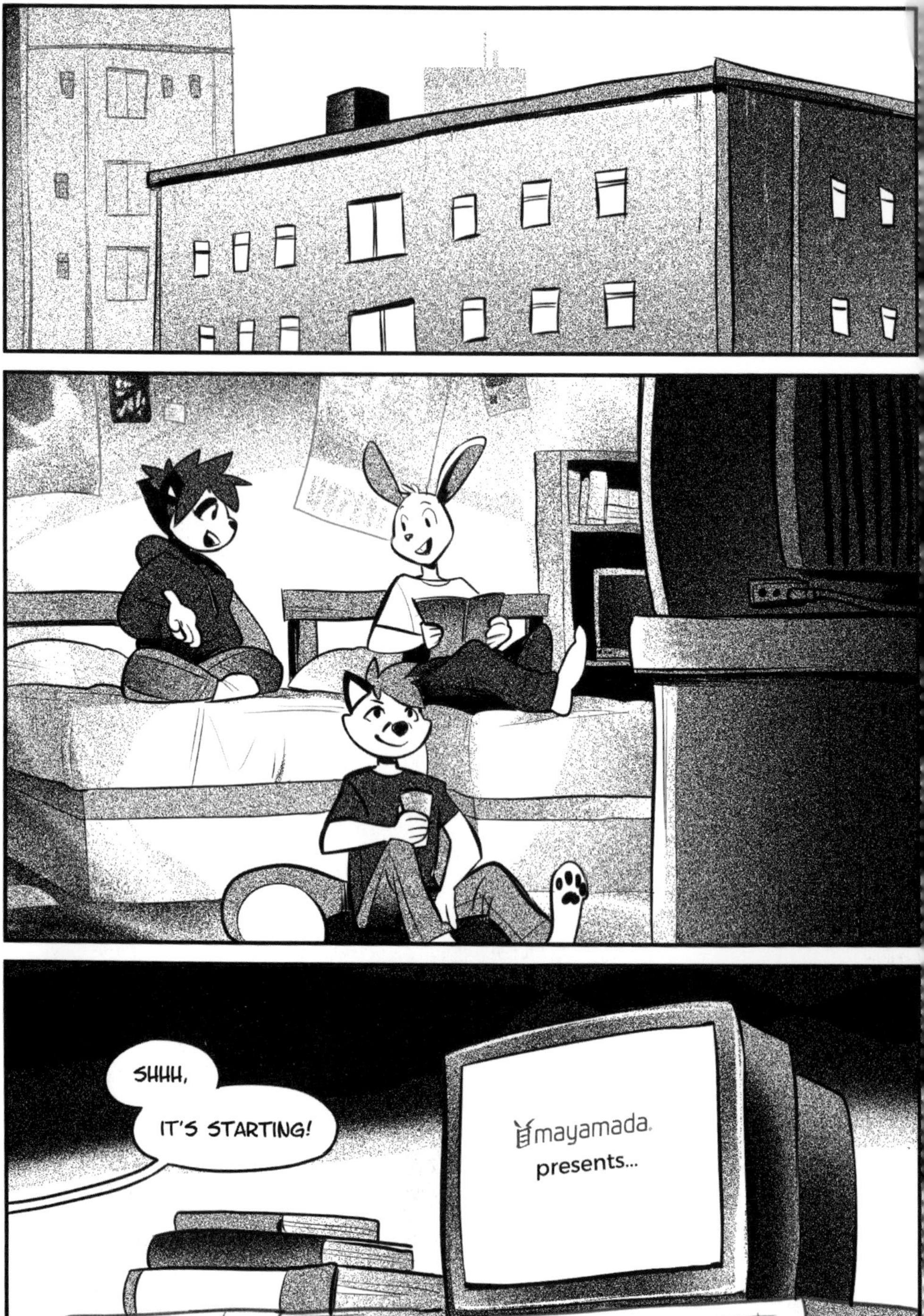
SHHH, IT'S STARTING!
mayamada presents...

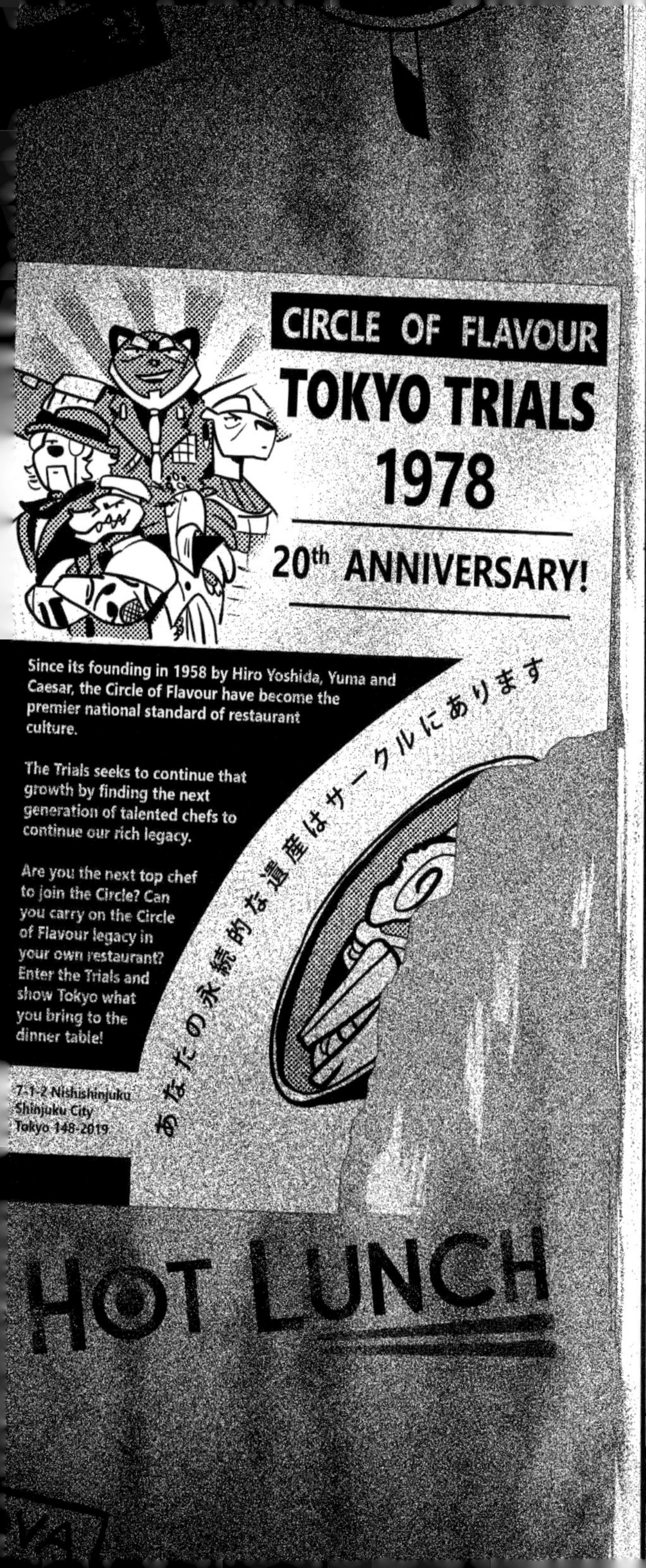
CIRCLE OF FLAVOUR
TOKYO TRIALS
1978
20th ANNIVERSARY!
Since its founding in 1958 by Hiro Yoshida, Yuma and Caesar, the Circle of Flavour have become the premier national standard of restaurant culture.
The Trials seeks to continue that growth by finding the next generation of talented chefs to continue our rich legacy.
Are you the next top chef to join the Circle? Can you carry on the Circle of Flavour legacy in your own restaurant? Enter the Trials and show Tokyo what you bring to the dinner table!
あなたの永続的な遺産はサークルにあります
7-1-2 Nishishinjuku
Shinjuku City
Tokyo 148-2019
HOT LUNCH

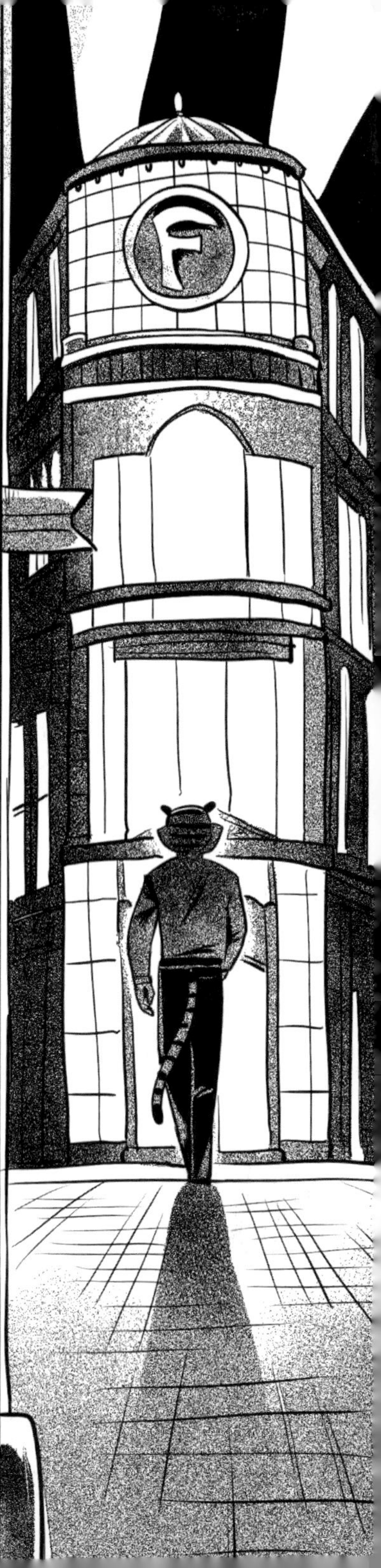

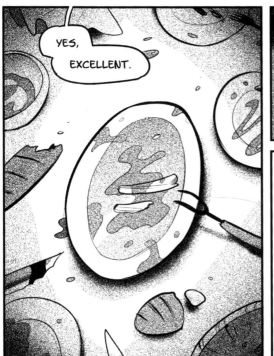

YES, EXCELLENT.

A SPLENDID MEAL, SORA.

THANK YOU.

NOW IF WE COULD HAVE THE TABLE CLEARED...

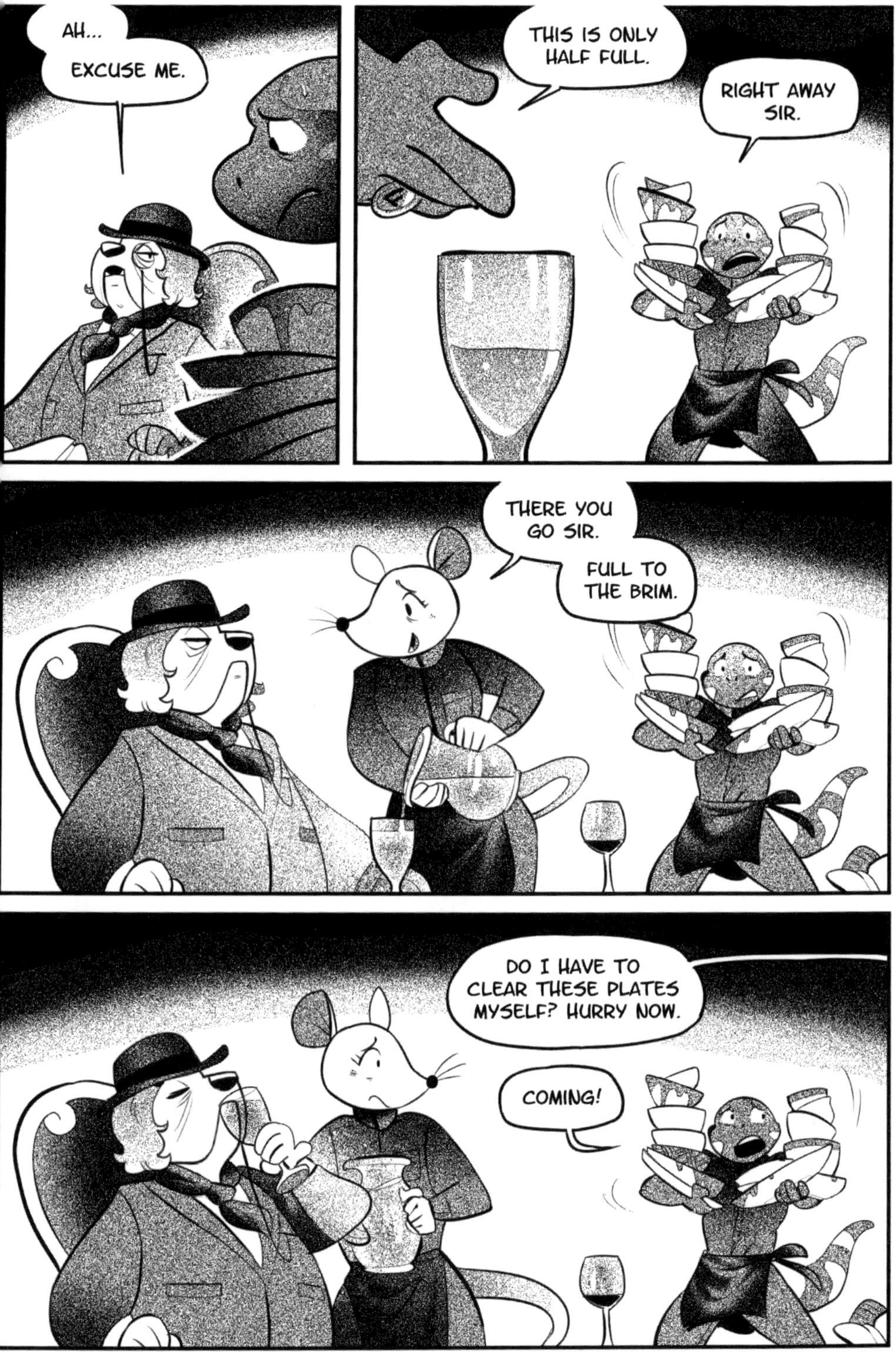
AH...
EXCUSE ME.
THIS IS ONLY HALF FULL.
RIGHT AWAY SIR.
THERE YOU GO SIR.
FULL TO THE BRIM.
DO I HAVE TO CLEAR THESE PLATES MYSELF? HURRY NOW.
COMING!

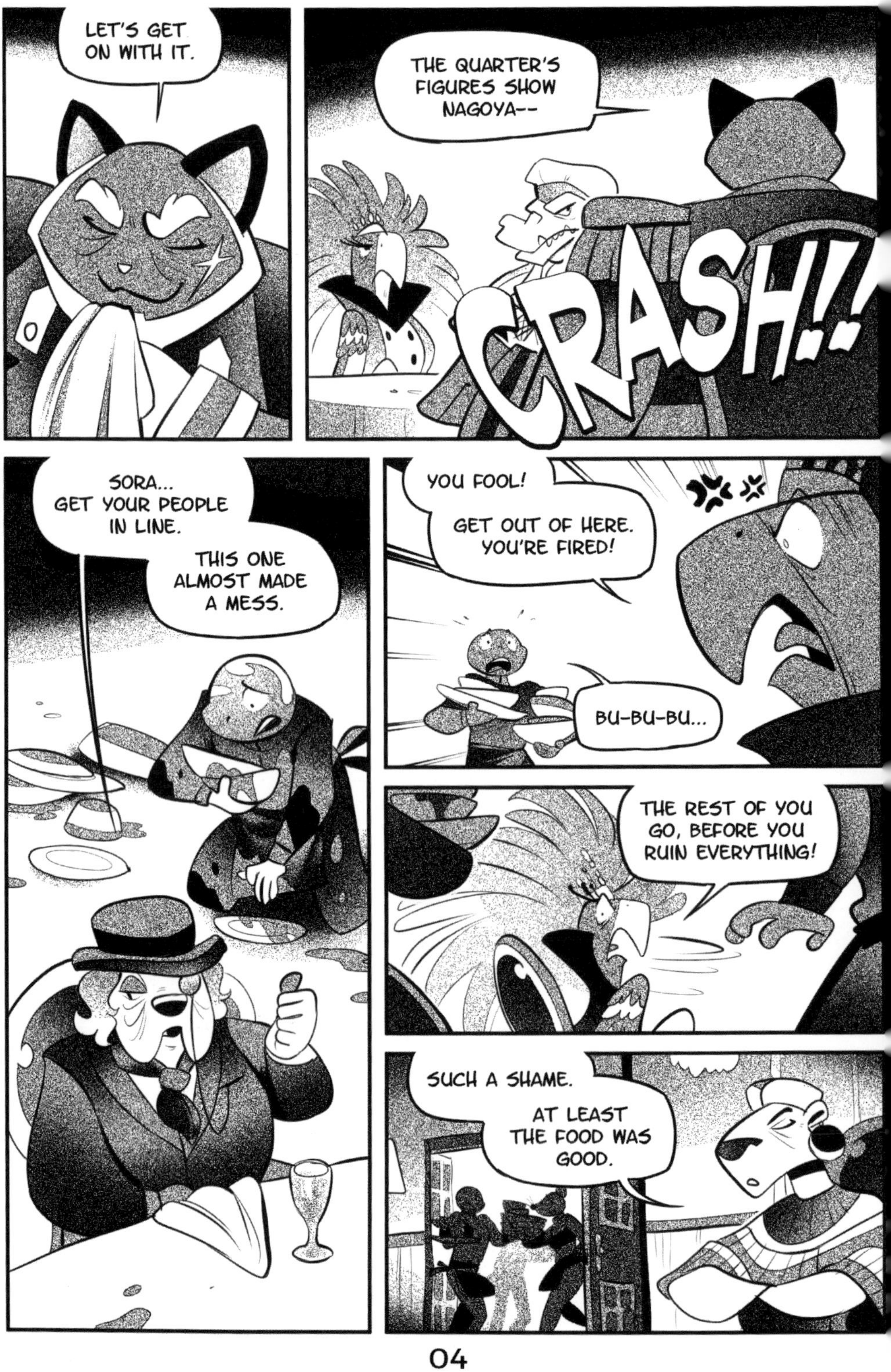
LET'S GET ON WITH IT.
THE QUARTER'S FIGURES SHOW NAGOYA--
CRASH!!
SORA... GET YOUR PEOPLE IN LINE.
THIS ONE ALMOST MADE A MESS.
YOU FOOL!
GET OUT OF HERE. YOU'RE FIRED!
BU-BU-BU...
THE REST OF YOU GO, BEFORE YOU RUIN EVERYTHING!
SUCH A SHAME.
AT LEAST THE FOOD WAS GOOD.

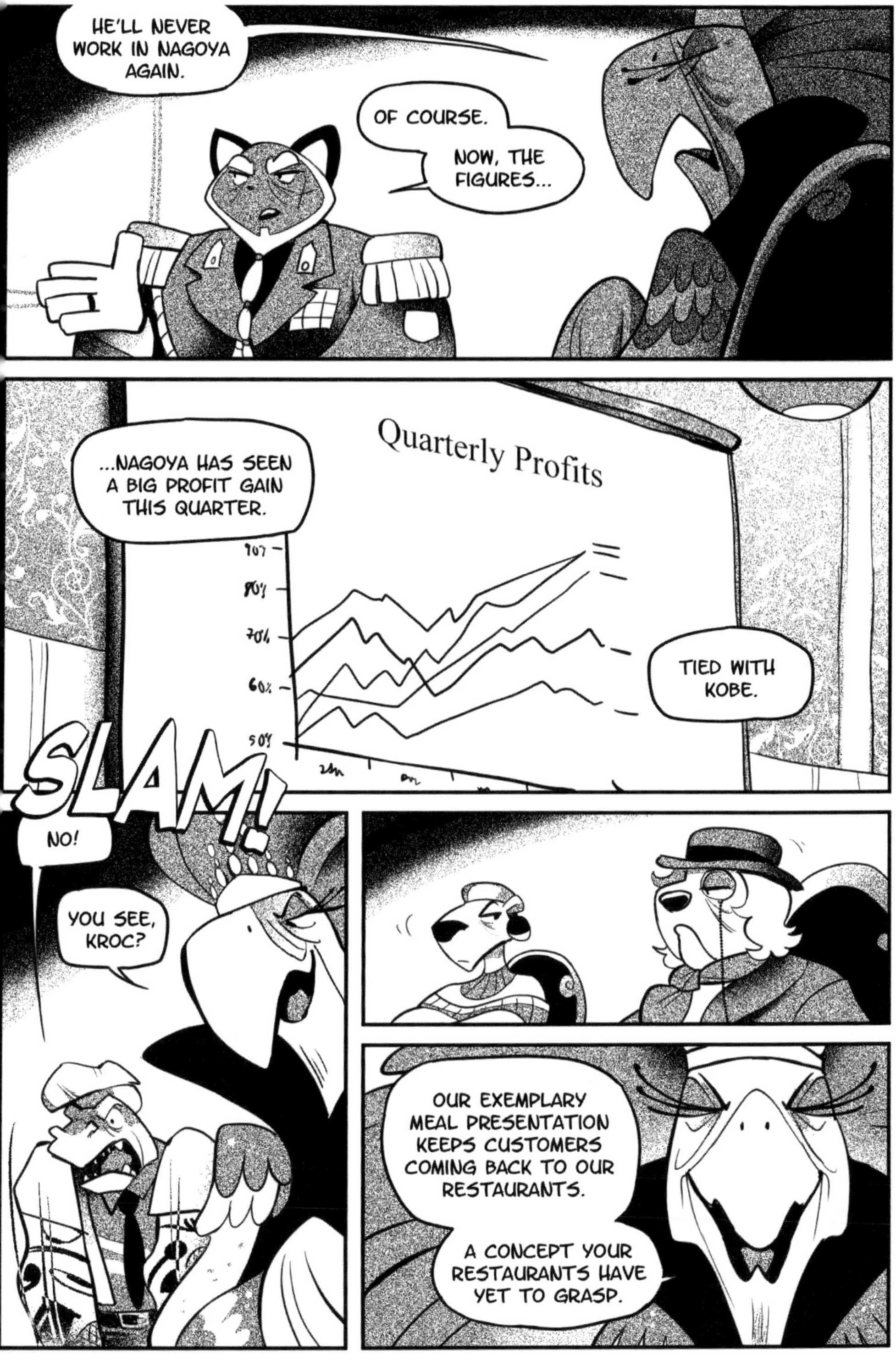

HE'LL NEVER WORK IN NAGOYA AGAIN.
OF COURSE.
NOW, THE FIGURES...
...NAGOYA HAS SEEN A BIG PROFIT GAIN THIS QUARTER.
Quarterly Profits
TIED WITH KOBE.
SLAM!
NO!
YOU SEE, KROC?
OUR EXEMPLARY MEAL PRESENTATION KEEPS CUSTOMERS COMING BACK TO OUR RESTAURANTS.
A CONCEPT YOUR RESTAURANTS HAVE YET TO GRASP.

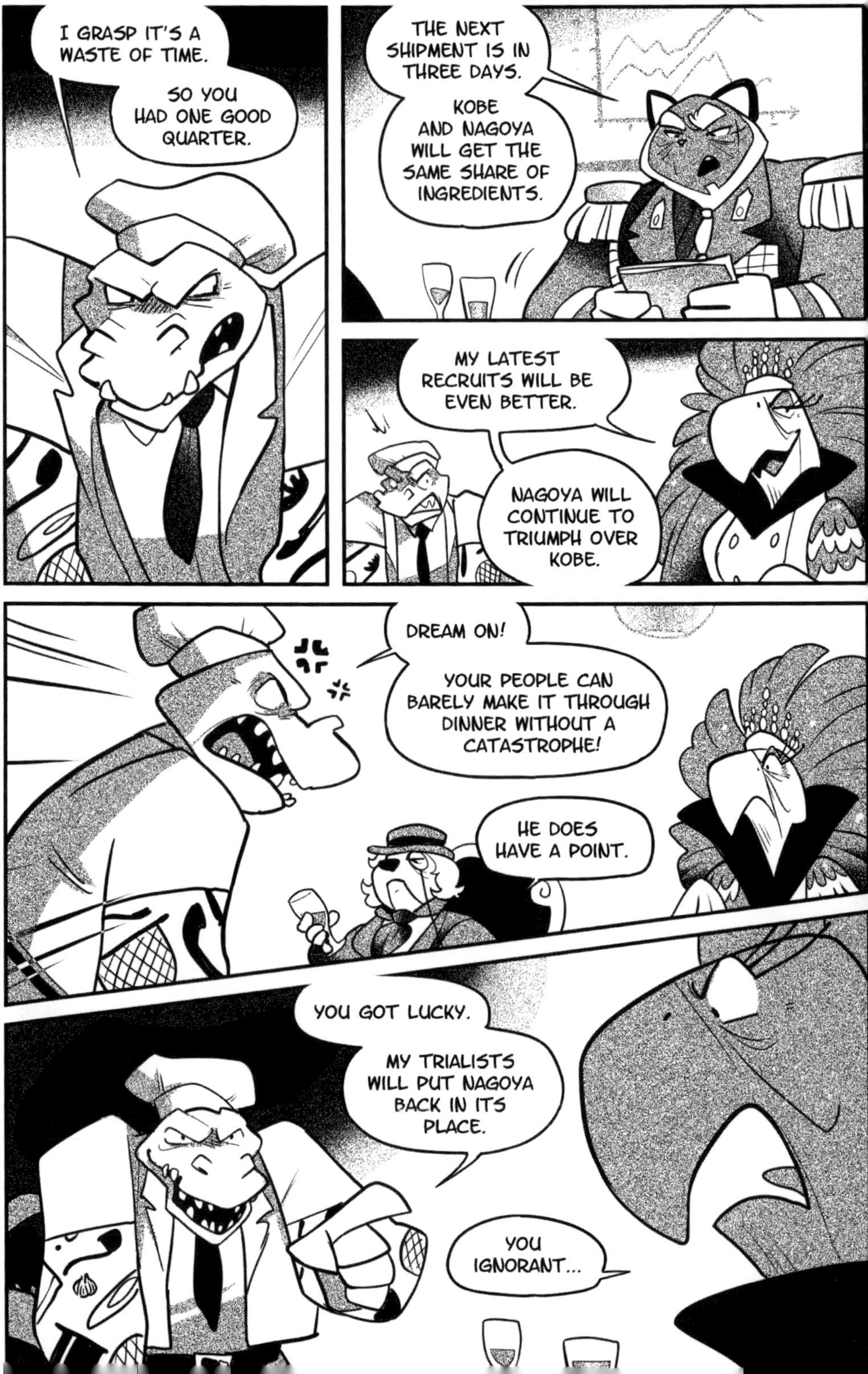
I GRASP IT'S A WASTE OF TIME.
SO YOU HAD ONE GOOD QUARTER.
THE NEXT SHIPMENT IS IN THREE DAYS.
KOBE AND NAGOYA WILL GET THE SAME SHARE OF INGREDIENTS.
MY LATEST RECRUITS WILL BE EVEN BETTER.
NAGOYA WILL CONTINUE TO TRIUMPH OVER KOBE.
DREAM ON!
YOUR PEOPLE CAN BARELY MAKE IT THROUGH DINNER WITHOUT A CATASTROPHE!
HE DOES HAVE A POINT.
YOU GOT LUCKY.
MY TRIALISTS WILL PUT NAGOYA BACK IN ITS PLACE.
YOU IGNORANT...

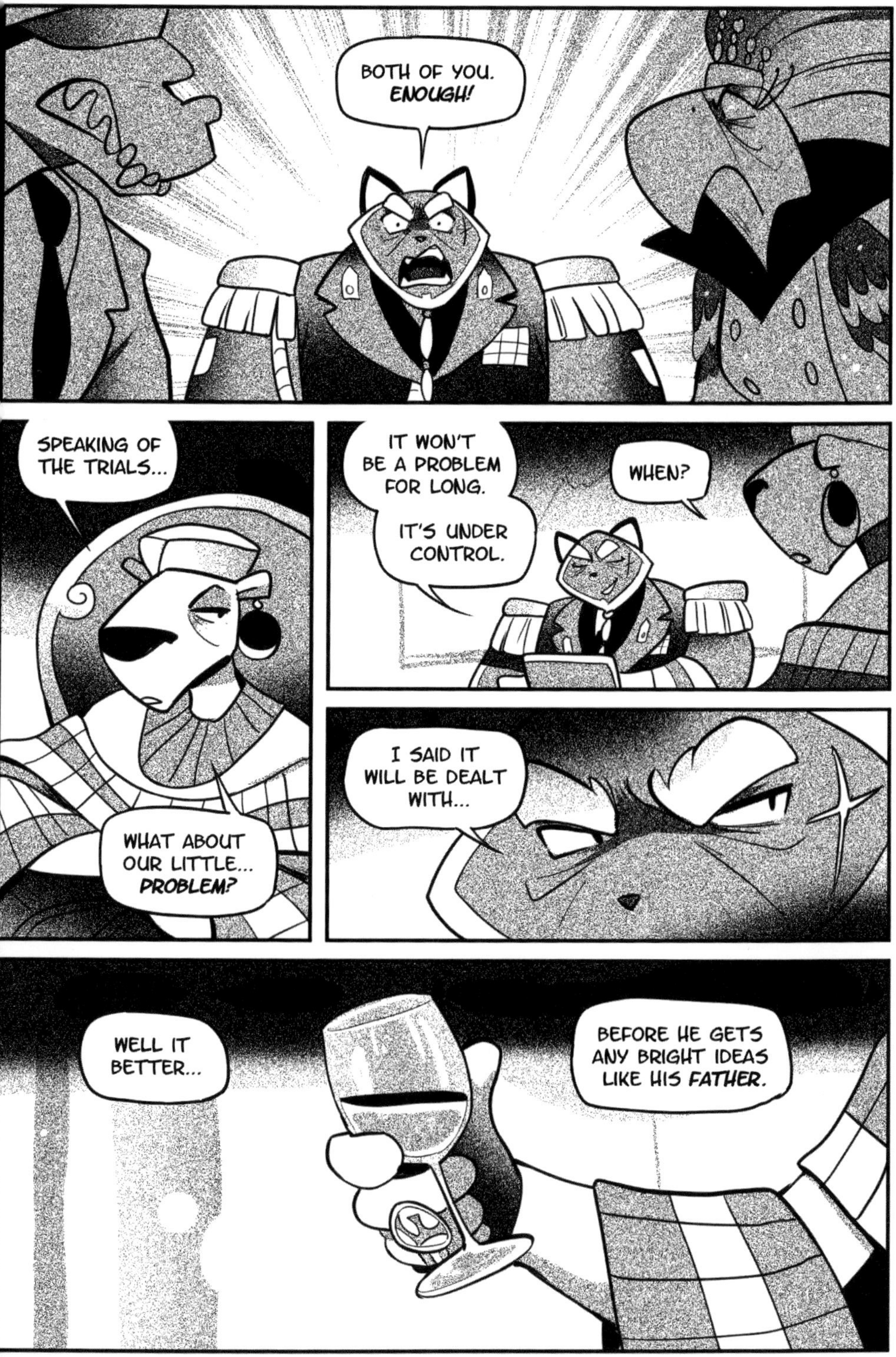
BOTH OF YOU. ENOUGH!
SPEAKING OF THE TRIALS...
WHAT ABOUT OUR LITTLE... PROBLEM?
IT WON'T BE A PROBLEM FOR LONG.
IT'S UNDER CONTROL.
WHEN?
I SAID IT WILL BE DEALT WITH...
WELL IT BETTER...
BEFORE HE GETS ANY BRIGHT IDEAS LIKE HIS FATHER.

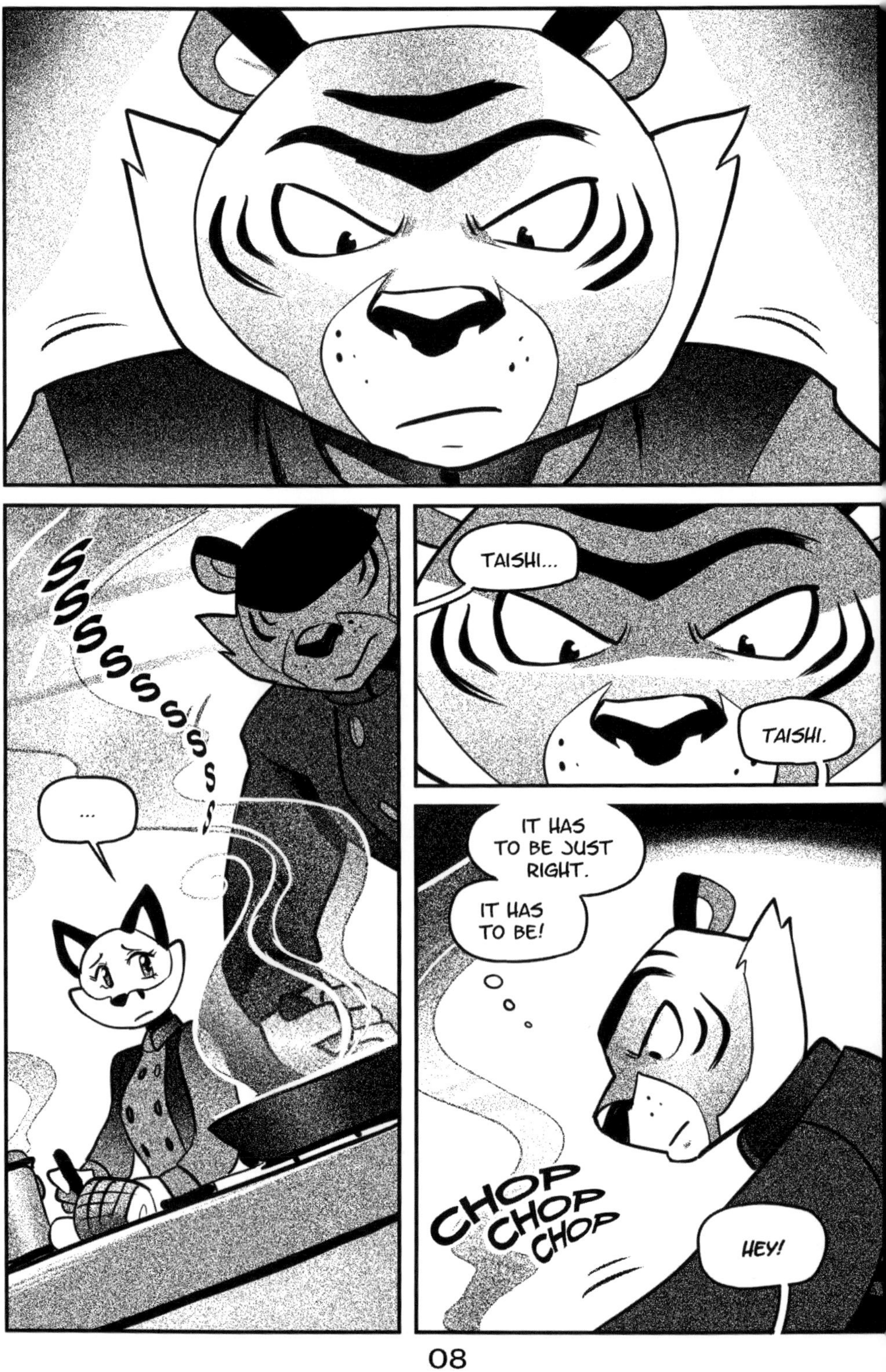

SSSSSSSSSS
...
TAISHI...
TAISHI.
IT HAS TO BE JUST RIGHT.
IT HAS TO BE!
CHOP CHOP CHOP
HEY!

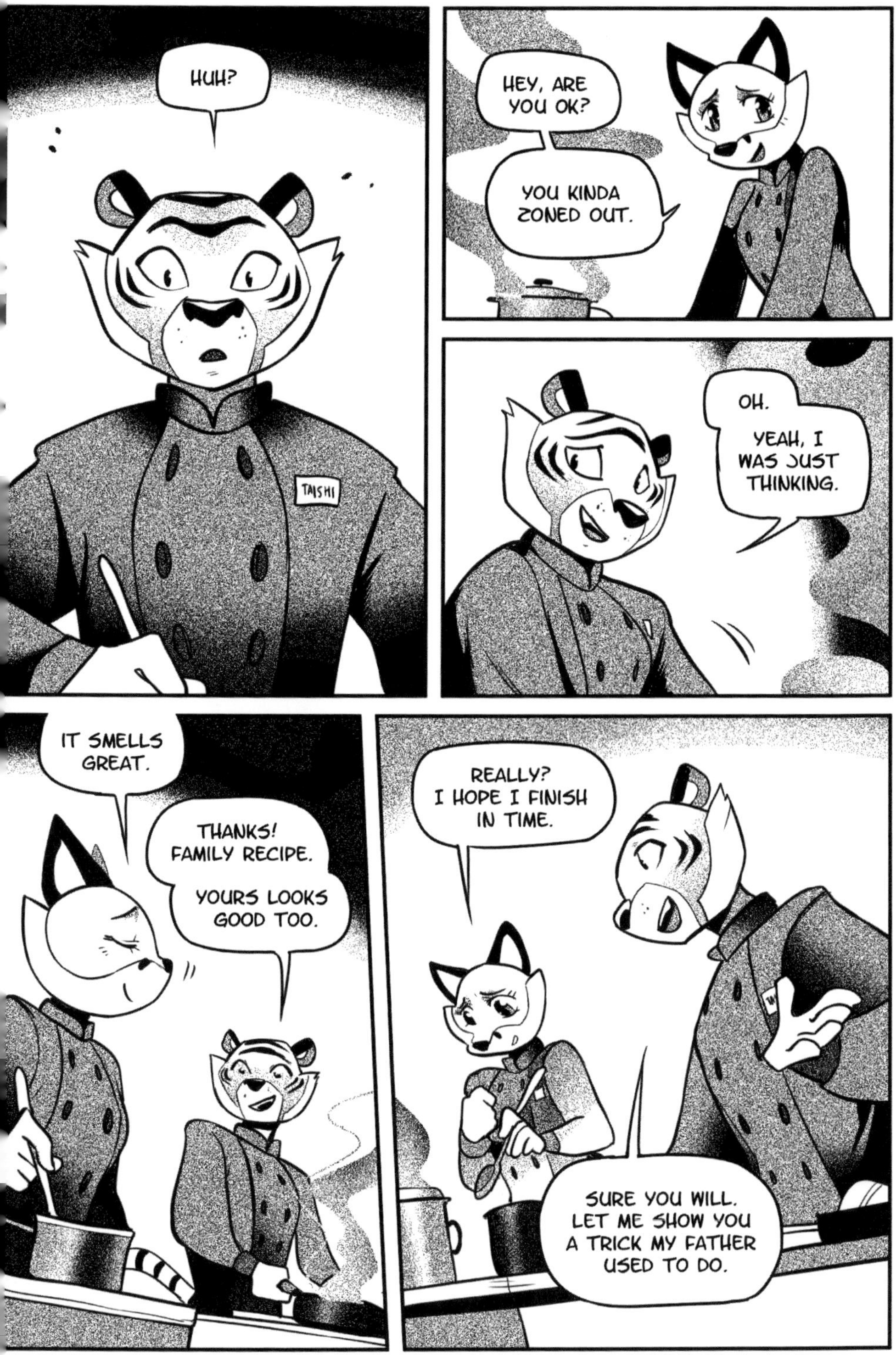

HUH?
TAISHI
HEY, ARE YOU OK?
YOU KINDA ZONED OUT.
OH.
YEAH, I WAS JUST THINKING.
IT SMELLS GREAT.
THANKS! FAMILY RECIPE.
YOURS LOOKS GOOD TOO.
REALLY? I HOPE I FINISH IN TIME.
SURE YOU WILL. LET ME SHOW YOU A TRICK MY FATHER USED TO DO.

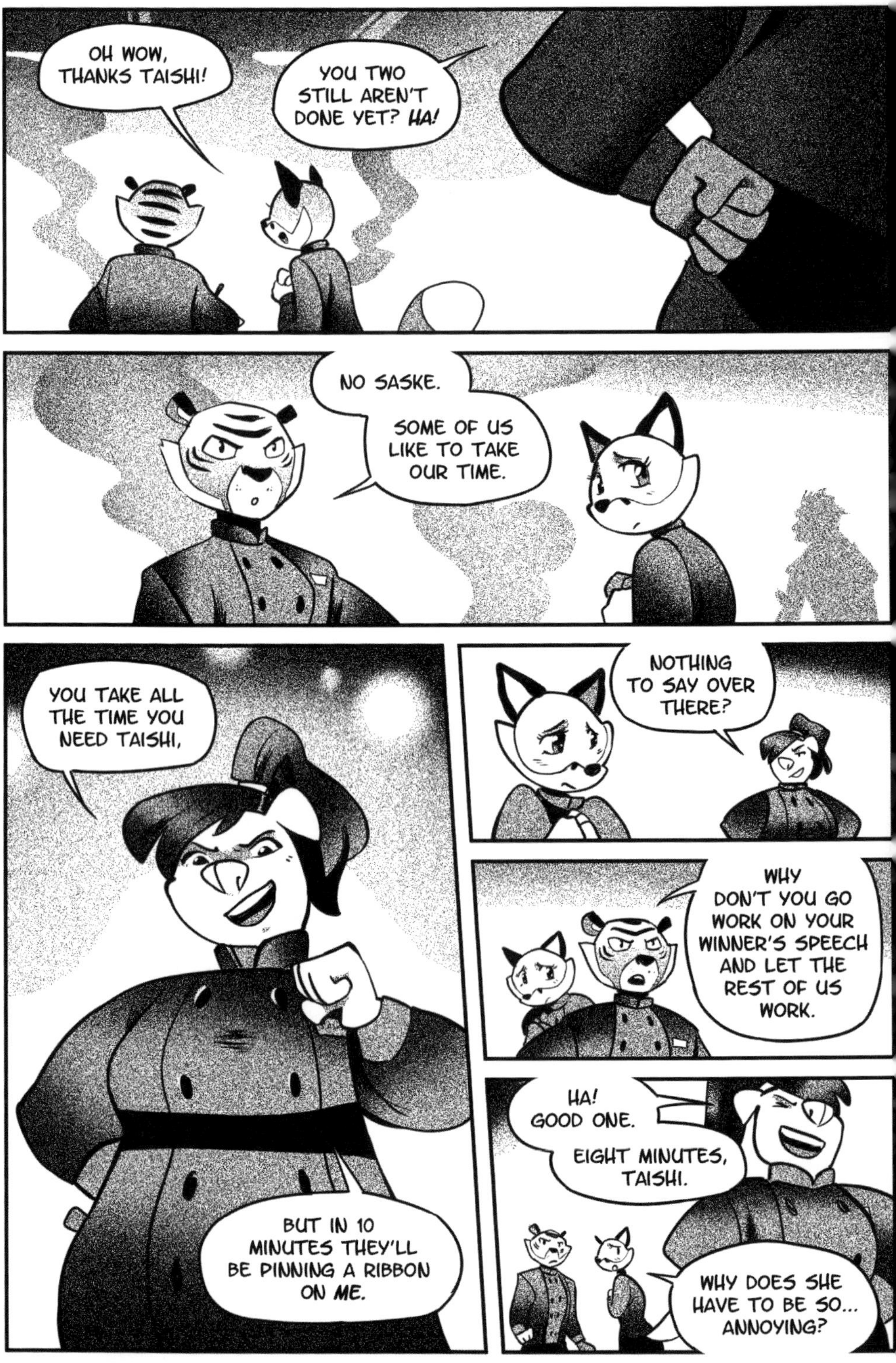
OH WOW, THANKS TAISHI!
YOU TWO STILL AREN'T DONE YET? HA!
NO SASKE.
SOME OF US LIKE TO TAKE OUR TIME.
YOU TAKE ALL THE TIME YOU NEED TAISHI,
BUT IN 10 MINUTES THEY'LL BE PINNING A RIBBON ON ME.
NOTHING TO SAY OVER THERE?
WHY DON'T YOU GO WORK ON YOUR WINNER'S SPEECH AND LET THE REST OF US WORK.
HA! GOOD ONE.
EIGHT MINUTES, TAISHI.
WHY DOES SHE HAVE TO BE SO... ANNOYING?

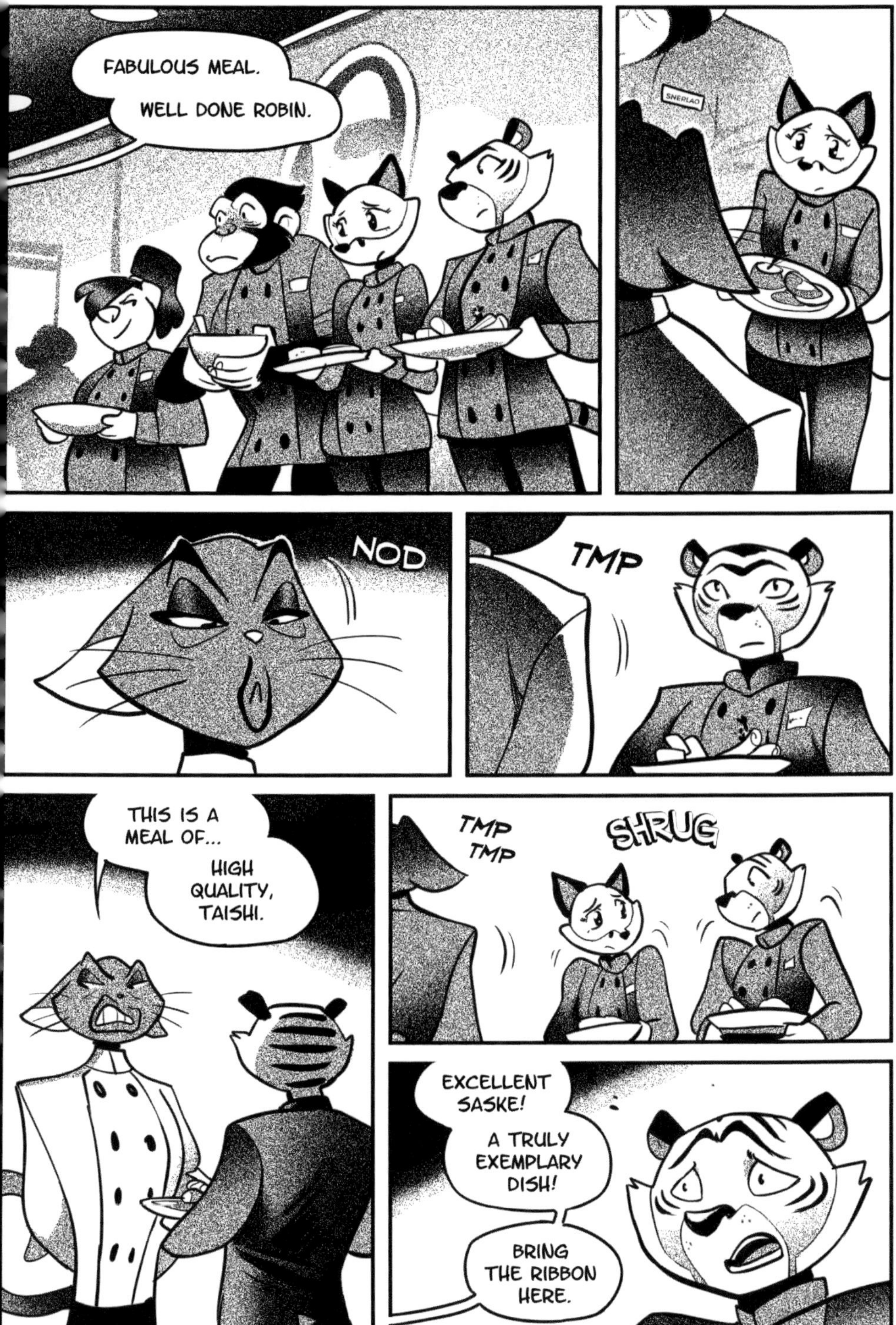

FABULOUS MEAL.
WELL DONE ROBIN.
SNERLAO
NOD
TMP
THIS IS A MEAL OF...
HIGH QUALITY, TAISHI.
TMP TMP
SHRUG
EXCELLENT SASKE!
A TRULY EXEMPLARY DISH!
BRING THE RIBBON HERE.

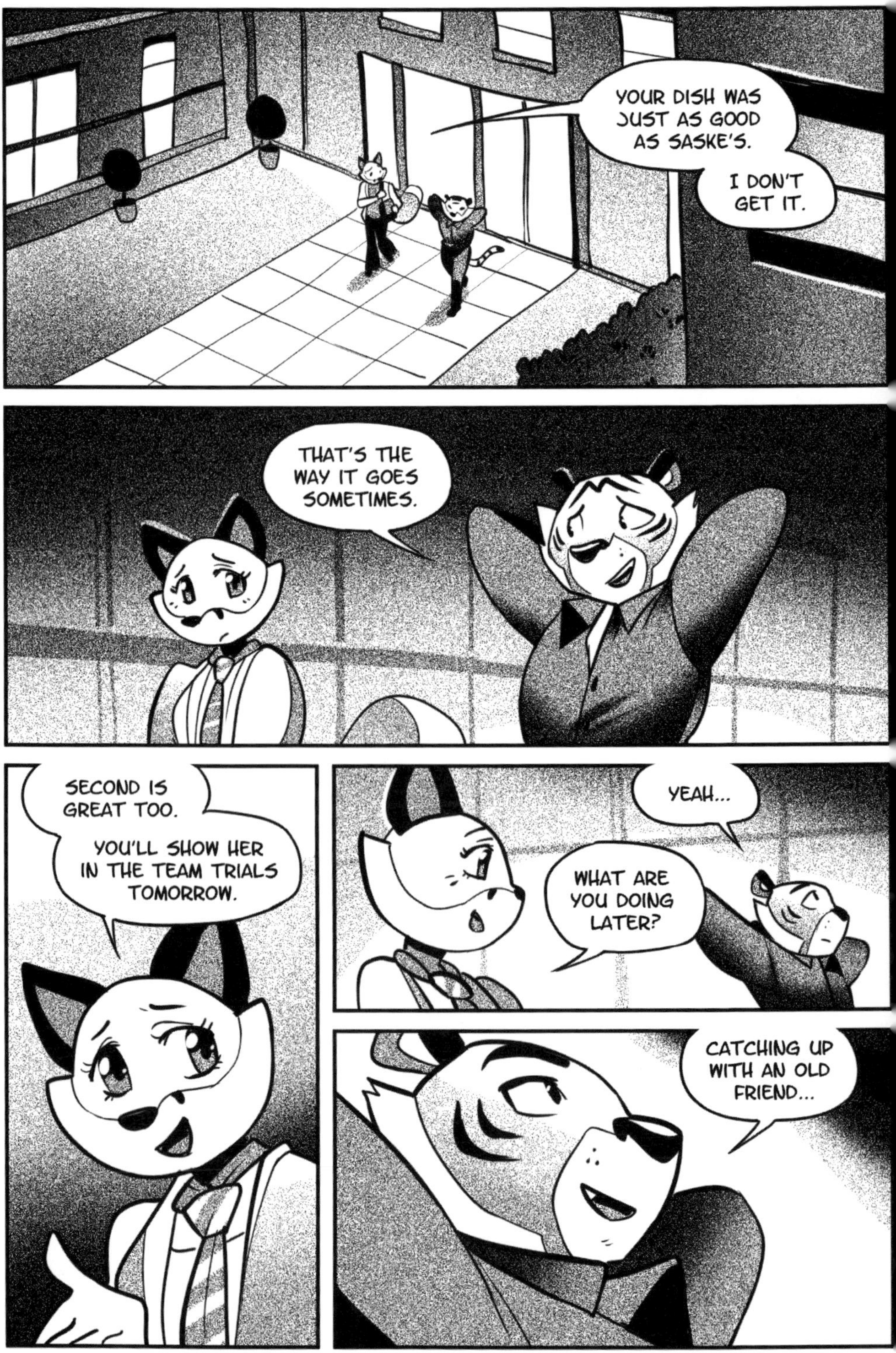
YOUR DISH WAS JUST AS GOOD AS SASKE'S.
I DON'T GET IT.
THAT'S THE WAY IT GOES SOMETIMES.
SECOND IS GREAT TOO.
YOU'LL SHOW HER IN THE TEAM TRIALS TOMORROW.
YEAH...
WHAT ARE YOU DOING LATER?
CATCHING UP WITH AN OLD FRIEND...

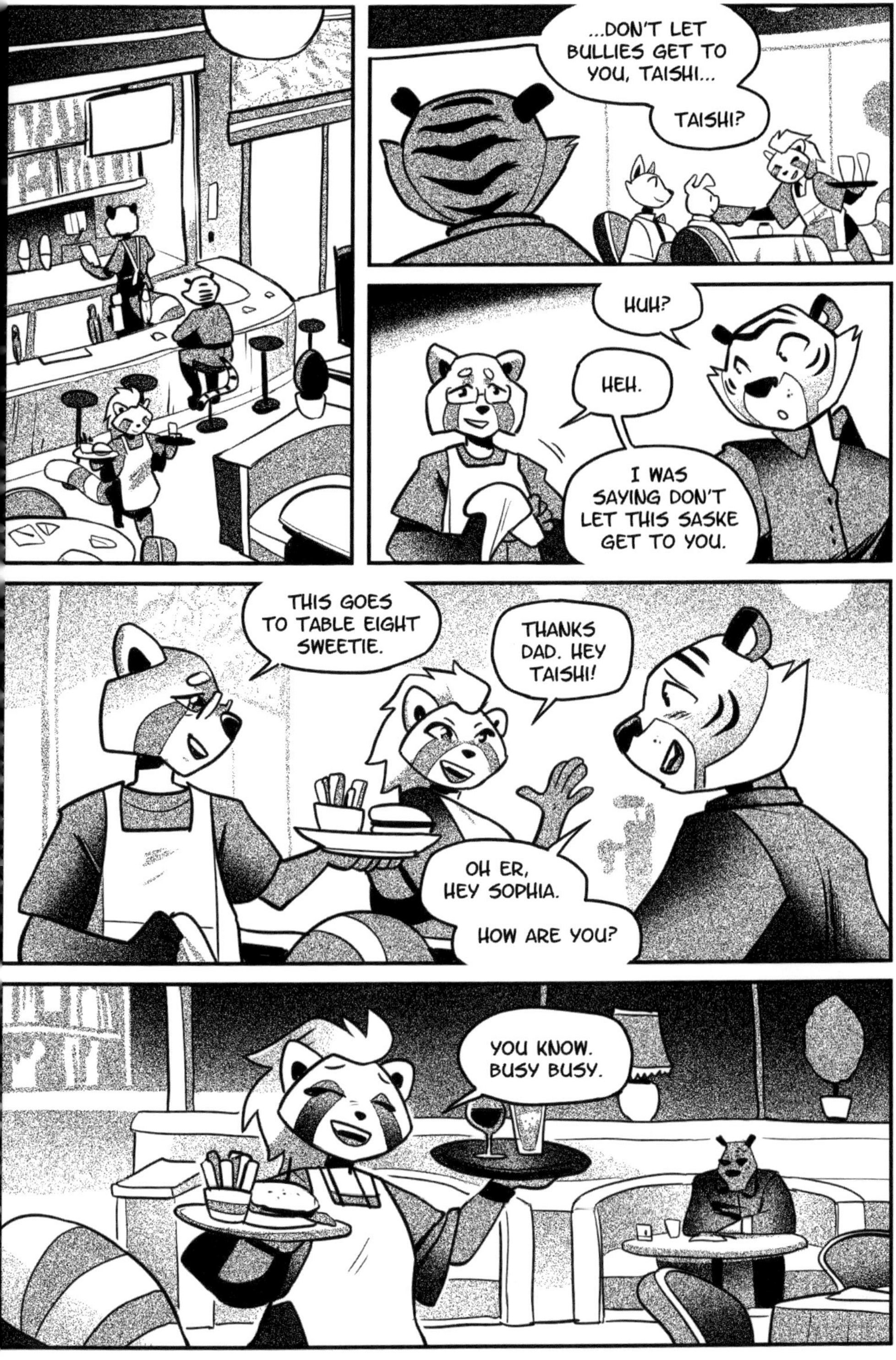
...DON'T LET BULLIES GET TO YOU, TAISHI...
TAISHI?
HUH?
HEH.
I WAS SAYING DON'T LET THIS SASKE GET TO YOU.
THIS GOES TO TABLE EIGHT SWEETIE.
THANKS DAD. HEY TAISHI!
OH ER, HEY SOPHIA.
HOW ARE YOU?
YOU KNOW. BUSY BUSY.

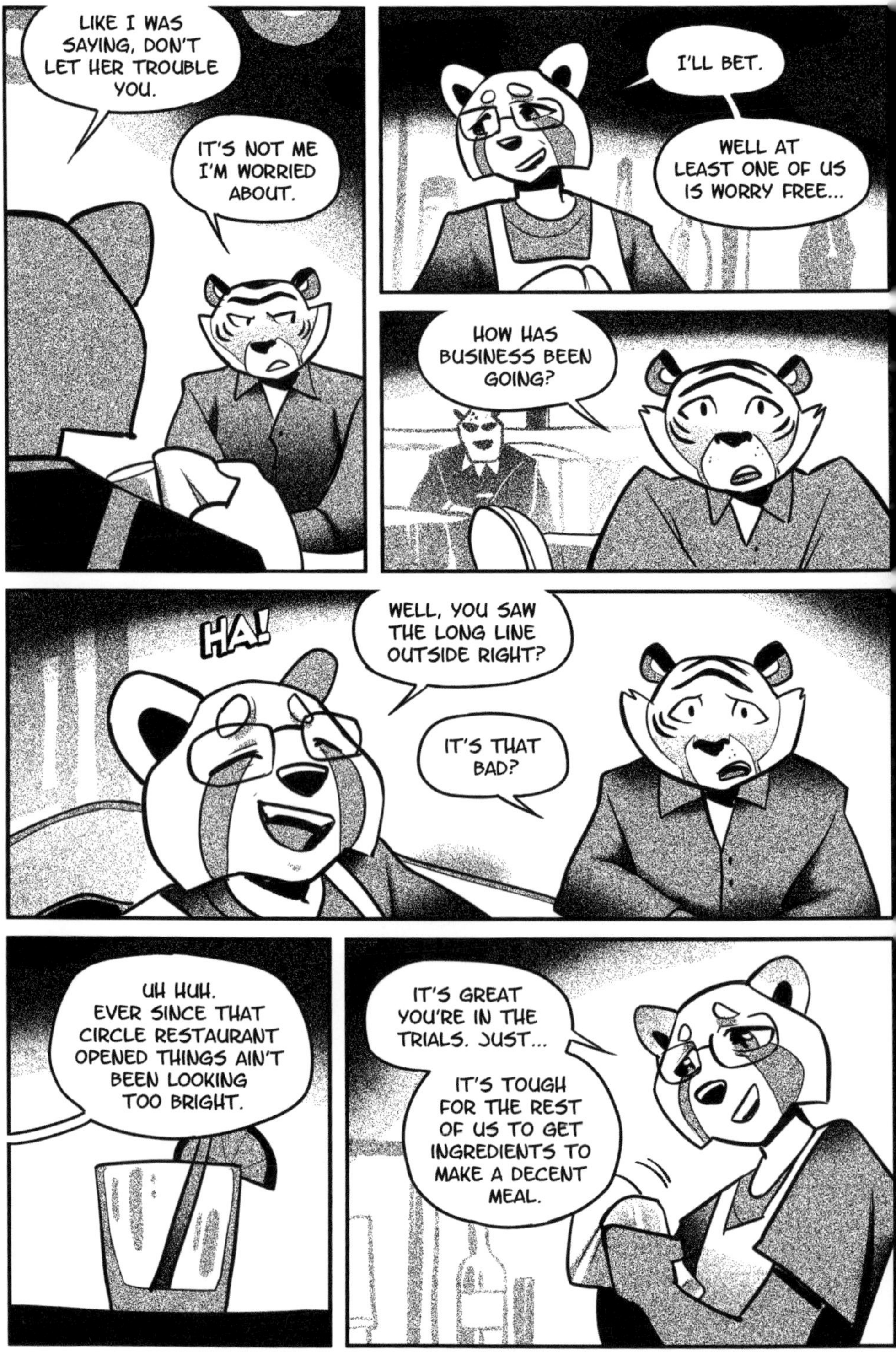

LIKE I WAS SAYING, DON'T LET HER TROUBLE YOU.
IT'S NOT ME I'M WORRIED ABOUT.
I'LL BET.
WELL AT LEAST ONE OF US IS WORRY FREE...
HOW HAS BUSINESS BEEN GOING?
HA!
WELL, YOU SAW THE LONG LINE OUTSIDE RIGHT?
IT'S THAT BAD?
UH HUH. EVER SINCE THAT CIRCLE RESTAURANT OPENED THINGS AIN'T BEEN LOOKING TOO BRIGHT.
IT'S GREAT YOU'RE IN THE TRIALS. JUST...
IT'S TOUGH FOR THE REST OF US TO GET INGREDIENTS TO MAKE A DECENT MEAL.

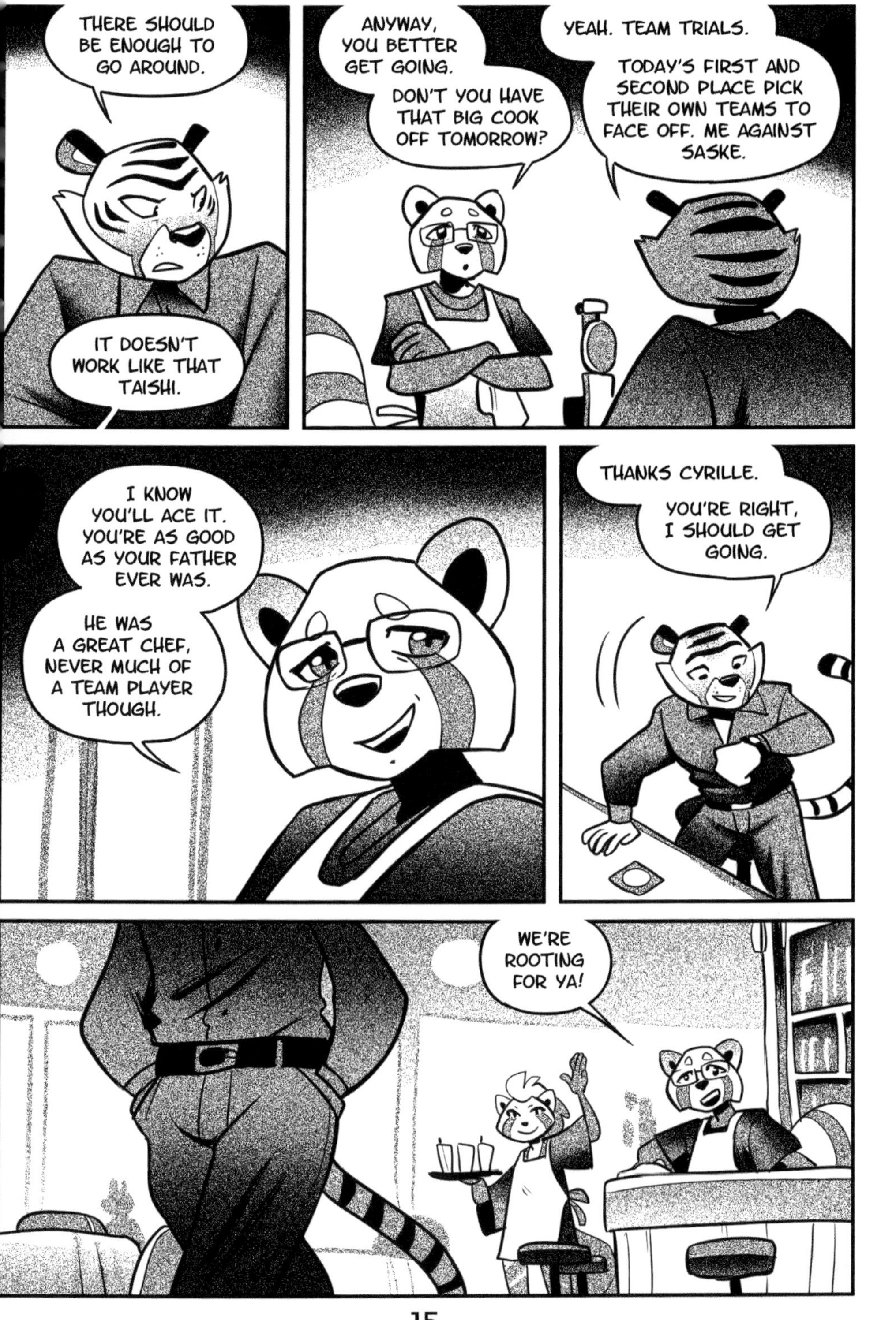
THERE SHOULD BE ENOUGH TO GO AROUND.
IT DOESN'T WORK LIKE THAT TAISHI.
ANYWAY, YOU BETTER GET GOING.
DON'T YOU HAVE THAT BIG COOK OFF TOMORROW?
YEAH. TEAM TRIALS.
TODAY'S FIRST AND SECOND PLACE PICK THEIR OWN TEAMS TO FACE OFF. ME AGAINST SASKE.
I KNOW YOU'LL ACE IT. YOU'RE AS GOOD AS YOUR FATHER EVER WAS.
HE WAS A GREAT CHEF, NEVER MUCH OF A TEAM PLAYER THOUGH.
THANKS CYRILLE.
YOU'RE RIGHT, I SHOULD GET GOING.
WE'RE ROOTING FOR YA!

I HEAR CAESAR HIMSELF WILL BE HERE TODAY TO WATCH OVER THE TRIALS.

NO WONDER SASKE'S BEEN ON HER BEST BEHAVIOUR...

WE'LL HAVE TO COOK UP SOMETHING SPECIAL TO--

WHAT THE...

WHERE DID ALL THIS COME FROM, EH?

HEY! GET OFF ME!

WHAT IS THIS?!

YOU'RE COMING WITH US, THIEF.

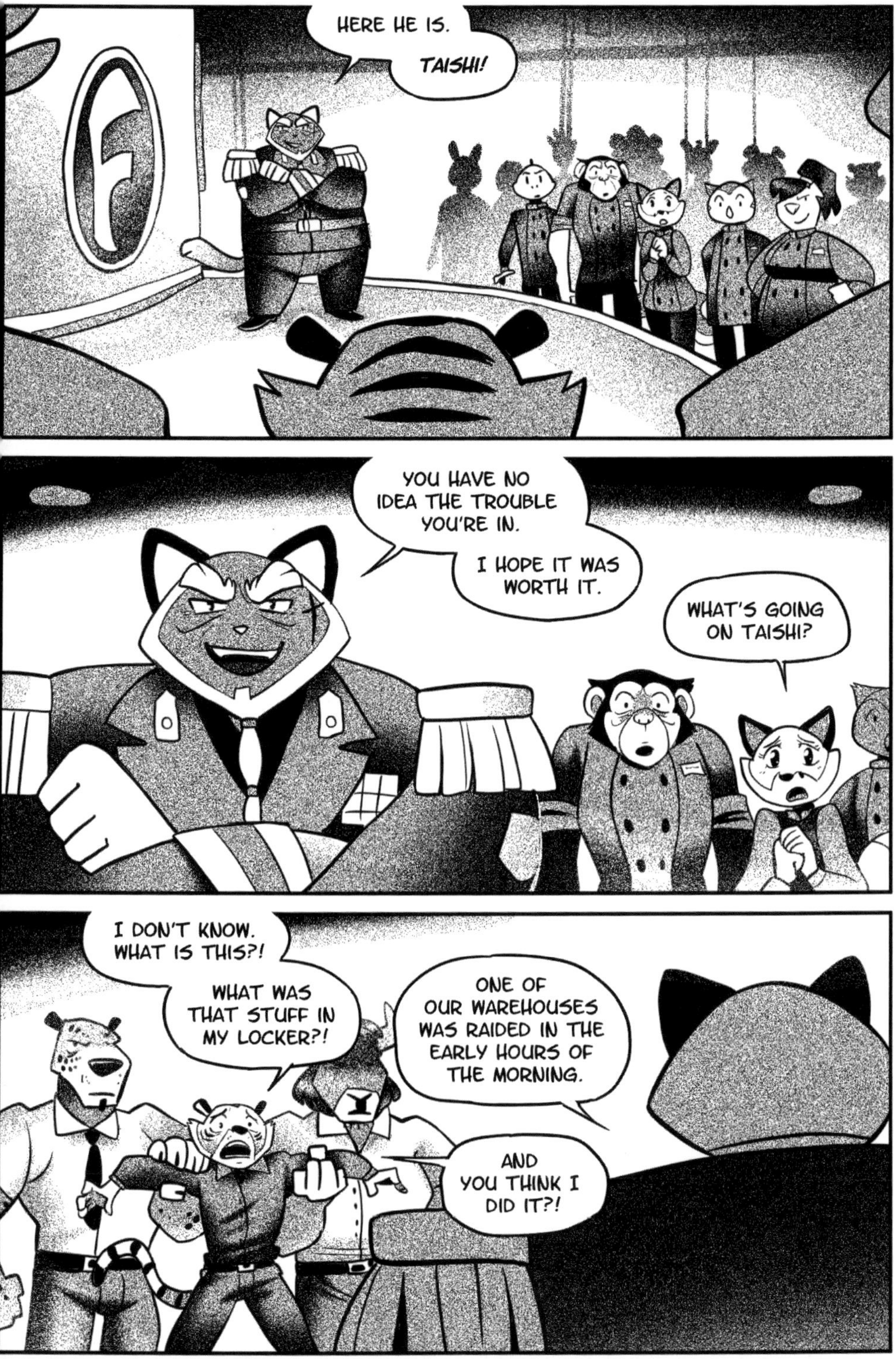
HERE HE IS.
TAISHI!
YOU HAVE NO IDEA THE TROUBLE YOU'RE IN.
I HOPE IT WAS WORTH IT.
WHAT'S GOING ON TAISHI?
I DON'T KNOW. WHAT IS THIS?!
WHAT WAS THAT STUFF IN MY LOCKER?!
ONE OF OUR WAREHOUSES WAS RAIDED IN THE EARLY HOURS OF THE MORNING.
AND YOU THINK I DID IT?!

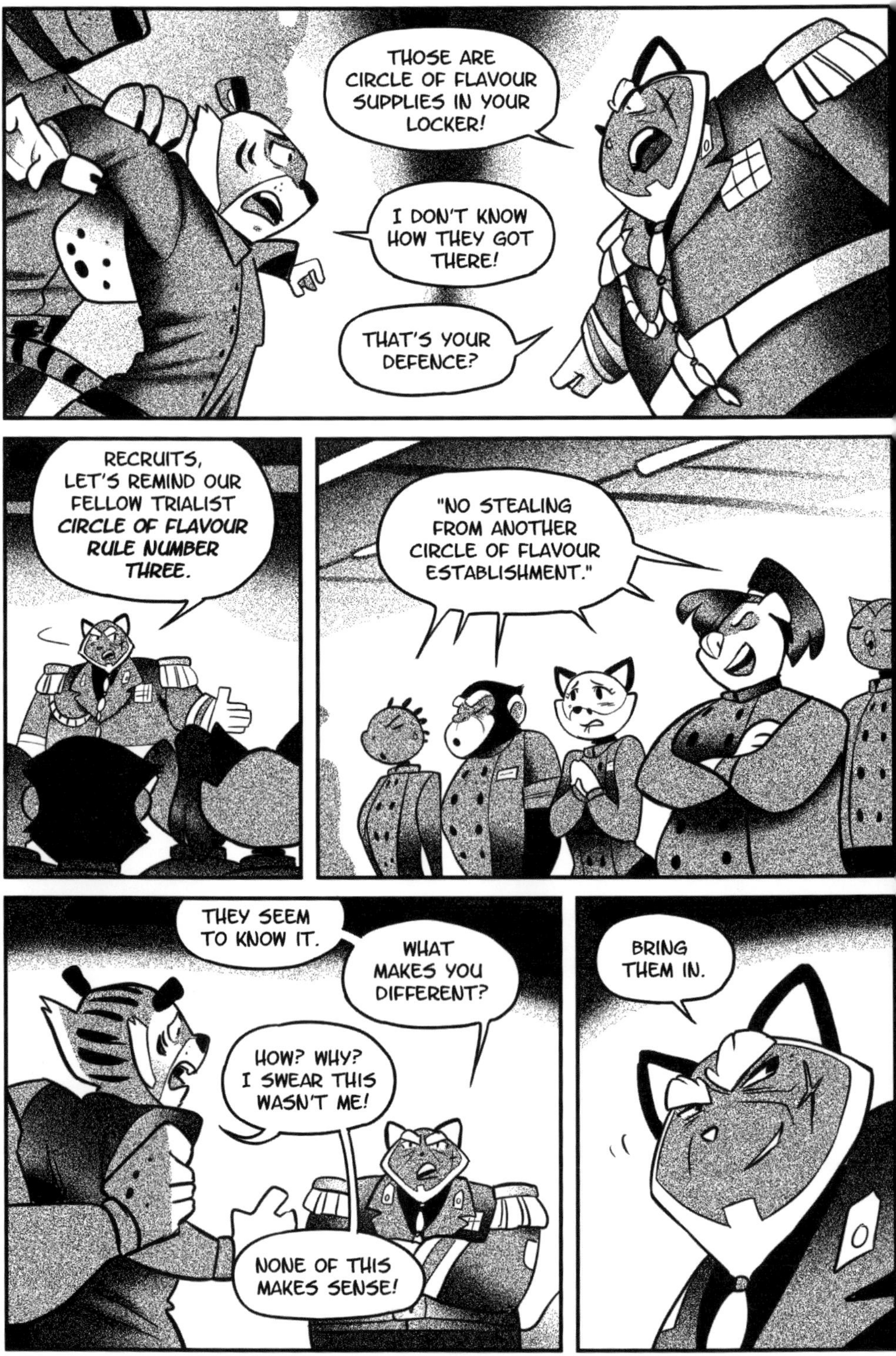
THOSE ARE CIRCLE OF FLAVOUR SUPPLIES IN YOUR LOCKER!
I DON'T KNOW HOW THEY GOT THERE!
THAT'S YOUR DEFENCE?
RECRUITS, LET'S REMIND OUR FELLOW TRIALIST **CIRCLE OF FLAVOUR RULE NUMBER THREE.**
"NO STEALING FROM ANOTHER CIRCLE OF FLAVOUR ESTABLISHMENT."
THEY SEEM TO KNOW IT.
WHAT MAKES YOU DIFFERENT?
HOW? WHY? I SWEAR THIS WASN'T ME!
NONE OF THIS MAKES SENSE!
BRING THEM IN.

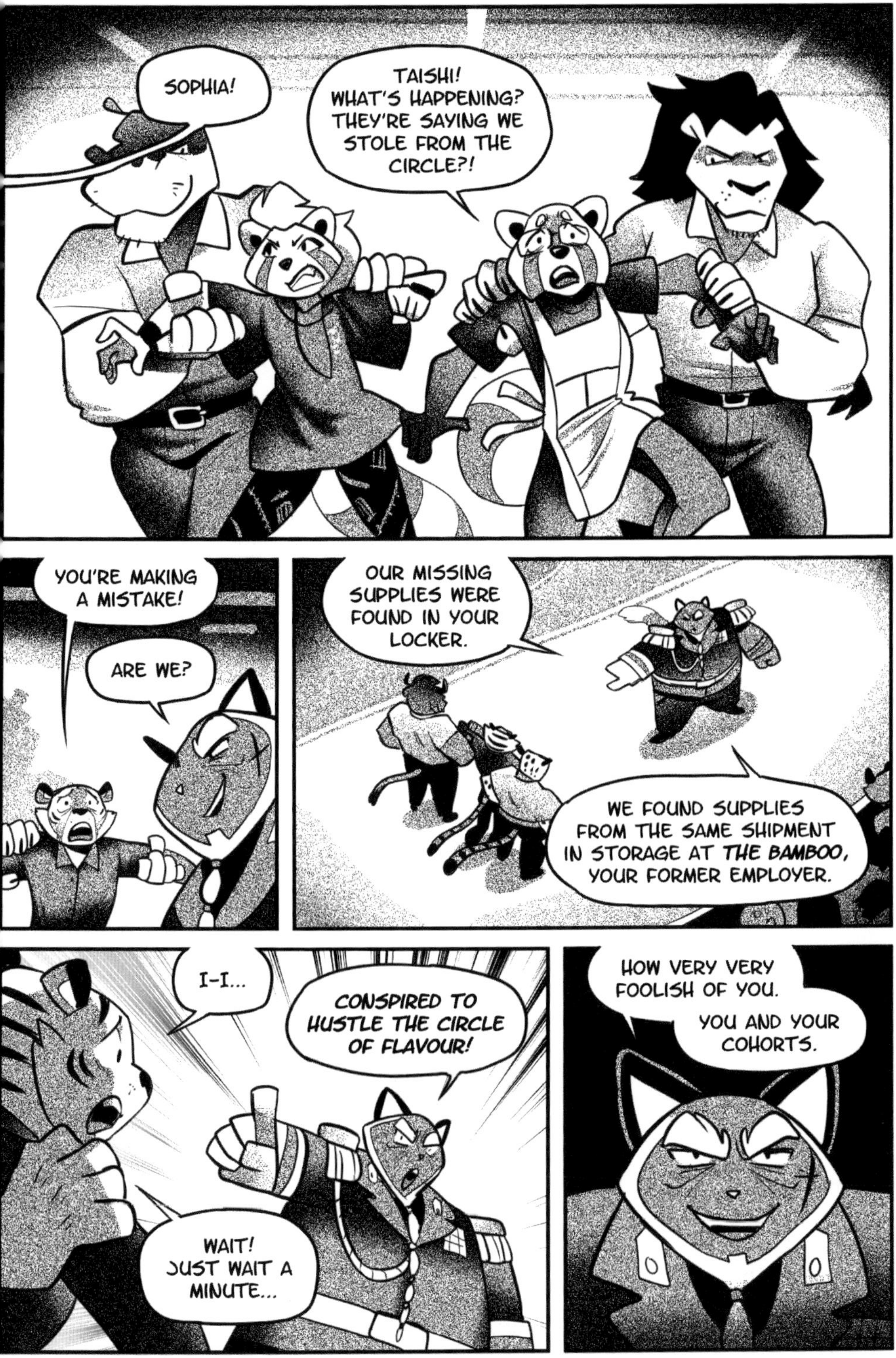

SOPHIA!
TAISHI! WHAT'S HAPPENING? THEY'RE SAYING WE STOLE FROM THE CIRCLE?!
YOU'RE MAKING A MISTAKE!
ARE WE?
OUR MISSING SUPPLIES WERE FOUND IN YOUR LOCKER.
WE FOUND SUPPLIES FROM THE SAME SHIPMENT IN STORAGE AT *THE BAMBOO*, YOUR FORMER EMPLOYER.
I-I...
CONSPIRED TO HUSTLE THE CIRCLE OF FLAVOUR!
WAIT! JUST WAIT A MINUTE...
HOW VERY VERY FOOLISH OF YOU.
YOU AND YOUR COHORTS.

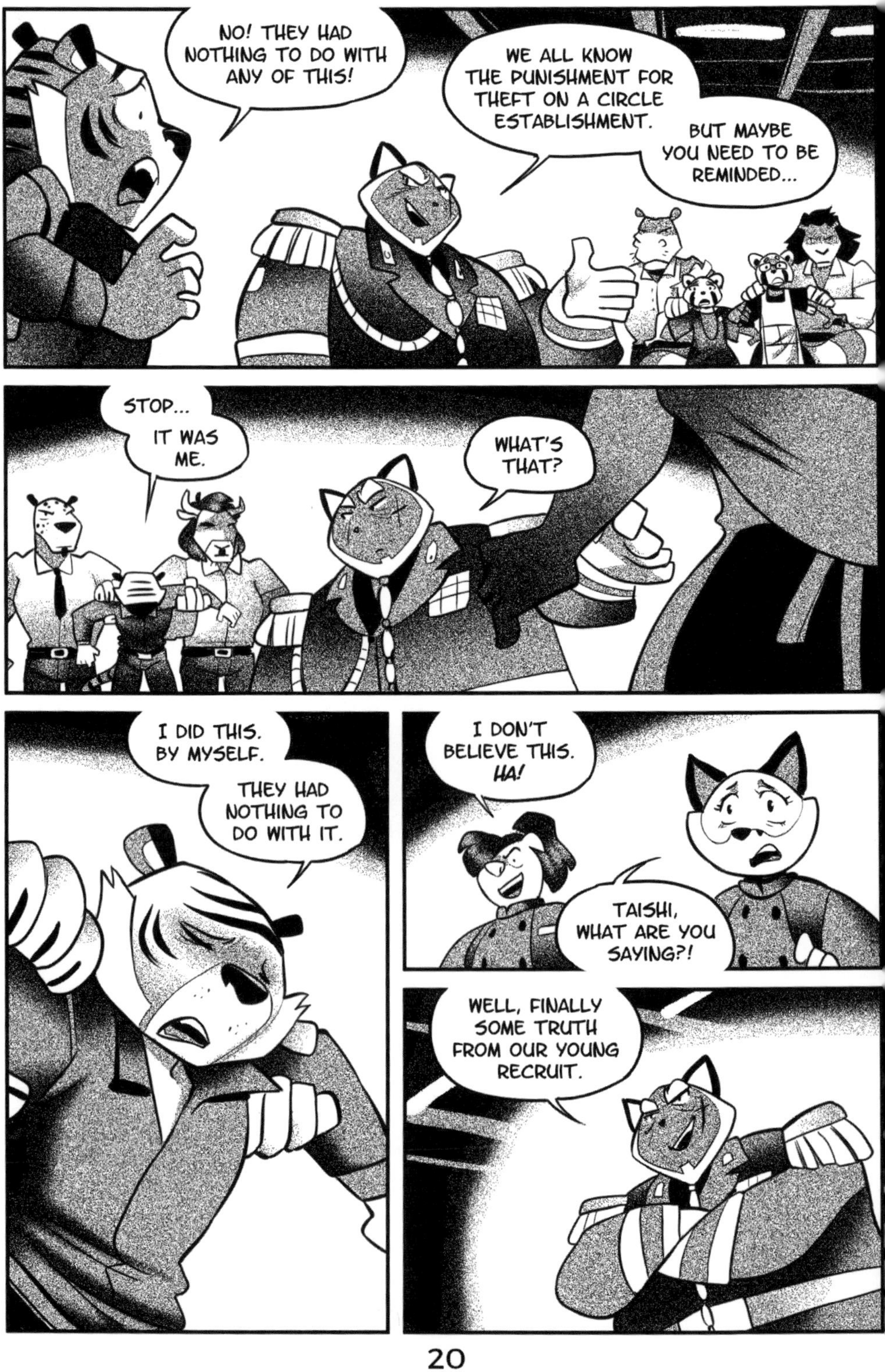
NO! THEY HAD NOTHING TO DO WITH ANY OF THIS!
WE ALL KNOW THE PUNISHMENT FOR THEFT ON A CIRCLE ESTABLISHMENT.
BUT MAYBE YOU NEED TO BE REMINDED...
STOP...
IT WAS ME.
WHAT'S THAT?
I DID THIS. BY MYSELF.
THEY HAD NOTHING TO DO WITH IT.
I DON'T BELIEVE THIS. HA!
TAISHI, WHAT ARE YOU SAYING?!
WELL, FINALLY SOME TRUTH FROM OUR YOUNG RECRUIT.

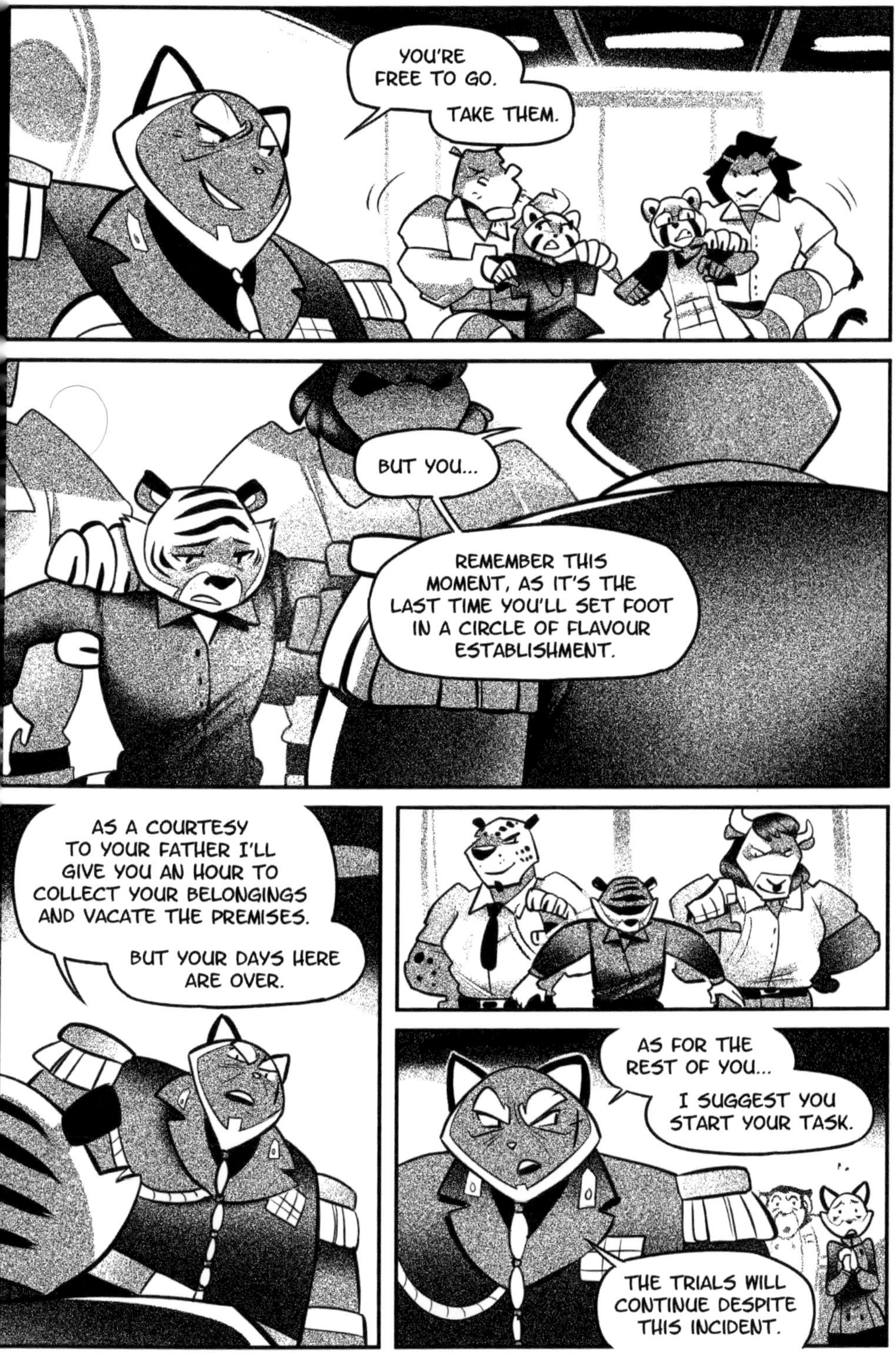
YOU'RE FREE TO GO.
TAKE THEM.
BUT YOU...
REMEMBER THIS MOMENT, AS IT'S THE LAST TIME YOU'LL SET FOOT IN A CIRCLE OF FLAVOUR ESTABLISHMENT.
AS A COURTESY TO YOUR FATHER I'LL GIVE YOU AN HOUR TO COLLECT YOUR BELONGINGS AND VACATE THE PREMISES.
BUT YOUR DAYS HERE ARE OVER.
AS FOR THE REST OF YOU...
I SUGGEST YOU START YOUR TASK.
THE TRIALS WILL CONTINUE DESPITE THIS INCIDENT.

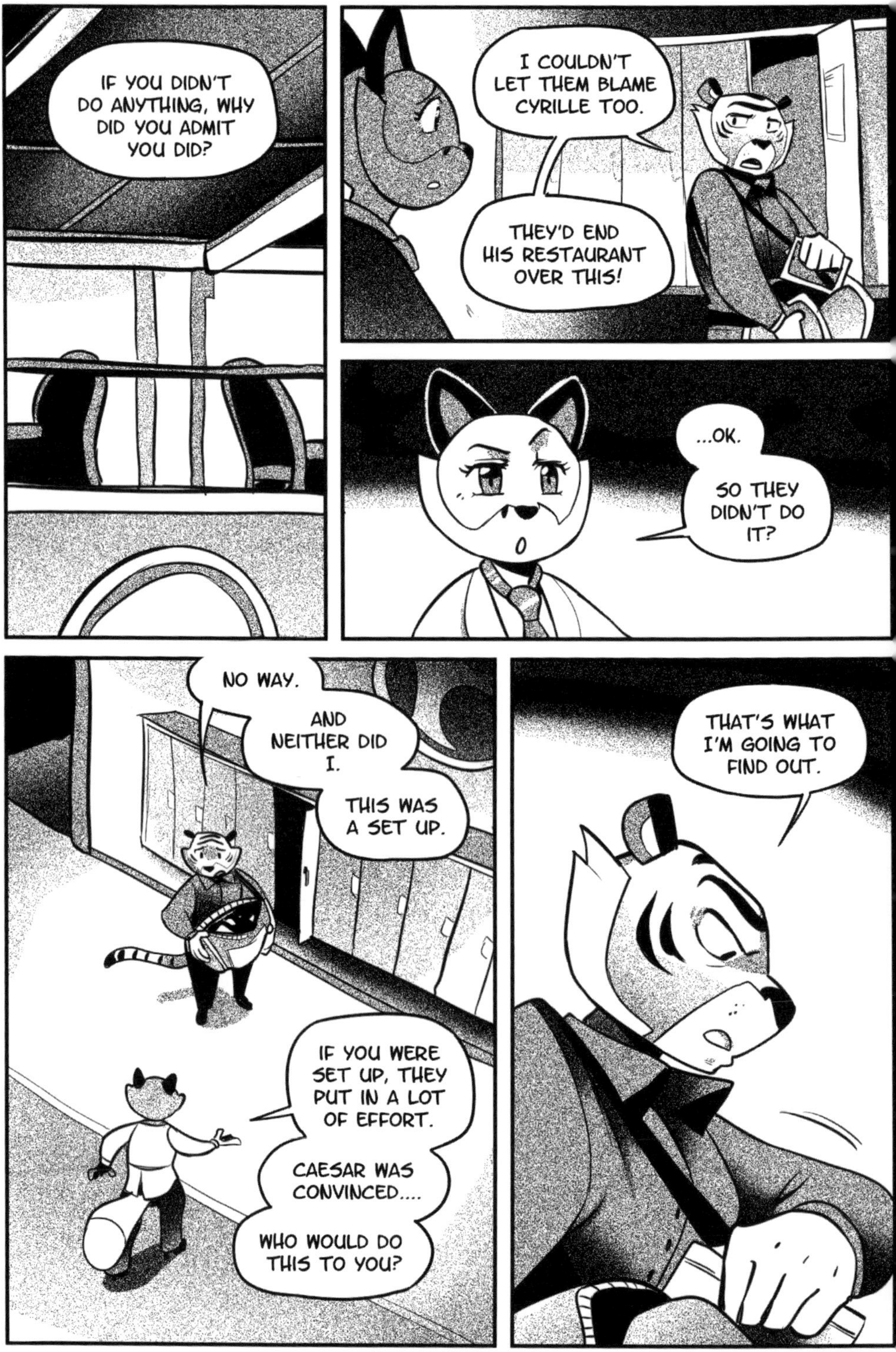
IF YOU DIDN'T DO ANYTHING, WHY DID YOU ADMIT YOU DID?
I COULDN'T LET THEM BLAME CYRILLE TOO.
THEY'D END HIS RESTAURANT OVER THIS!
...OK.
SO THEY DIDN'T DO IT?
NO WAY.
AND NEITHER DID I.
THIS WAS A SET UP.
IF YOU WERE SET UP, THEY PUT IN A LOT OF EFFORT.
CAESAR WAS CONVINCED....
WHO WOULD DO THIS TO YOU?
THAT'S WHAT I'M GOING TO FIND OUT.

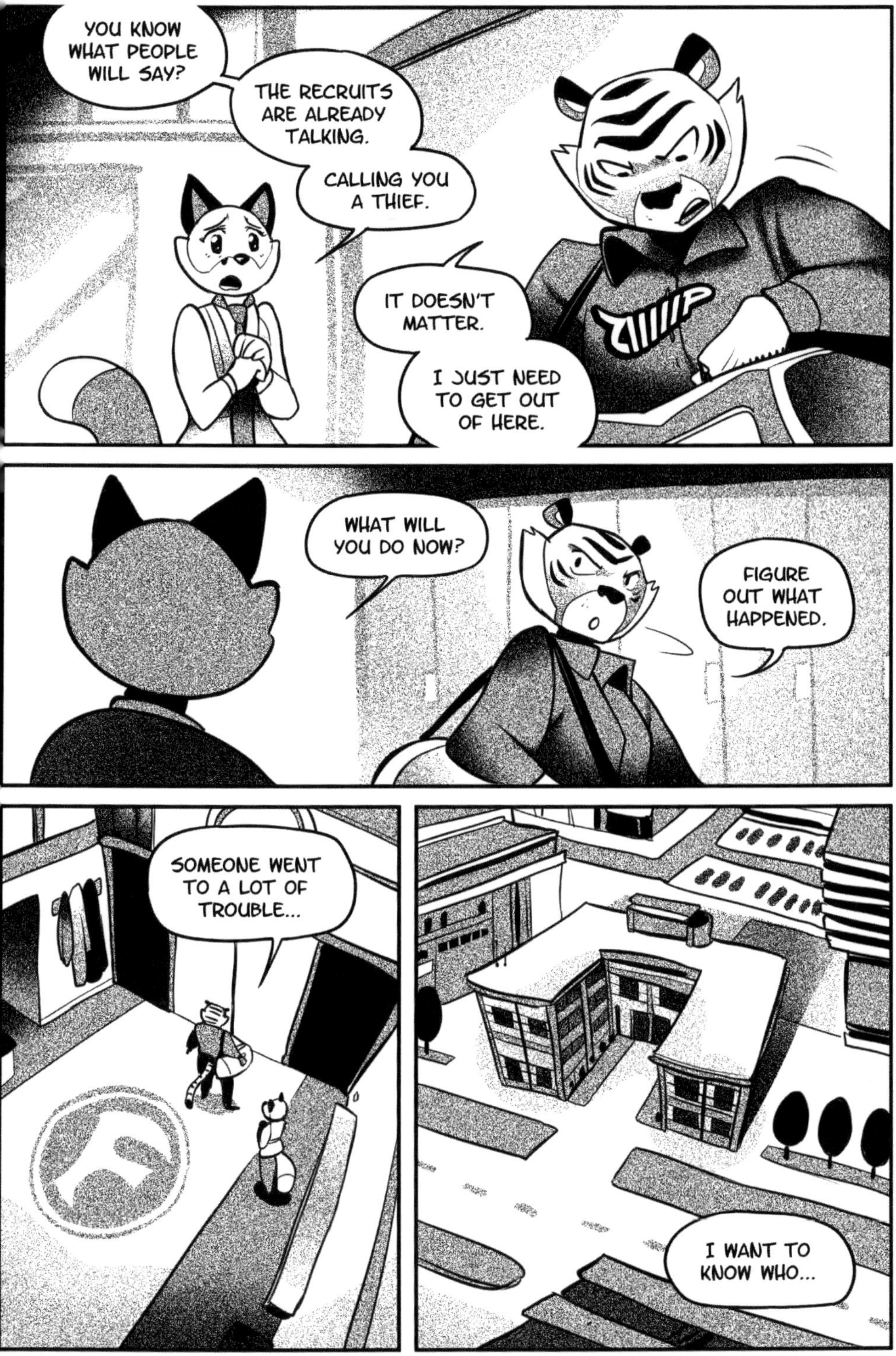
YOU KNOW WHAT PEOPLE WILL SAY?
THE RECRUITS ARE ALREADY TALKING.
CALLING YOU A THIEF.
IT DOESN'T MATTER.
I JUST NEED TO GET OUT OF HERE.
WHAT WILL YOU DO NOW?
FIGURE OUT WHAT HAPPENED.
SOMEONE WENT TO A LOT OF TROUBLE...
I WANT TO KNOW WHO...

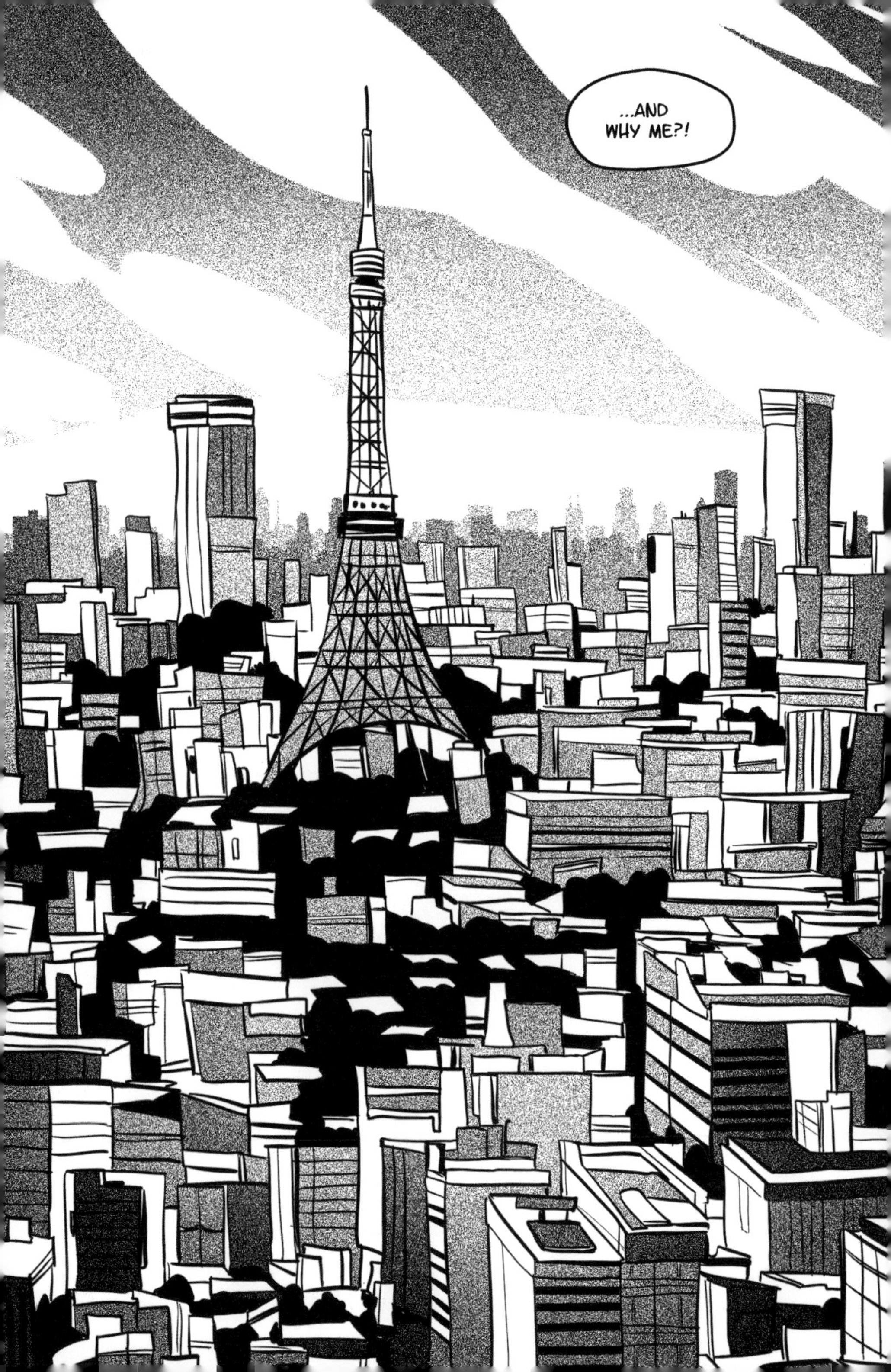
...AND WHY ME?!

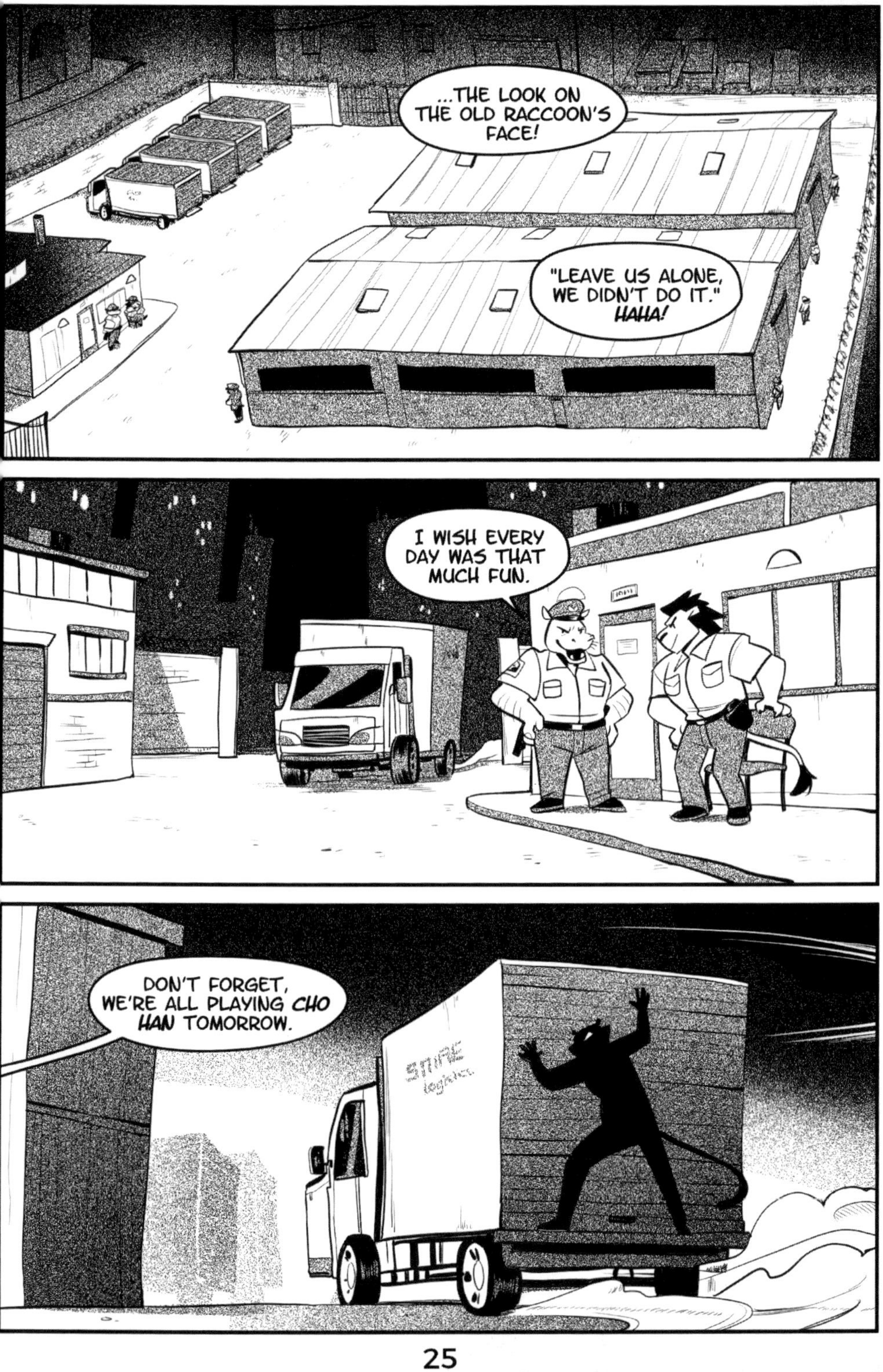
...THE LOOK ON THE OLD RACCOON'S FACE!
"LEAVE US ALONE, WE DIDN'T DO IT." *HAHA!*
I WISH EVERY DAY WAS THAT MUCH FUN.
DON'T FORGET, WE'RE ALL PLAYING *CHO HAN* TOMORROW.

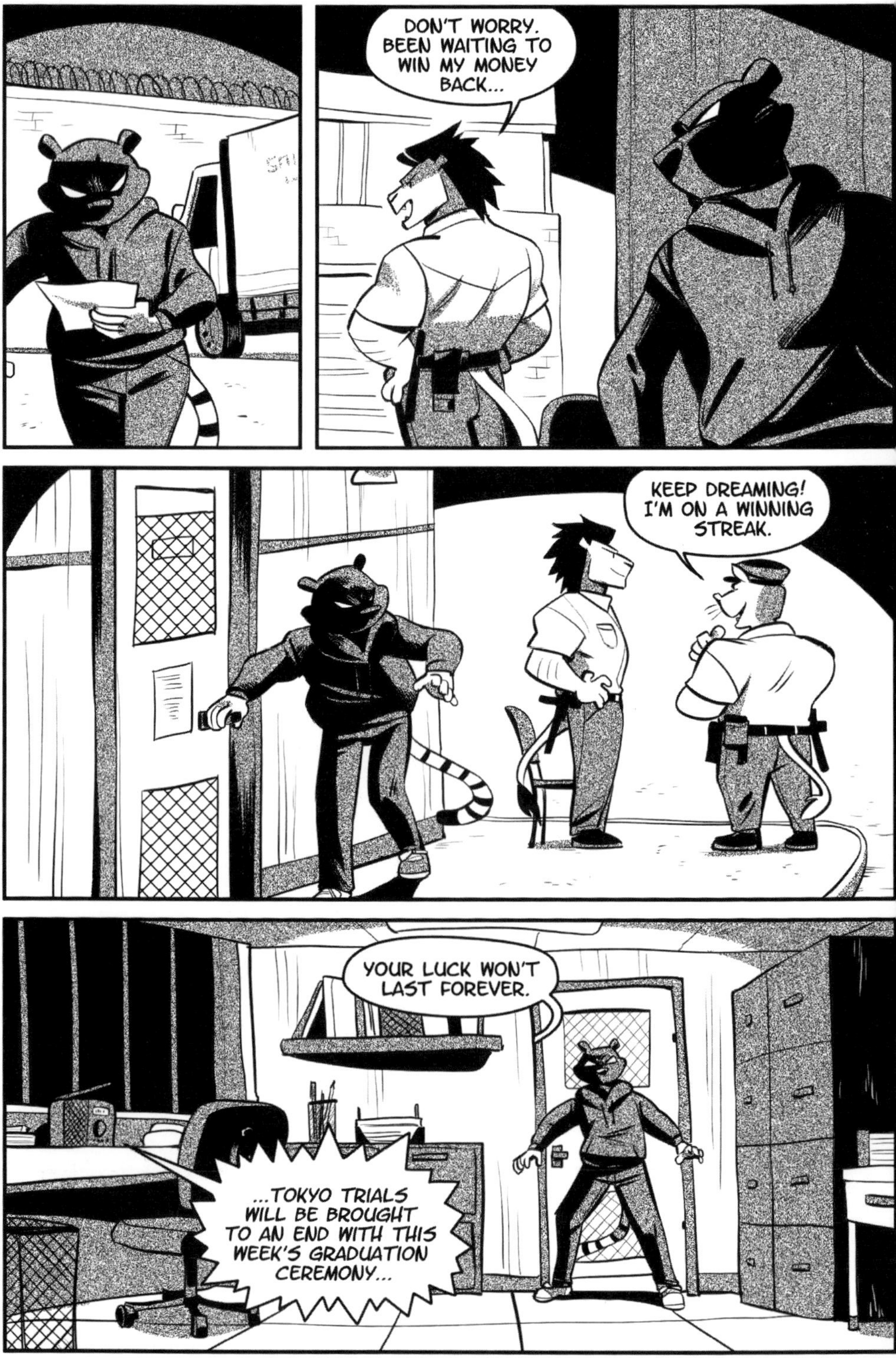
DON'T WORRY. BEEN WAITING TO WIN MY MONEY BACK...
KEEP DREAMING! I'M ON A WINNING STREAK.
YOUR LUCK WON'T LAST FOREVER.
...TOKYO TRIALS WILL BE BROUGHT TO AN END WITH THIS WEEK'S GRADUATION CEREMONY...

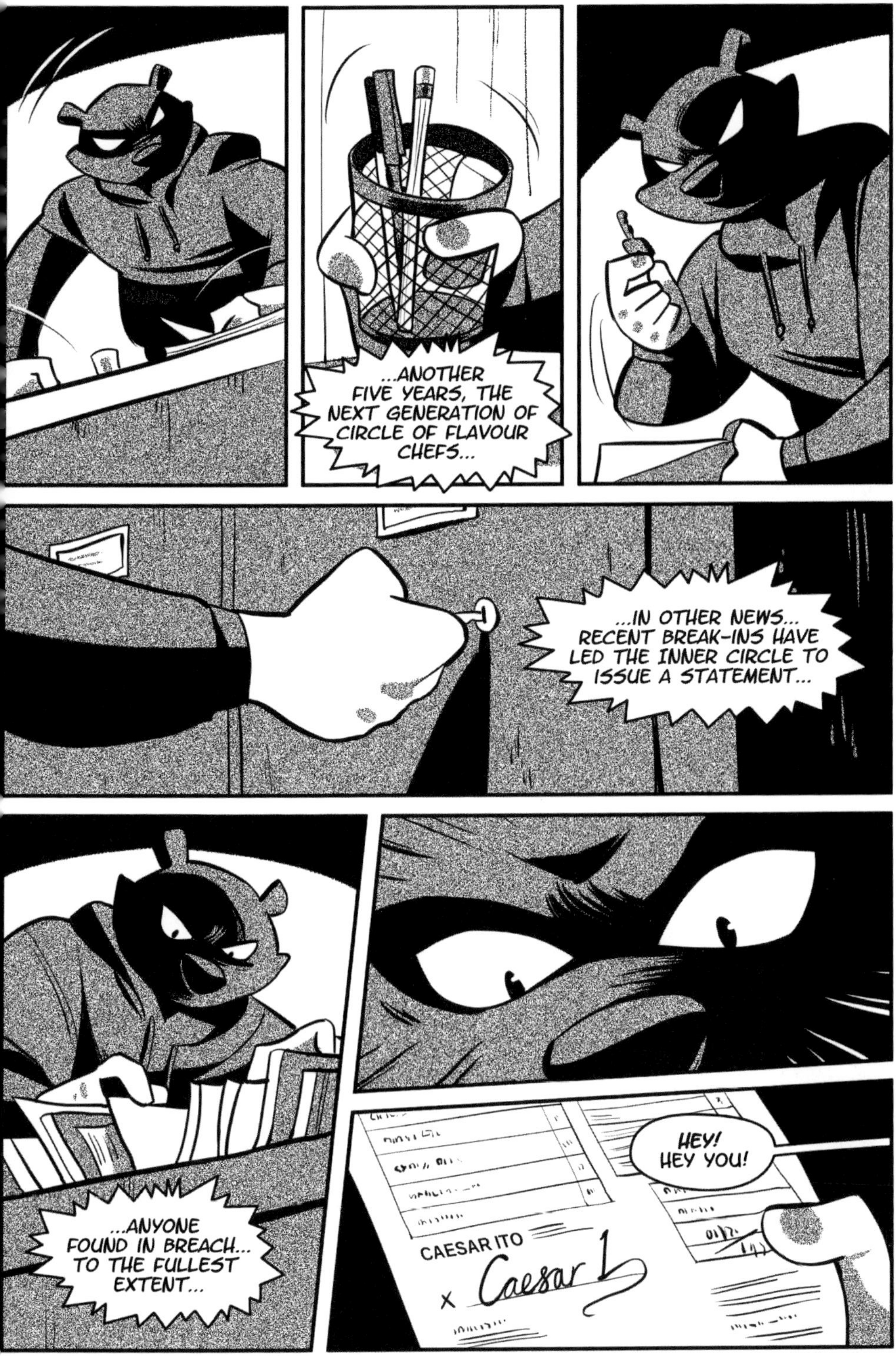
...ANOTHER FIVE YEARS, THE NEXT GENERATION OF CIRCLE OF FLAVOUR CHEFS...
...IN OTHER NEWS... RECENT BREAK-INS HAVE LED THE INNER CIRCLE TO ISSUE A STATEMENT...
...ANYONE FOUND IN BREACH... TO THE FULLEST EXTENT...
HEY! HEY YOU!
CAESAR ITO
x Caesar I

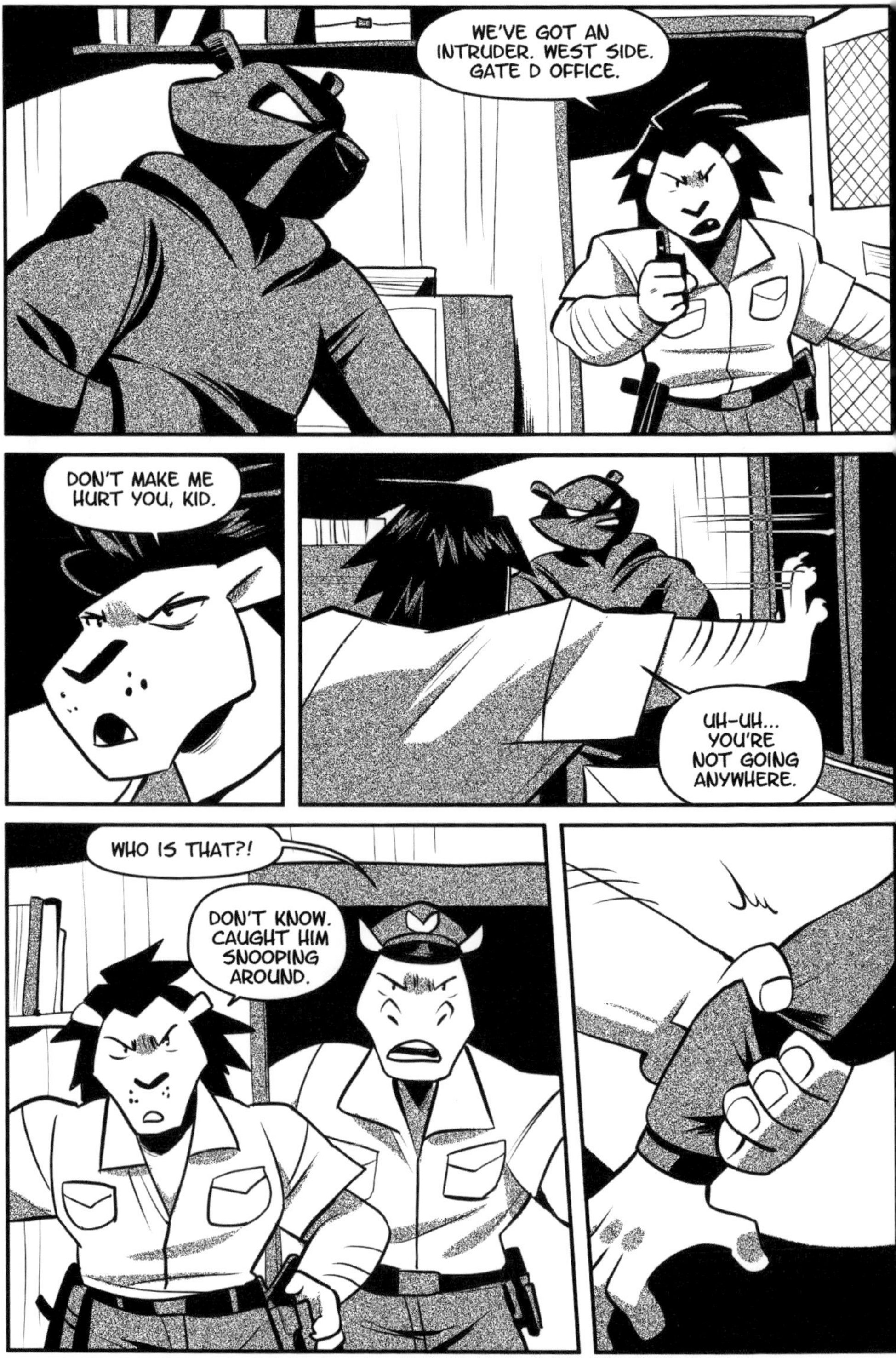
WE'VE GOT AN INTRUDER. WEST SIDE. GATE D OFFICE.
DON'T MAKE ME HURT YOU, KID.
UH-UH... YOU'RE NOT GOING ANYWHERE.
WHO IS THAT?!
DON'T KNOW. CAUGHT HIM SNOOPING AROUND.

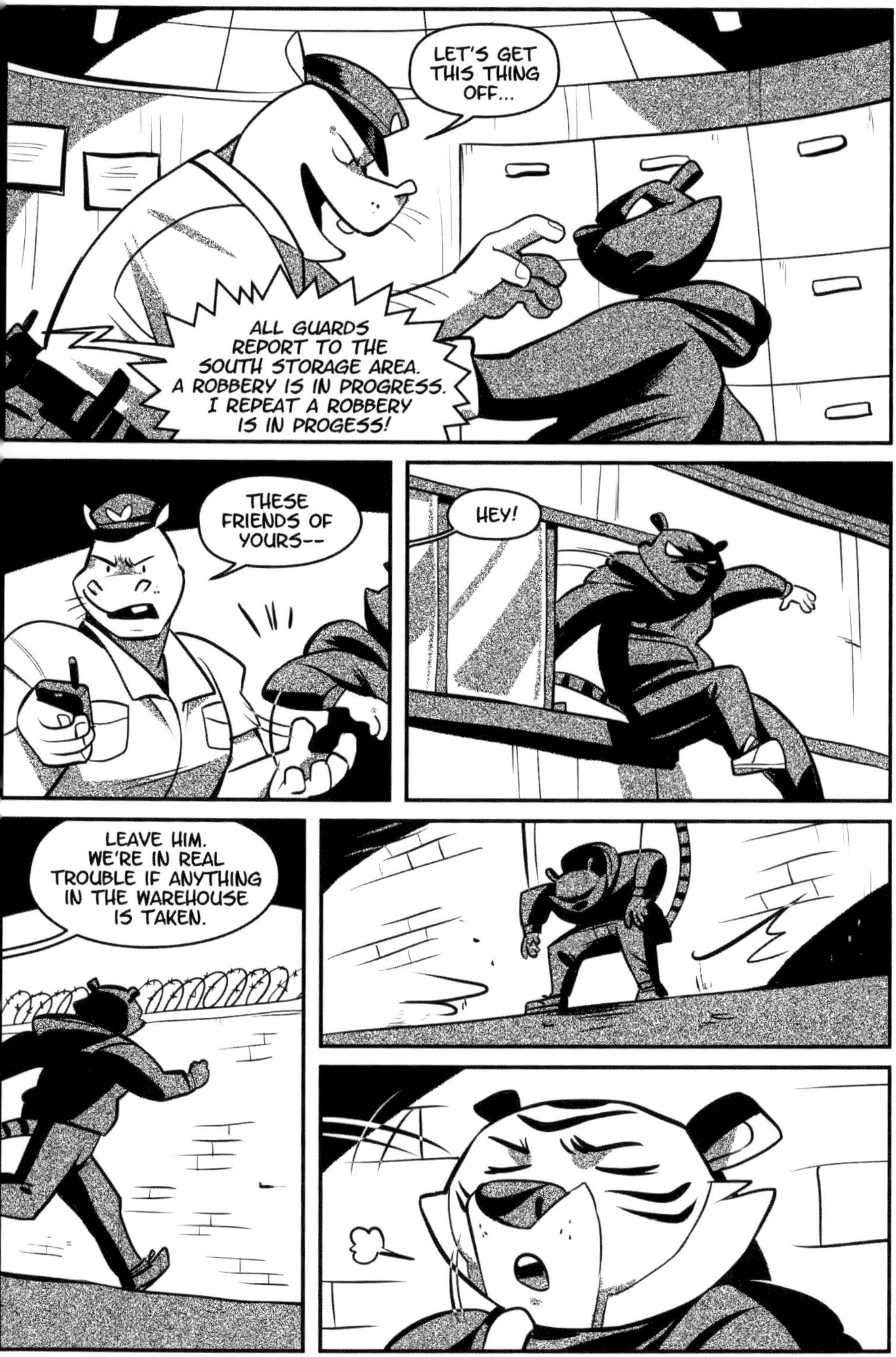
LET'S GET THIS THING OFF...
ALL GUARDS REPORT TO THE SOUTH STORAGE AREA. A ROBBERY IS IN PROGRESS. I REPEAT A ROBBERY IS IN PROGESS!
THESE FRIENDS OF YOURS--
HEY!
LEAVE HIM. WE'RE IN REAL TROUBLE IF ANYTHING IN THE WAREHOUSE IS TAKEN.

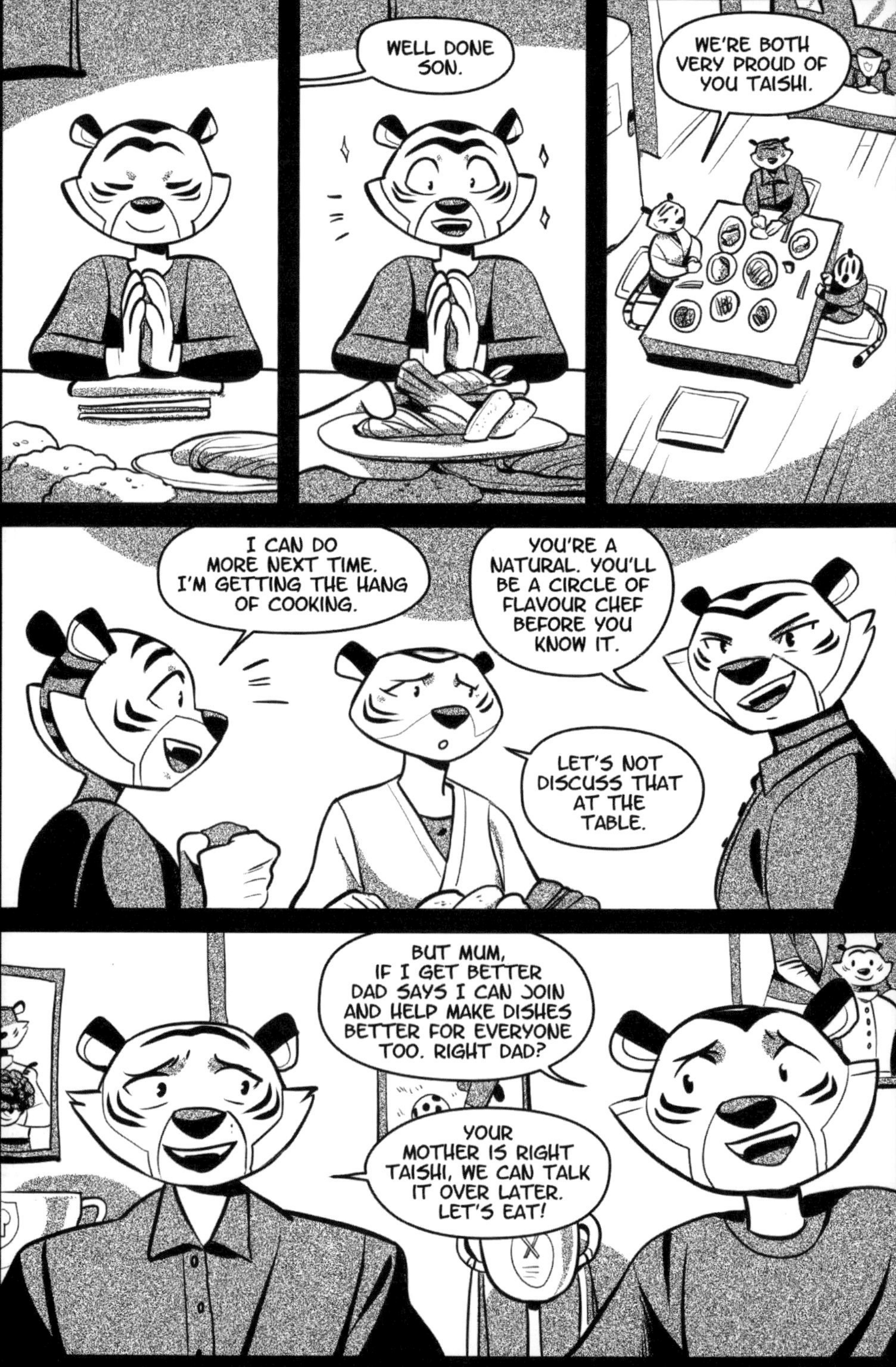
WELL DONE SON.
WE'RE BOTH VERY PROUD OF YOU TAISHI.
I CAN DO MORE NEXT TIME. I'M GETTING THE HANG OF COOKING.
YOU'RE A NATURAL. YOU'LL BE A CIRCLE OF FLAVOUR CHEF BEFORE YOU KNOW IT.
LET'S NOT DISCUSS THAT AT THE TABLE.
BUT MUM, IF I GET BETTER DAD SAYS I CAN JOIN AND HELP MAKE DISHES BETTER FOR EVERYONE TOO. RIGHT DAD?
YOUR MOTHER IS RIGHT TAISHI, WE CAN TALK IT OVER LATER. LET'S EAT!

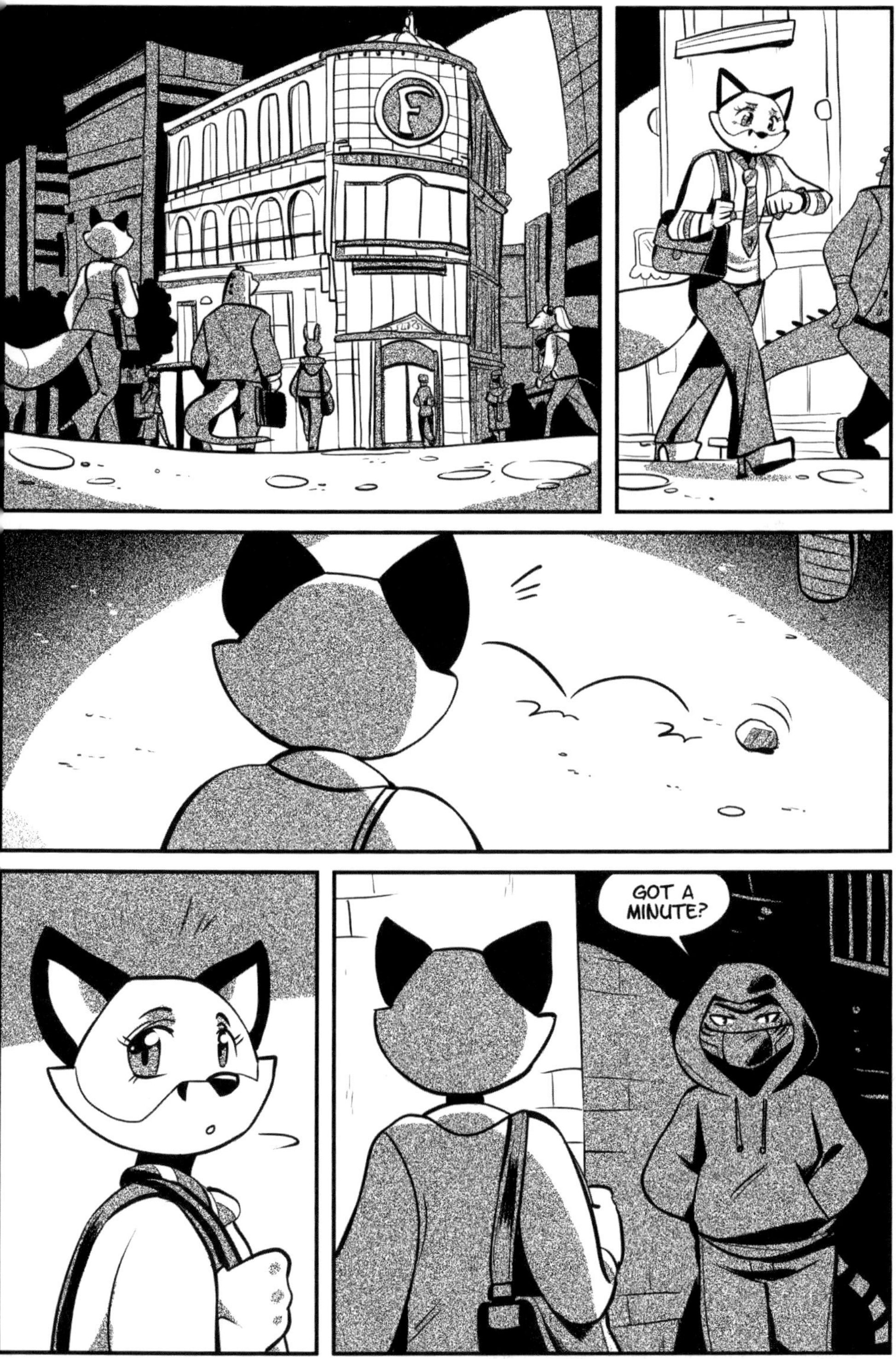
GOT A MINUTE?

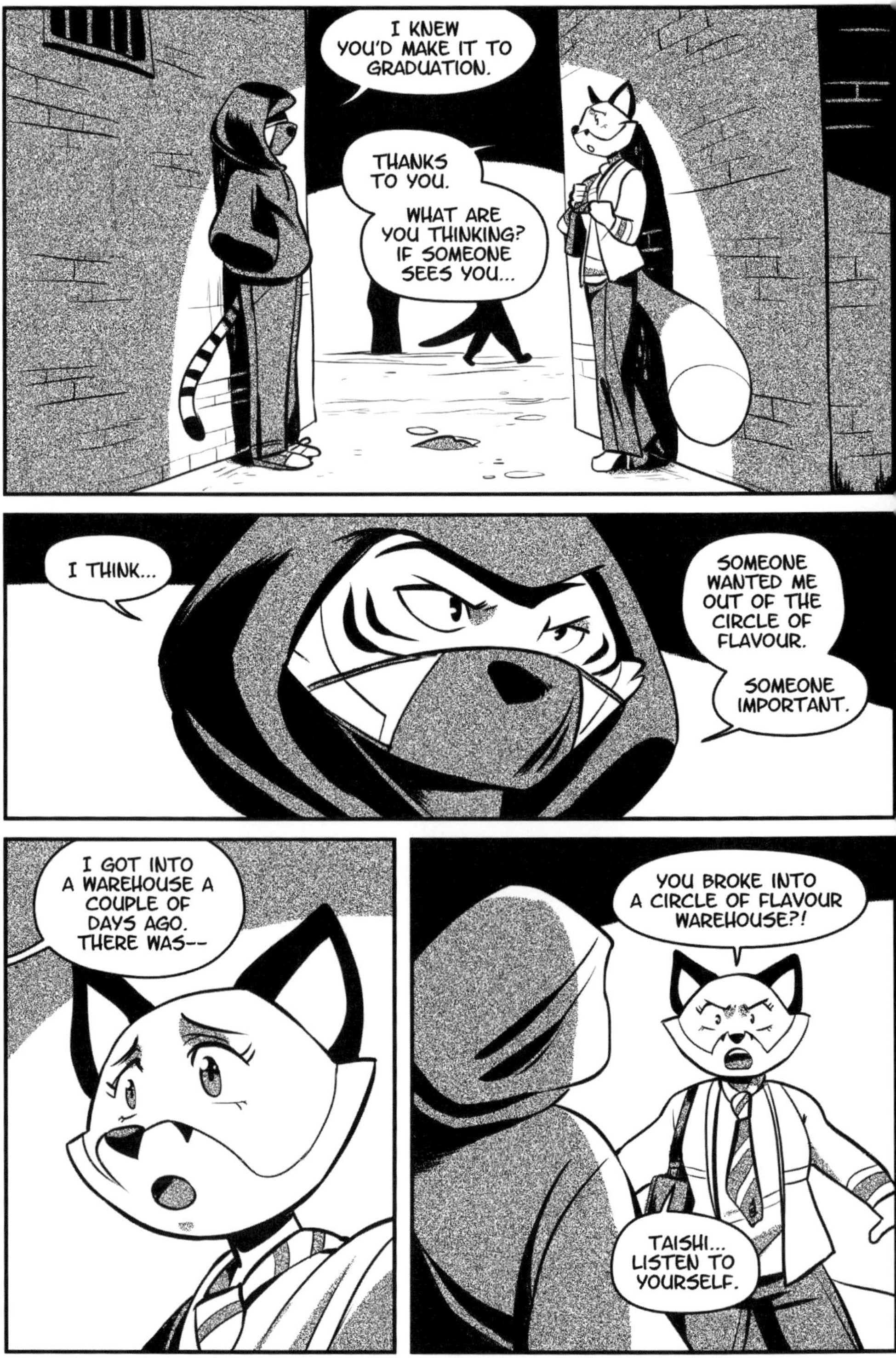

I KNEW YOU'D MAKE IT TO GRADUATION.
THANKS TO YOU.
WHAT ARE YOU THINKING? IF SOMEONE SEES YOU...
I THINK...
SOMEONE WANTED ME OUT OF THE CIRCLE OF FLAVOUR.
SOMEONE IMPORTANT.
I GOT INTO A WAREHOUSE A COUPLE OF DAYS AGO. THERE WAS--
YOU BROKE INTO A CIRCLE OF FLAVOUR WAREHOUSE?!
TAISHI... LISTEN TO YOURSELF.

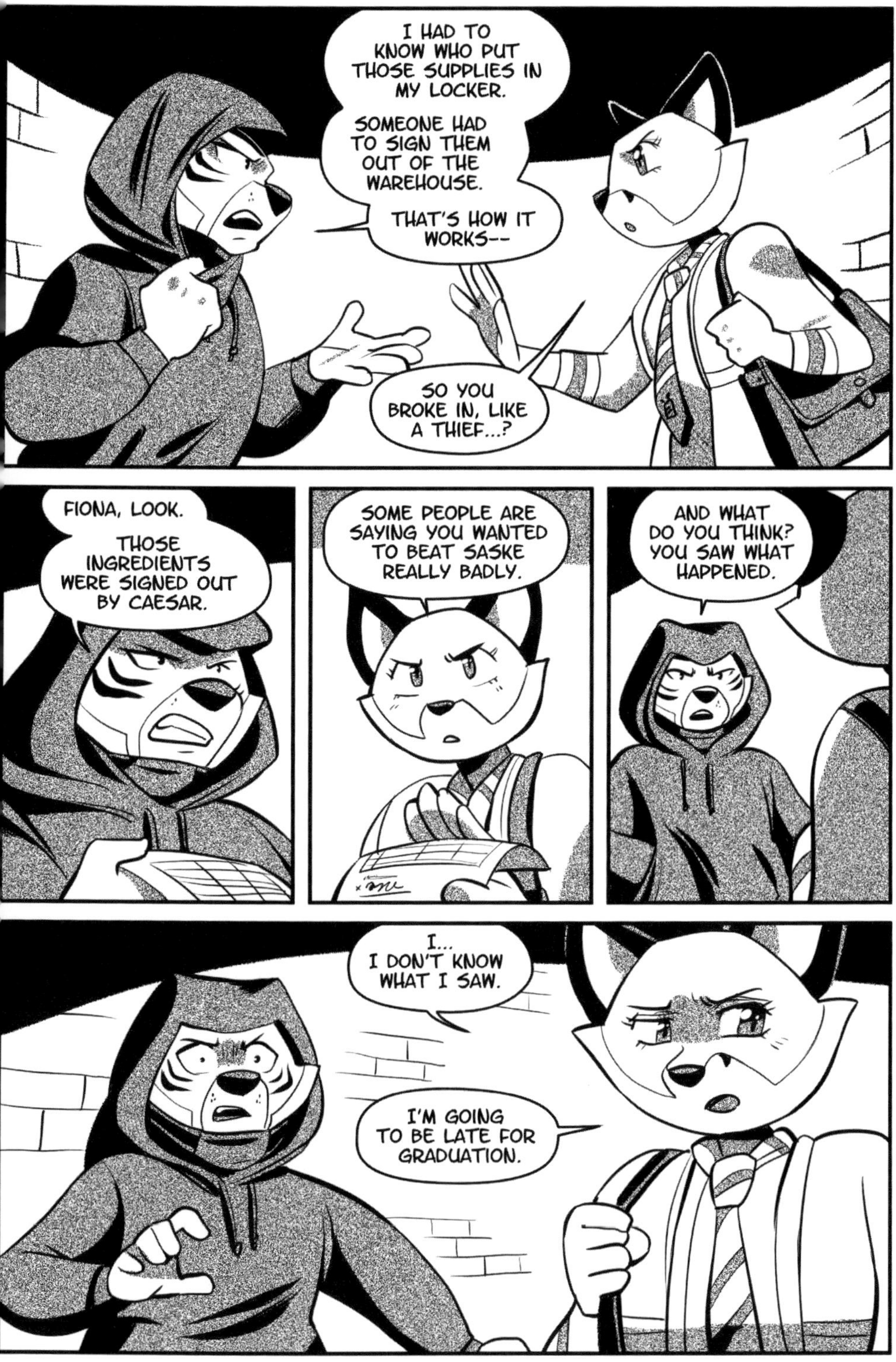
I HAD TO KNOW WHO PUT THOSE SUPPLIES IN MY LOCKER.
SOMEONE HAD TO SIGN THEM OUT OF THE WAREHOUSE.
THAT'S HOW IT WORKS--
SO YOU BROKE IN, LIKE A THIEF...?
FIONA, LOOK.
THOSE INGREDIENTS WERE SIGNED OUT BY CAESAR.
SOME PEOPLE ARE SAYING YOU WANTED TO BEAT SASKE REALLY BADLY.
AND WHAT DO YOU THINK? YOU SAW WHAT HAPPENED.
I... I DON'T KNOW WHAT I SAW.
I'M GOING TO BE LATE FOR GRADUATION.

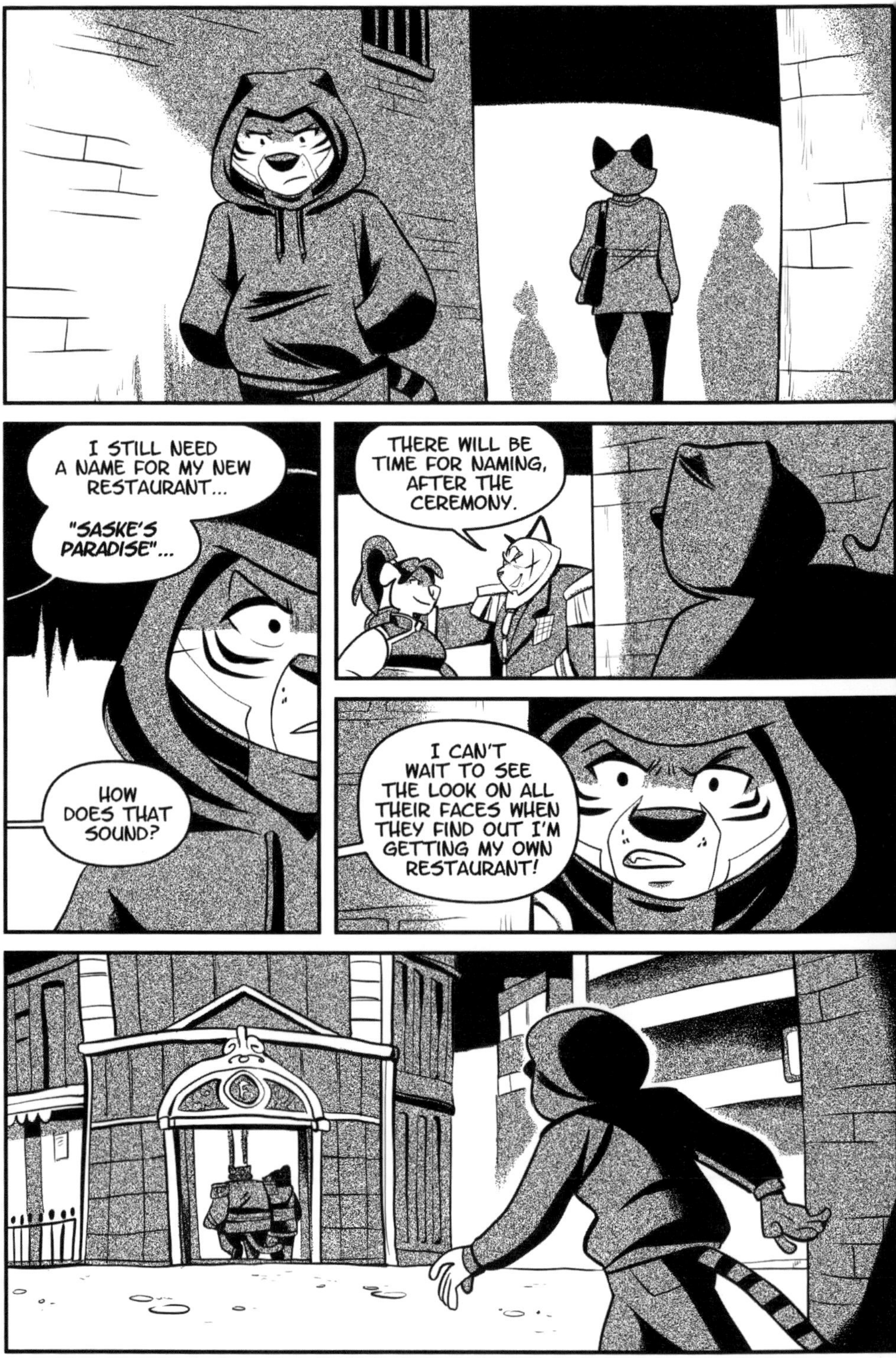
I STILL NEED A NAME FOR MY NEW RESTAURANT...
"SASKE'S PARADISE"...
HOW DOES THAT SOUND?
THERE WILL BE TIME FOR NAMING, AFTER THE CEREMONY.
I CAN'T WAIT TO SEE THE LOOK ON ALL THEIR FACES WHEN THEY FIND OUT I'M GETTING MY OWN RESTAURANT!

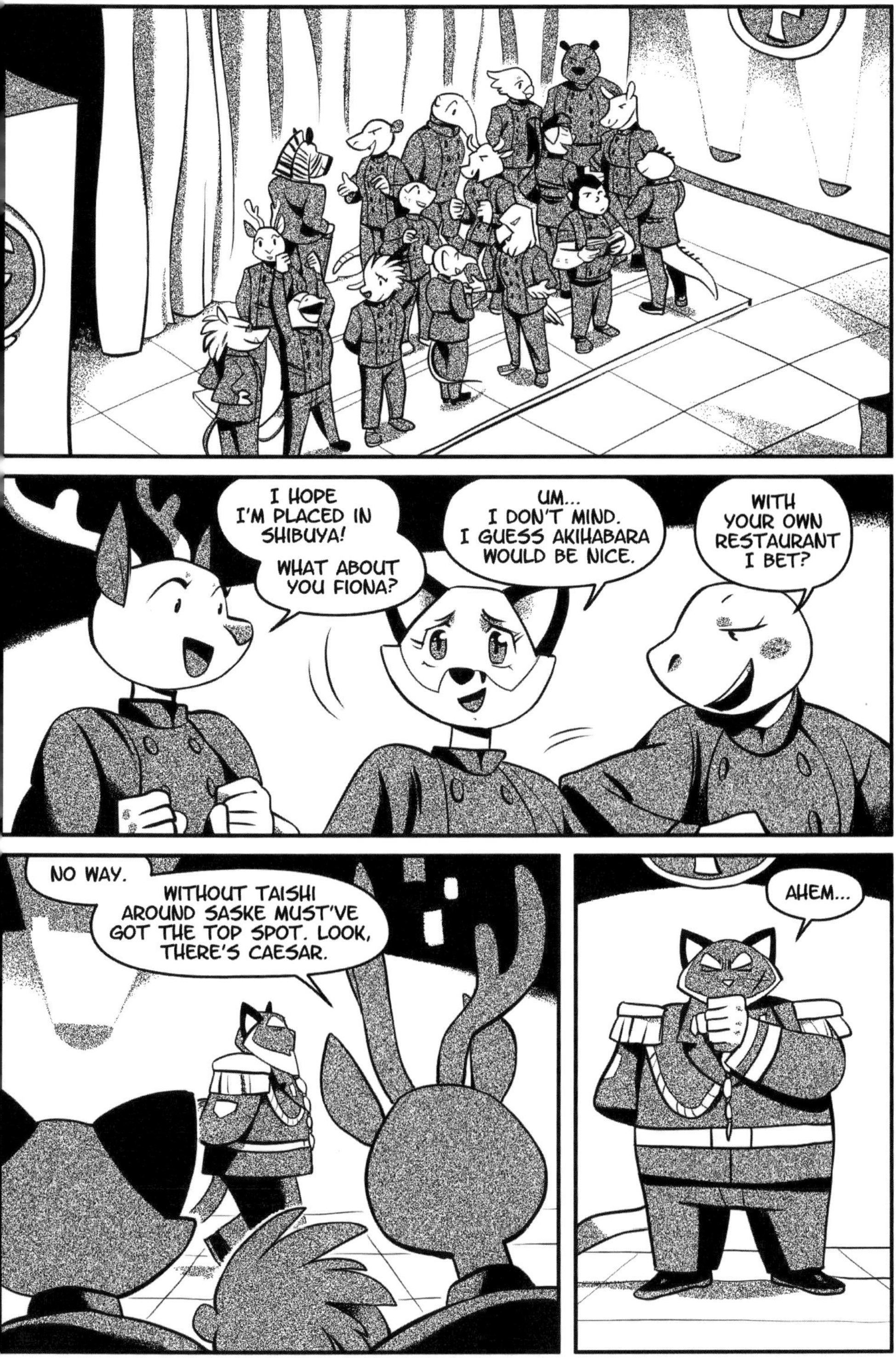

I HOPE I'M PLACED IN SHIBUYA!
WHAT ABOUT YOU FIONA?
UM... I DON'T MIND. I GUESS AKIHABARA WOULD BE NICE.
WITH YOUR OWN RESTAURANT I BET?
NO WAY.
WITHOUT TAISHI AROUND SASKE MUST'VE GOT THE TOP SPOT. LOOK, THERE'S CAESAR.
AHEM...

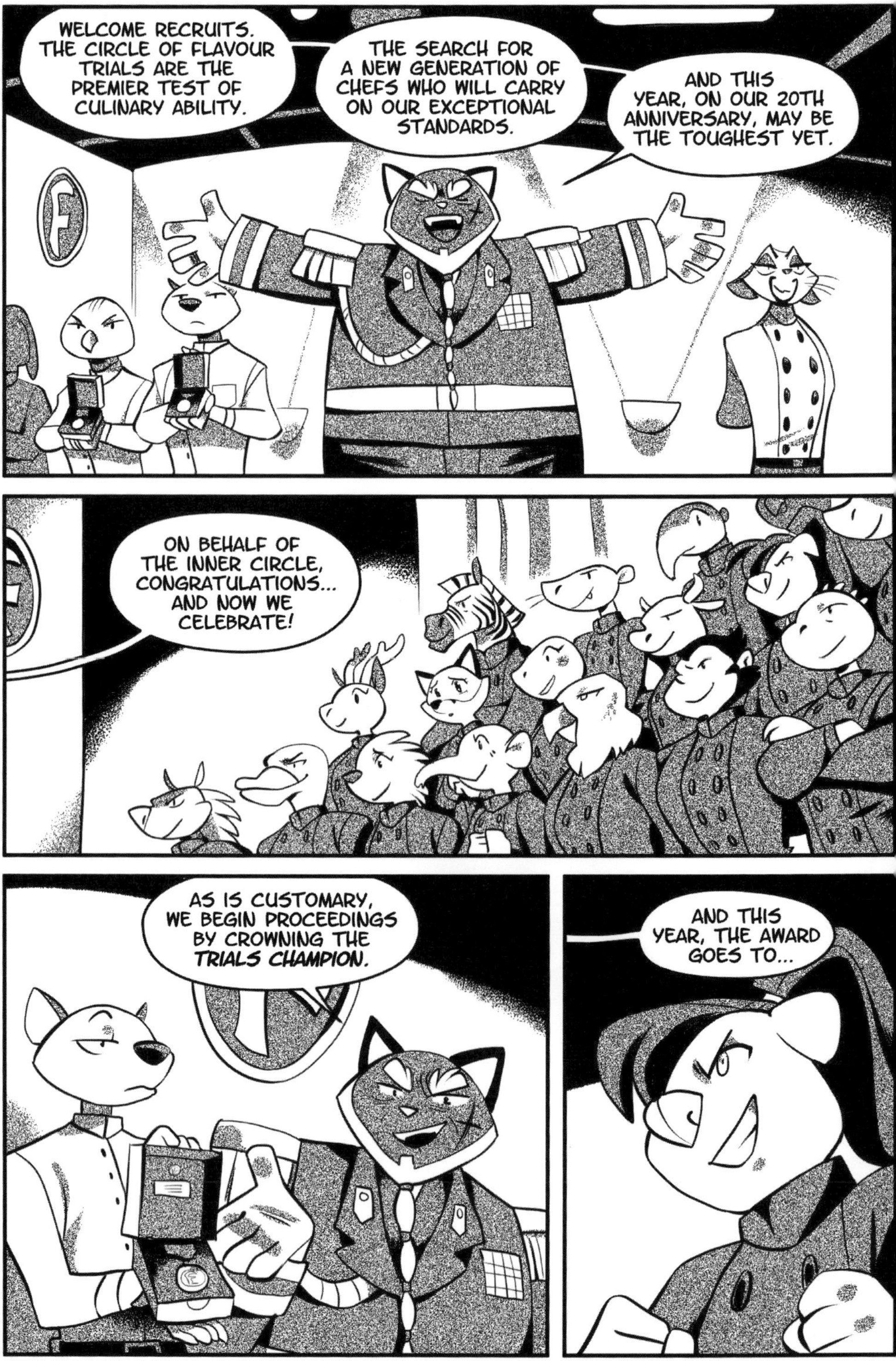
WELCOME RECRUITS. THE CIRCLE OF FLAVOUR TRIALS ARE THE PREMIER TEST OF CULINARY ABILITY.
THE SEARCH FOR A NEW GENERATION OF CHEFS WHO WILL CARRY ON OUR EXCEPTIONAL STANDARDS.
AND THIS YEAR, ON OUR 20TH ANNIVERSARY, MAY BE THE TOUGHEST YET.
ON BEHALF OF THE INNER CIRCLE, CONGRATULATIONS... AND NOW WE CELEBRATE!
AS IS CUSTOMARY, WE BEGIN PROCEEDINGS BY CROWNING THE *TRIALS CHAMPION*.
AND THIS YEAR, THE AWARD GOES TO...

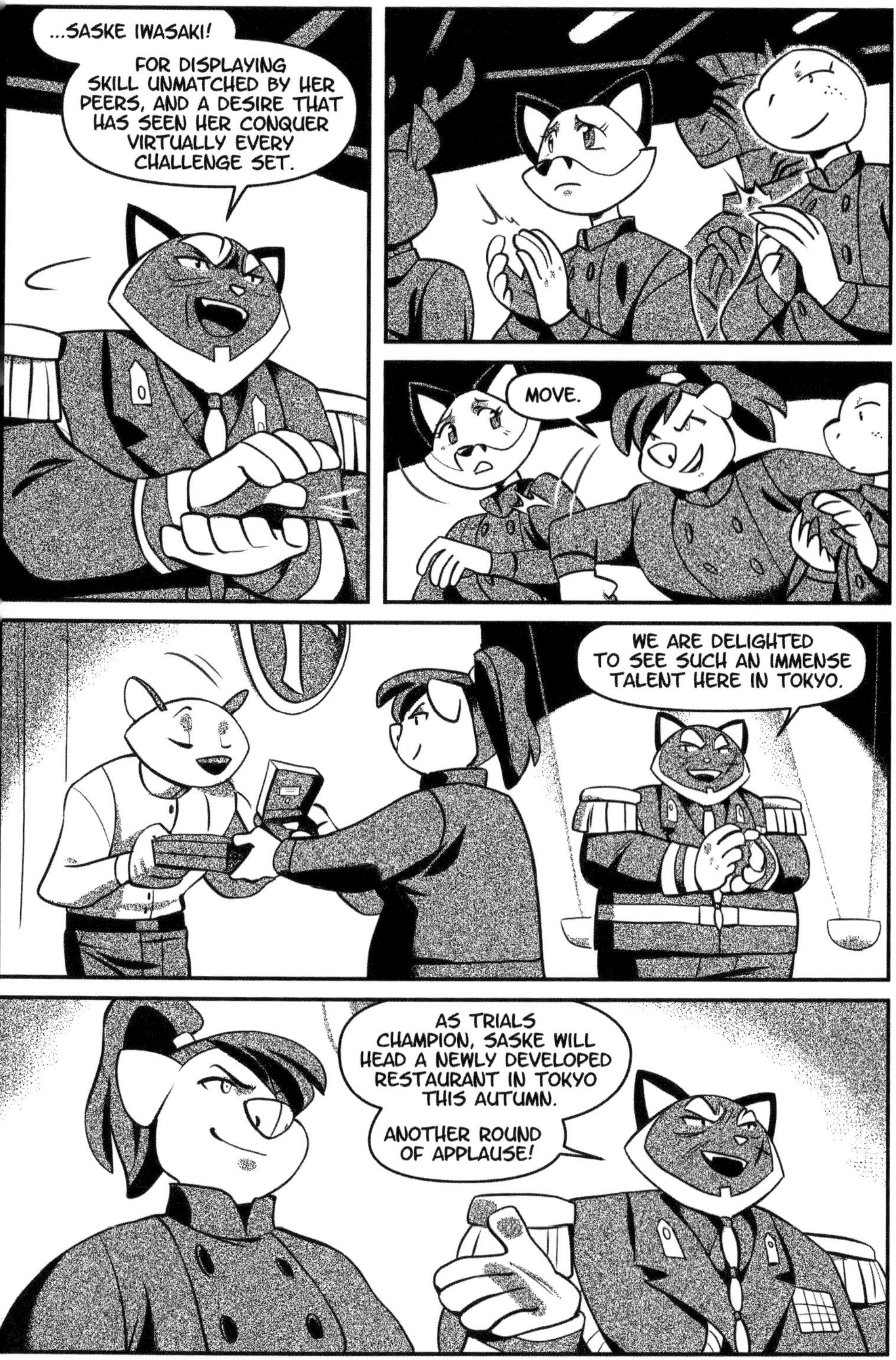
...SASKE IWASAKI!
FOR DISPLAYING SKILL UNMATCHED BY HER PEERS, AND A DESIRE THAT HAS SEEN HER CONQUER VIRTUALLY EVERY CHALLENGE SET.
MOVE.
WE ARE DELIGHTED TO SEE SUCH AN IMMENSE TALENT HERE IN TOKYO.
AS TRIALS CHAMPION, SASKE WILL HEAD A NEWLY DEVELOPED RESTAURANT IN TOKYO THIS AUTUMN.
ANOTHER ROUND OF APPLAUSE!

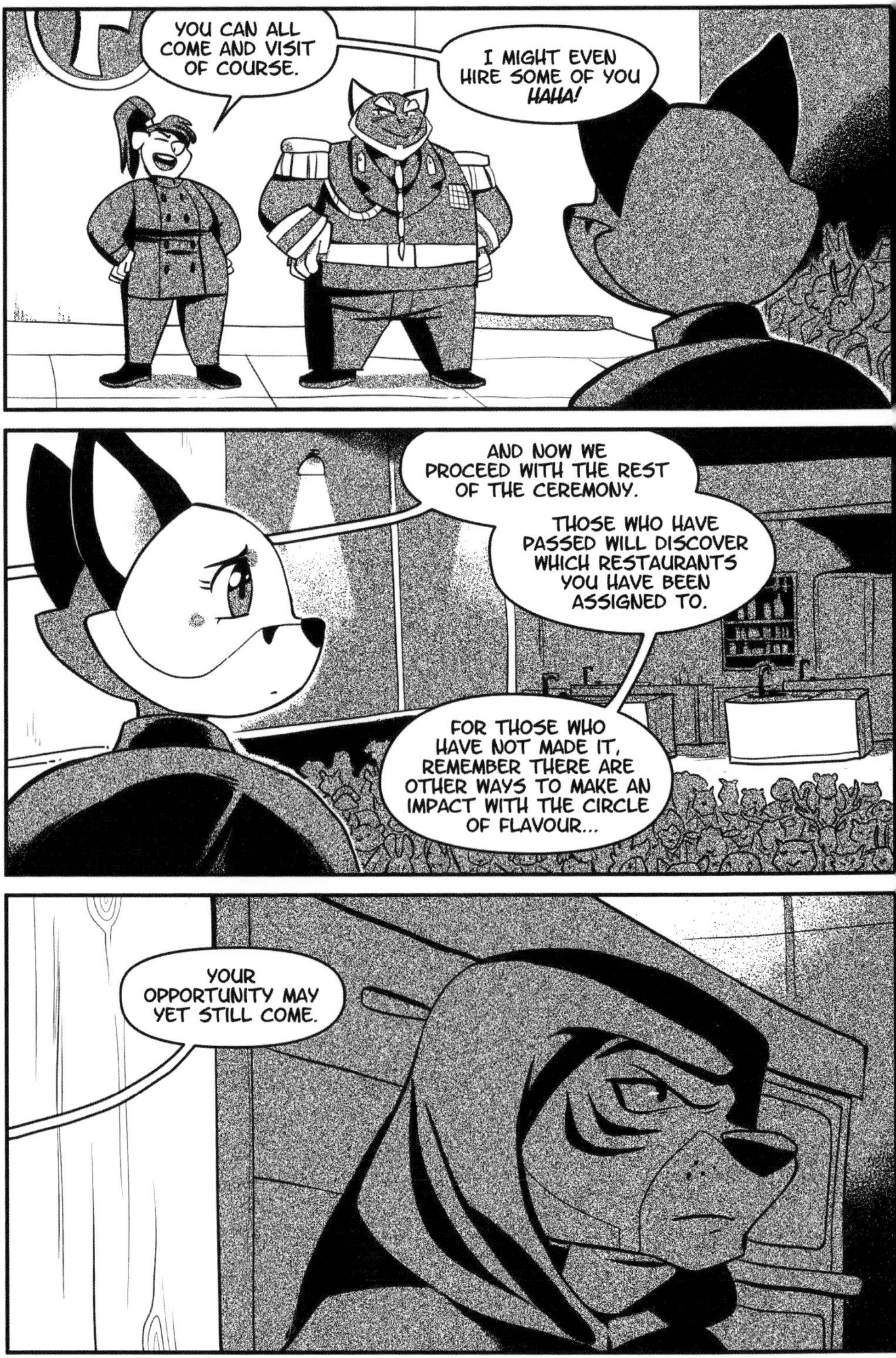
YOU CAN ALL COME AND VISIT OF COURSE.
I MIGHT EVEN HIRE SOME OF YOU *HAHA!*
AND NOW WE PROCEED WITH THE REST OF THE CEREMONY.
THOSE WHO HAVE PASSED WILL DISCOVER WHICH RESTAURANTS YOU HAVE BEEN ASSIGNED TO.
FOR THOSE WHO HAVE NOT MADE IT, REMEMBER THERE ARE OTHER WAYS TO MAKE AN IMPACT WITH THE CIRCLE OF FLAVOUR...
YOUR OPPORTUNITY MAY YET STILL COME.

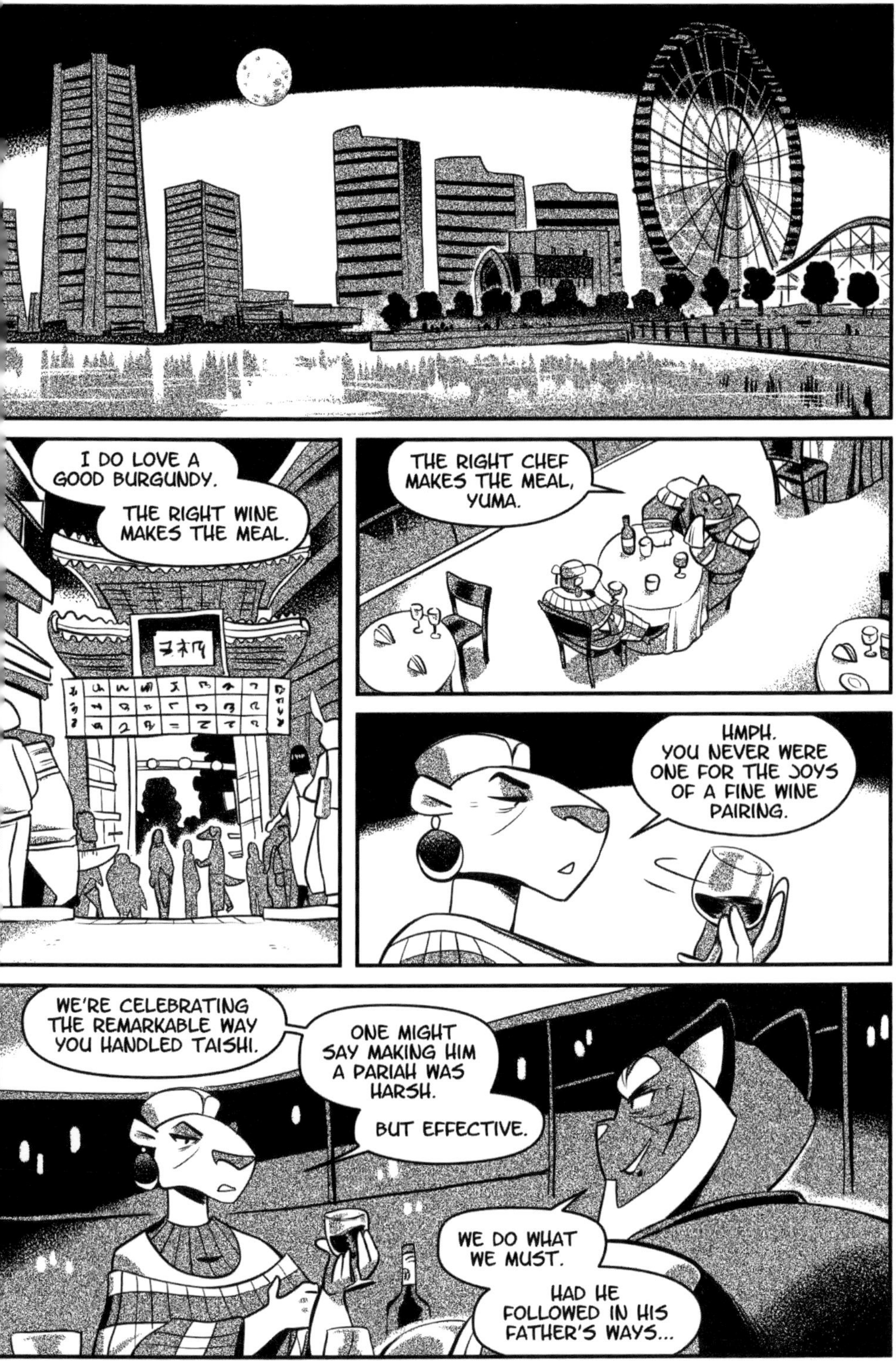

I DO LOVE A GOOD BURGUNDY.
THE RIGHT WINE MAKES THE MEAL.
THE RIGHT CHEF MAKES THE MEAL, YUMA.
HMPH. YOU NEVER WERE ONE FOR THE JOYS OF A FINE WINE PAIRING.
WE'RE CELEBRATING THE REMARKABLE WAY YOU HANDLED TAISHI.
ONE MIGHT SAY MAKING HIM A PARIAH WAS HARSH.
BUT EFFECTIVE.
WE DO WHAT WE MUST.
HAD HE FOLLOWED IN HIS FATHER'S WAYS...

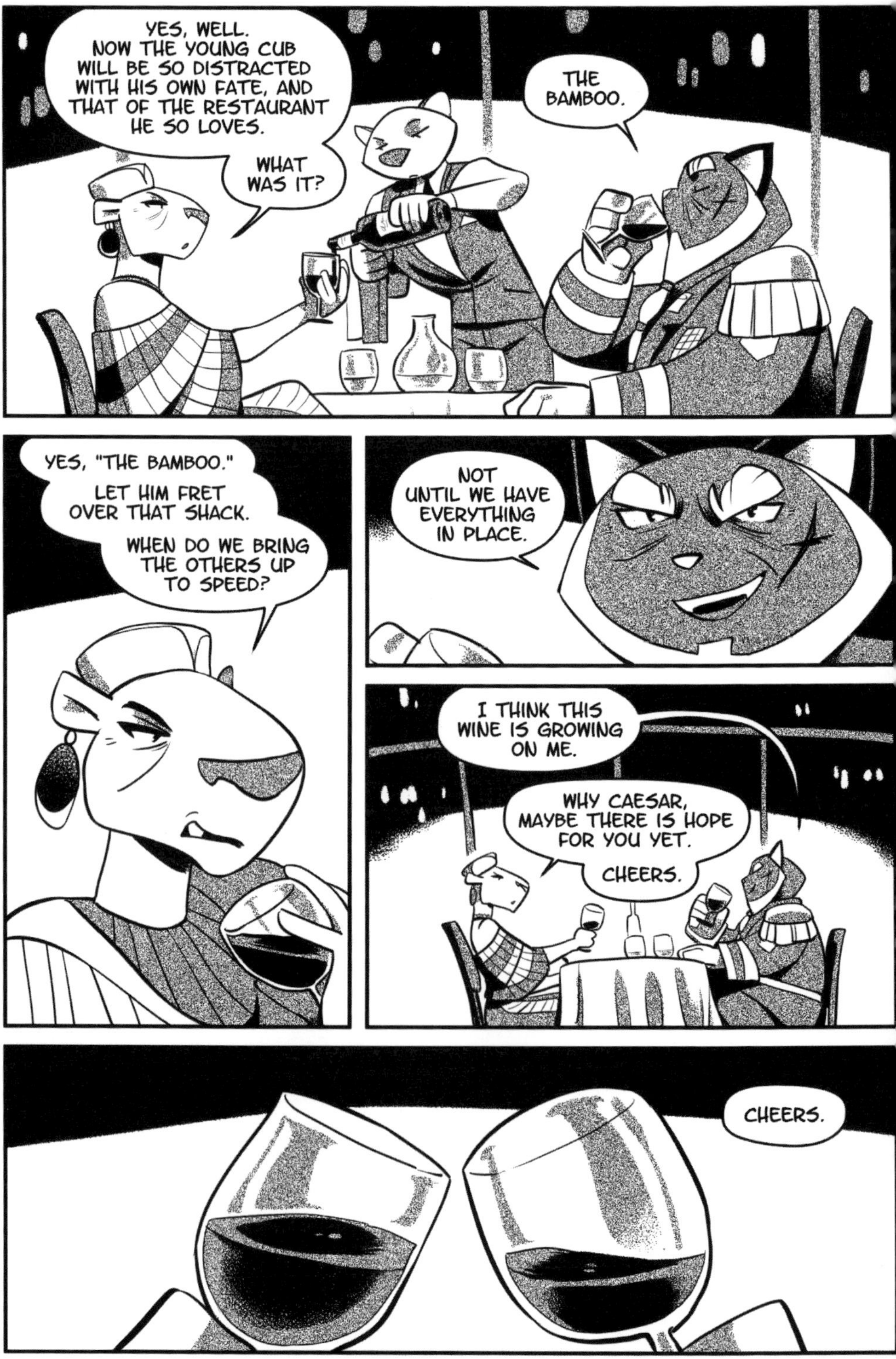
YES, WELL. NOW THE YOUNG CUB WILL BE SO DISTRACTED WITH HIS OWN FATE, AND THAT OF THE RESTAURANT HE SO LOVES.
WHAT WAS IT?
THE BAMBOO.
YES, "THE BAMBOO."
LET HIM FRET OVER THAT SHACK.
WHEN DO WE BRING THE OTHERS UP TO SPEED?
NOT UNTIL WE HAVE EVERYTHING IN PLACE.
I THINK THIS WINE IS GROWING ON ME.
WHY CAESAR, MAYBE THERE IS HOPE FOR YOU YET.
CHEERS.
CHEERS.

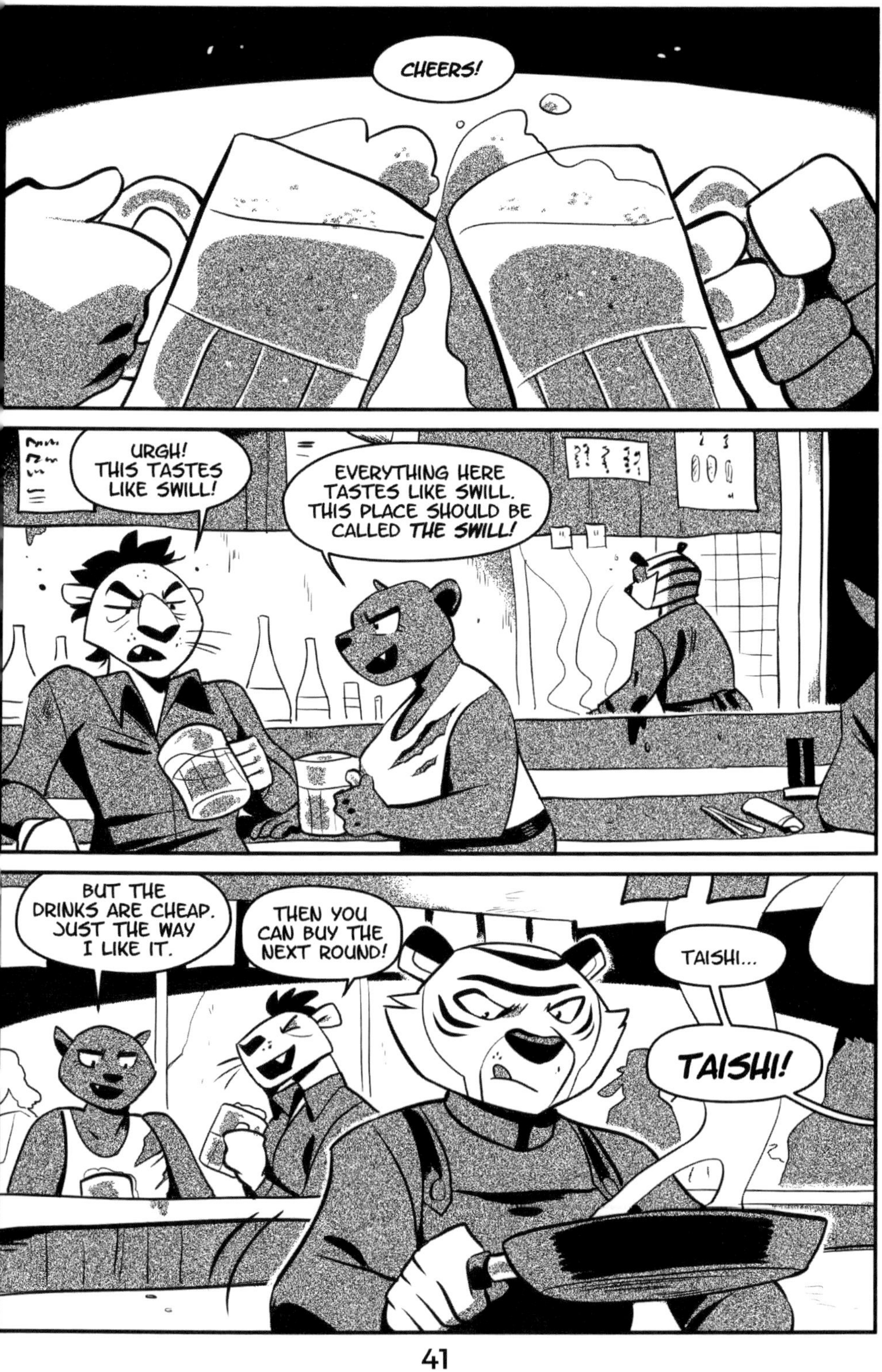
CHEERS!
URGH! THIS TASTES LIKE SWILL!
EVERYTHING HERE TASTES LIKE SWILL. THIS PLACE SHOULD BE CALLED THE SWILL!
BUT THE DRINKS ARE CHEAP. JUST THE WAY I LIKE IT.
THEN YOU CAN BUY THE NEXT ROUND!
TAISHI...
TAISHI!

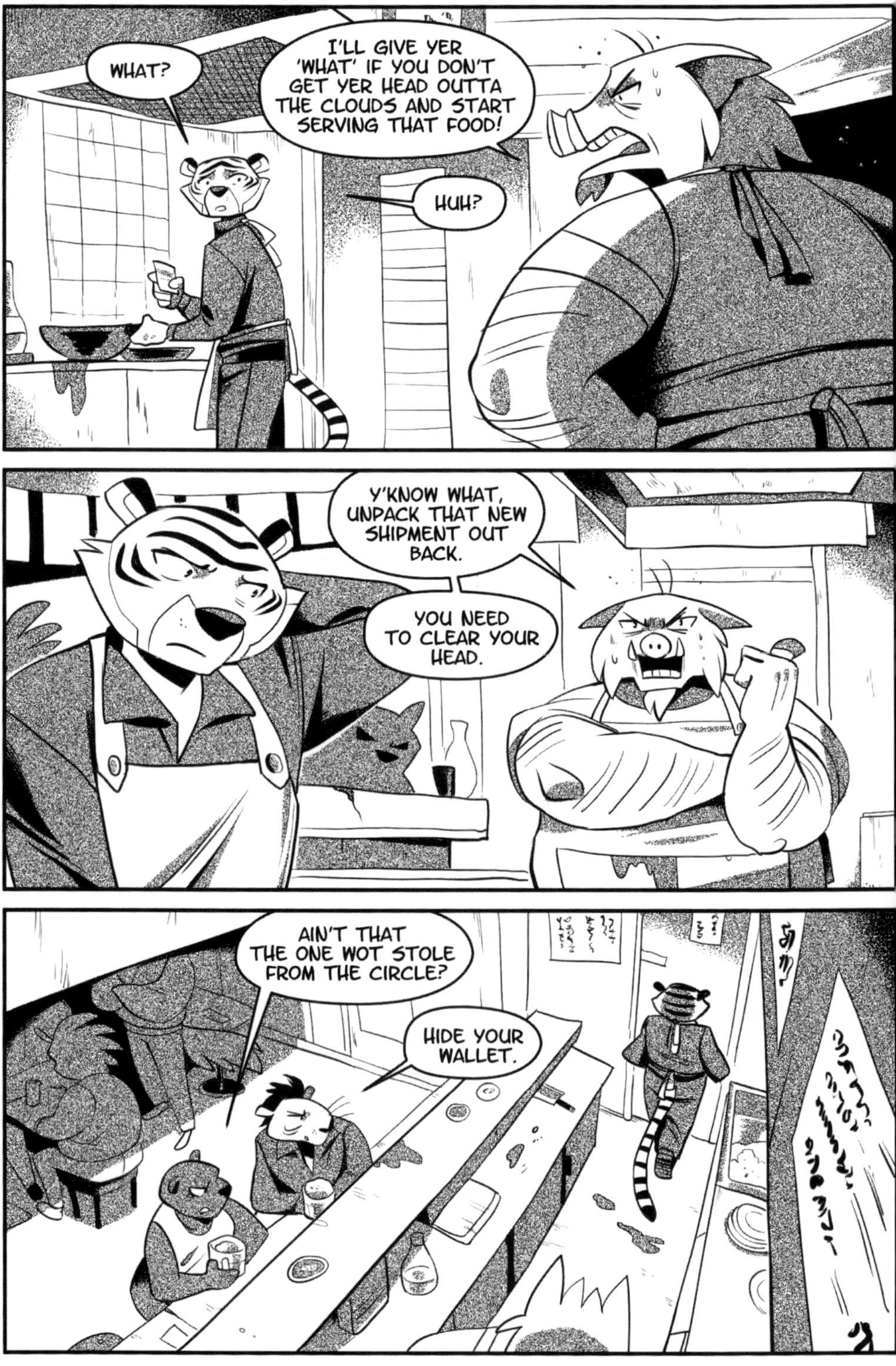
WHAT?
I'LL GIVE YER 'WHAT' IF YOU DON'T GET YER HEAD OUTTA THE CLOUDS AND START SERVING THAT FOOD!
HUH?
Y'KNOW WHAT, UNPACK THAT NEW SHIPMENT OUT BACK.
YOU NEED TO CLEAR YOUR HEAD.
AIN'T THAT THE ONE WOT STOLE FROM THE CIRCLE?
HIDE YOUR WALLET.

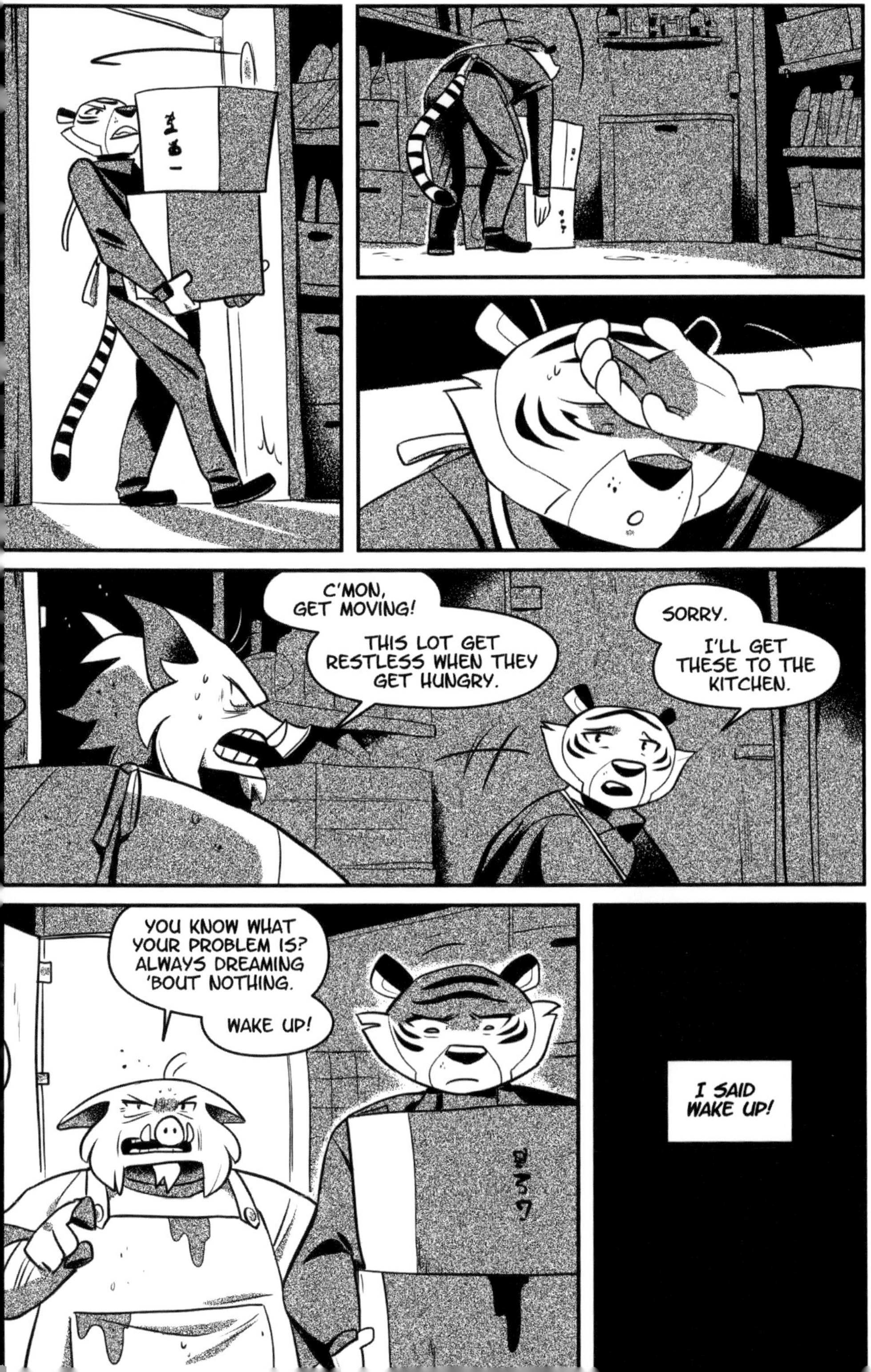
C'MON, GET MOVING!
THIS LOT GET RESTLESS WHEN THEY GET HUNGRY.
SORRY.
I'LL GET THESE TO THE KITCHEN.
YOU KNOW WHAT YOUR PROBLEM IS? ALWAYS DREAMING 'BOUT NOTHING.
WAKE UP!
I SAID WAKE UP!

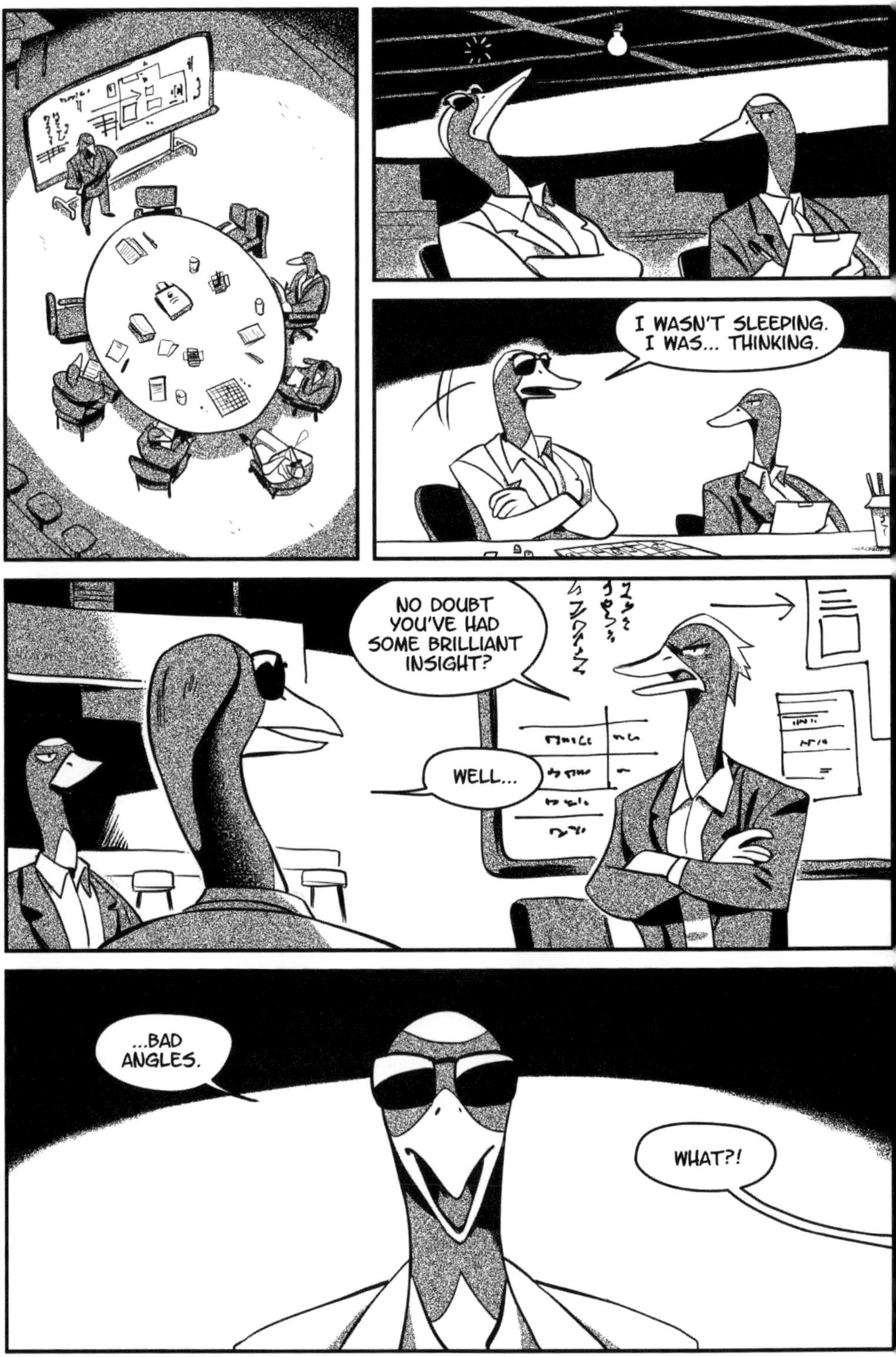
I WASN'T SLEEPING. I WAS... THINKING.
NO DOUBT YOU'VE HAD SOME BRILLIANT INSIGHT?
WELL...
...BAD ANGLES.
WHAT?!

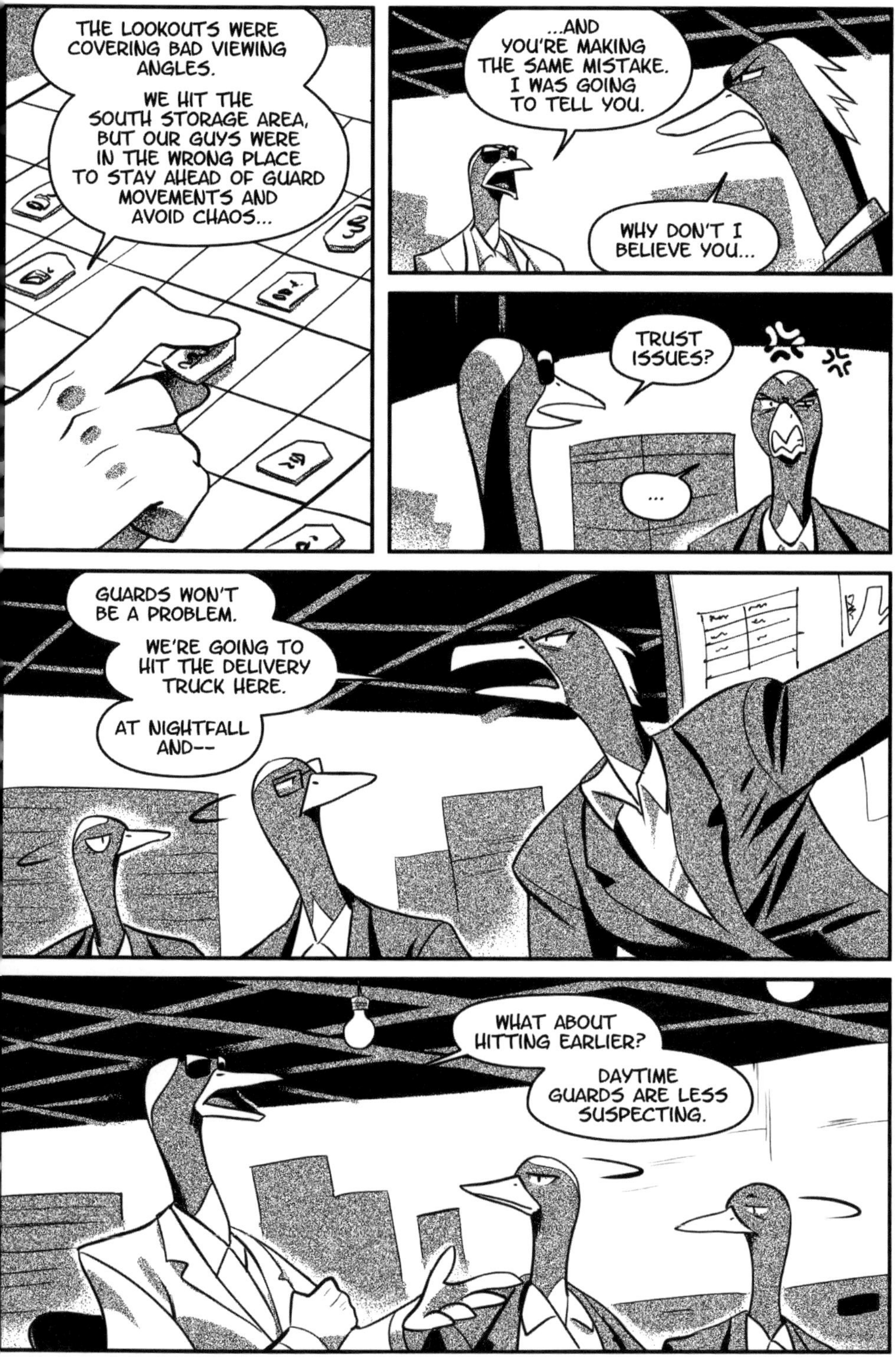
THE LOOKOUTS WERE COVERING BAD VIEWING ANGLES.
WE HIT THE SOUTH STORAGE AREA, BUT OUR GUYS WERE IN THE WRONG PLACE TO STAY AHEAD OF GUARD MOVEMENTS AND AVOID CHAOS...
...AND YOU'RE MAKING THE SAME MISTAKE. I WAS GOING TO TELL YOU.
WHY DON'T I BELIEVE YOU...
TRUST ISSUES?
...
GUARDS WON'T BE A PROBLEM.
WE'RE GOING TO HIT THE DELIVERY TRUCK HERE.
AT NIGHTFALL AND--
WHAT ABOUT HITTING EARLIER?
DAYTIME GUARDS ARE LESS SUSPECTING.

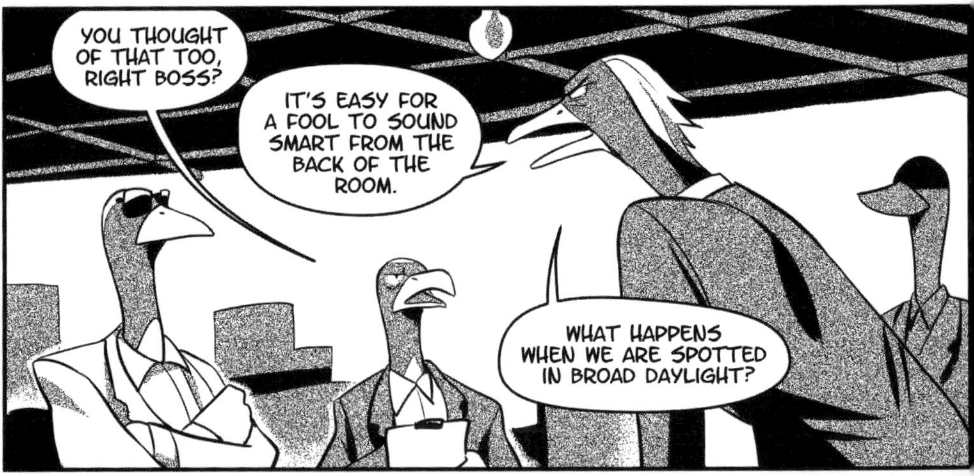
YOU THOUGHT OF THAT TOO, RIGHT BOSS?
IT'S EASY FOR A FOOL TO SOUND SMART FROM THE BACK OF THE ROOM.
WHAT HAPPENS WHEN WE ARE SPOTTED IN BROAD DAYLIGHT?

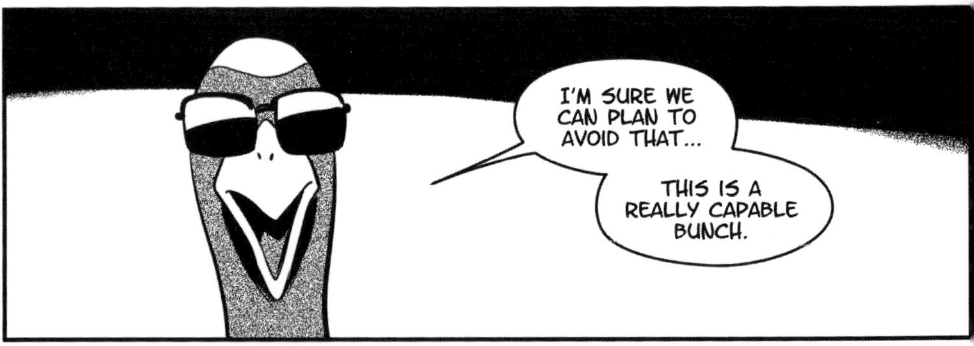
I'M SURE WE CAN PLAN TO AVOID THAT...
THIS IS A REALLY CAPABLE BUNCH.

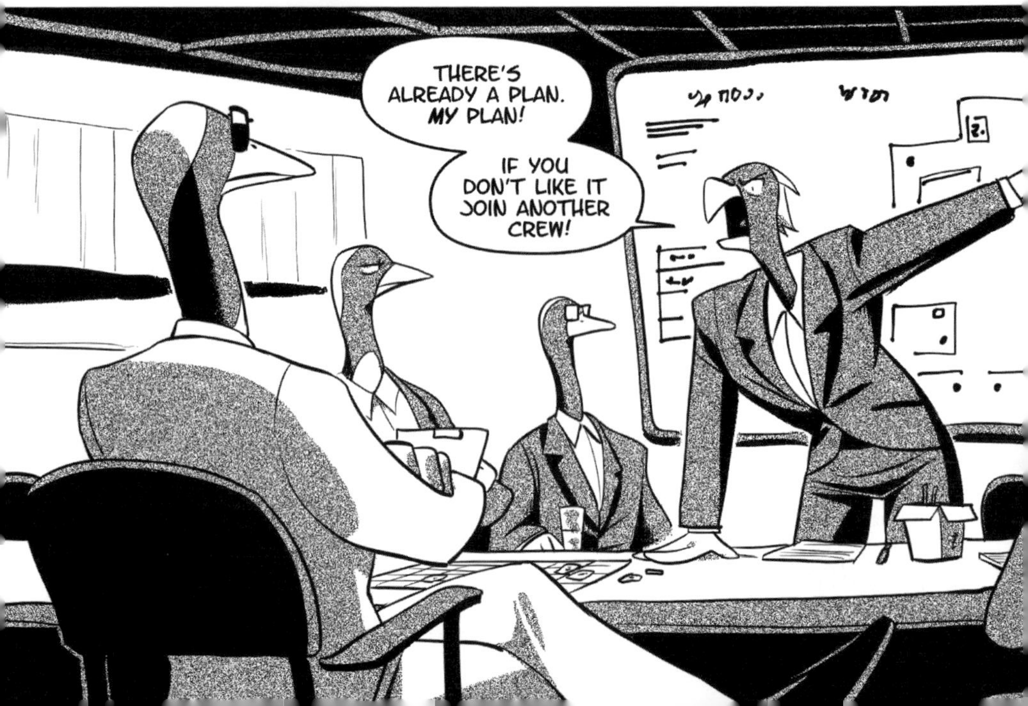
THERE'S ALREADY A PLAN. *MY PLAN!*
IF YOU DON'T LIKE IT JOIN ANOTHER CREW!

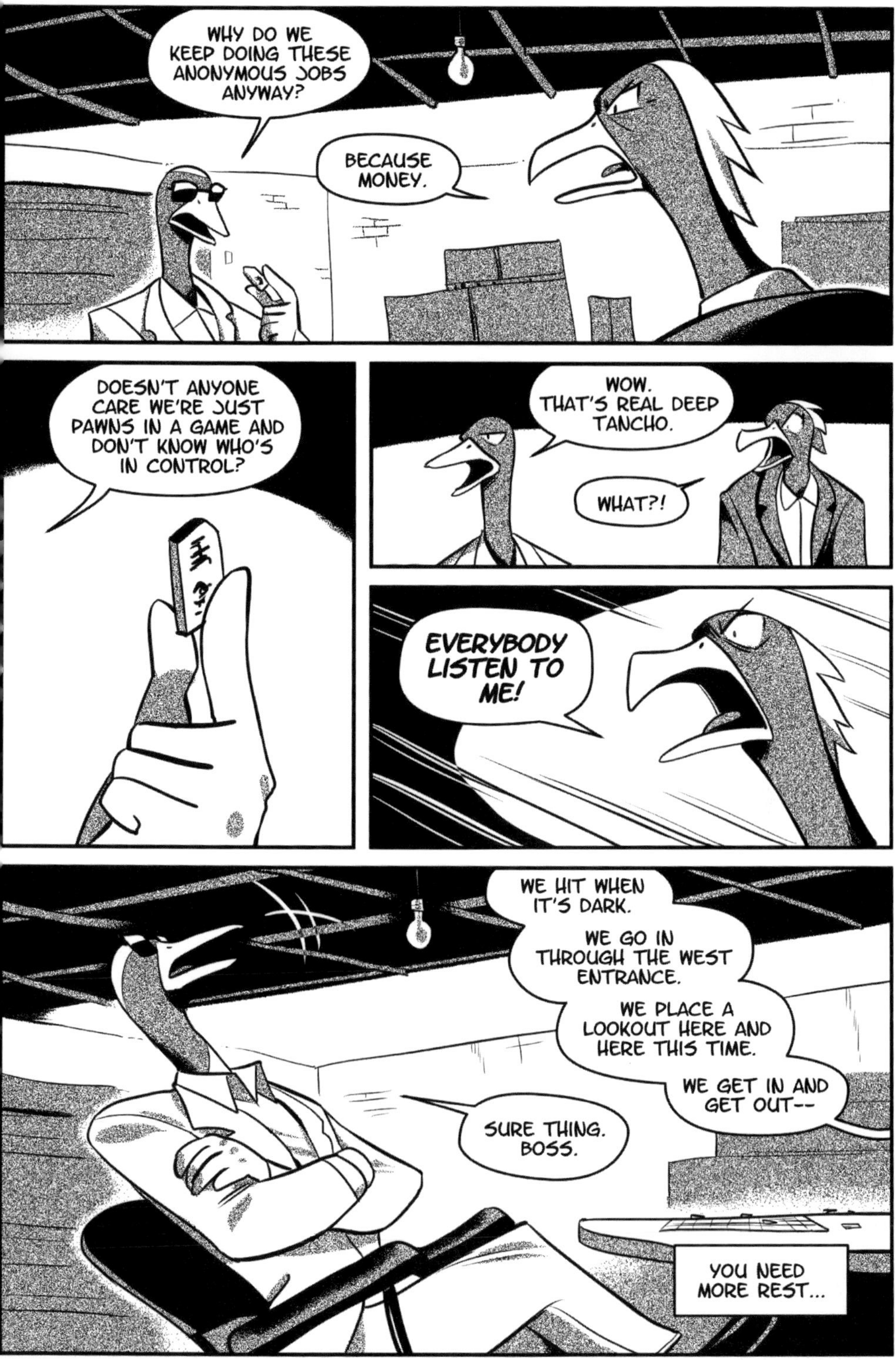
WHY DO WE KEEP DOING THESE ANONYMOUS JOBS ANYWAY?
BECAUSE MONEY.
DOESN'T ANYONE CARE WE'RE JUST PAWNS IN A GAME AND DON'T KNOW WHO'S IN CONTROL?
WOW. THAT'S REAL DEEP TANCHO.
WHAT?!
EVERYBODY LISTEN TO ME!
WE HIT WHEN IT'S DARK.
WE GO IN THROUGH THE WEST ENTRANCE.
WE PLACE A LOOKOUT HERE AND HERE THIS TIME.
WE GET IN AND GET OUT--
SURE THING. BOSS.
YOU NEED MORE REST...

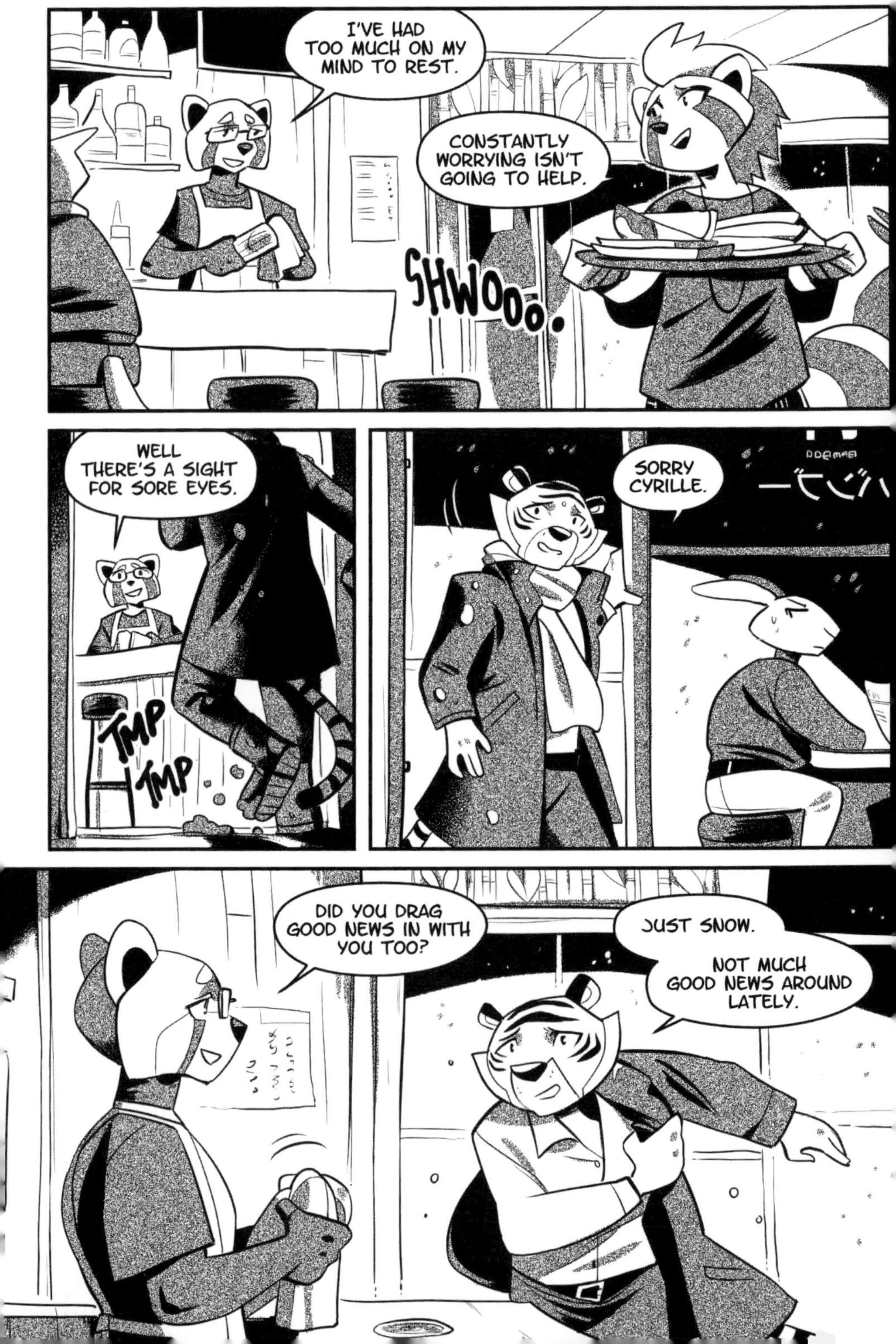
I'VE HAD TOO MUCH ON MY MIND TO REST.
CONSTANTLY WORRYING ISN'T GOING TO HELP.
SHWOOO.
WELL THERE'S A SIGHT FOR SORE EYES.
TMP TMP
SORRY CYRILLE.
DID YOU DRAG GOOD NEWS IN WITH YOU TOO?
JUST SNOW.
NOT MUCH GOOD NEWS AROUND LATELY.

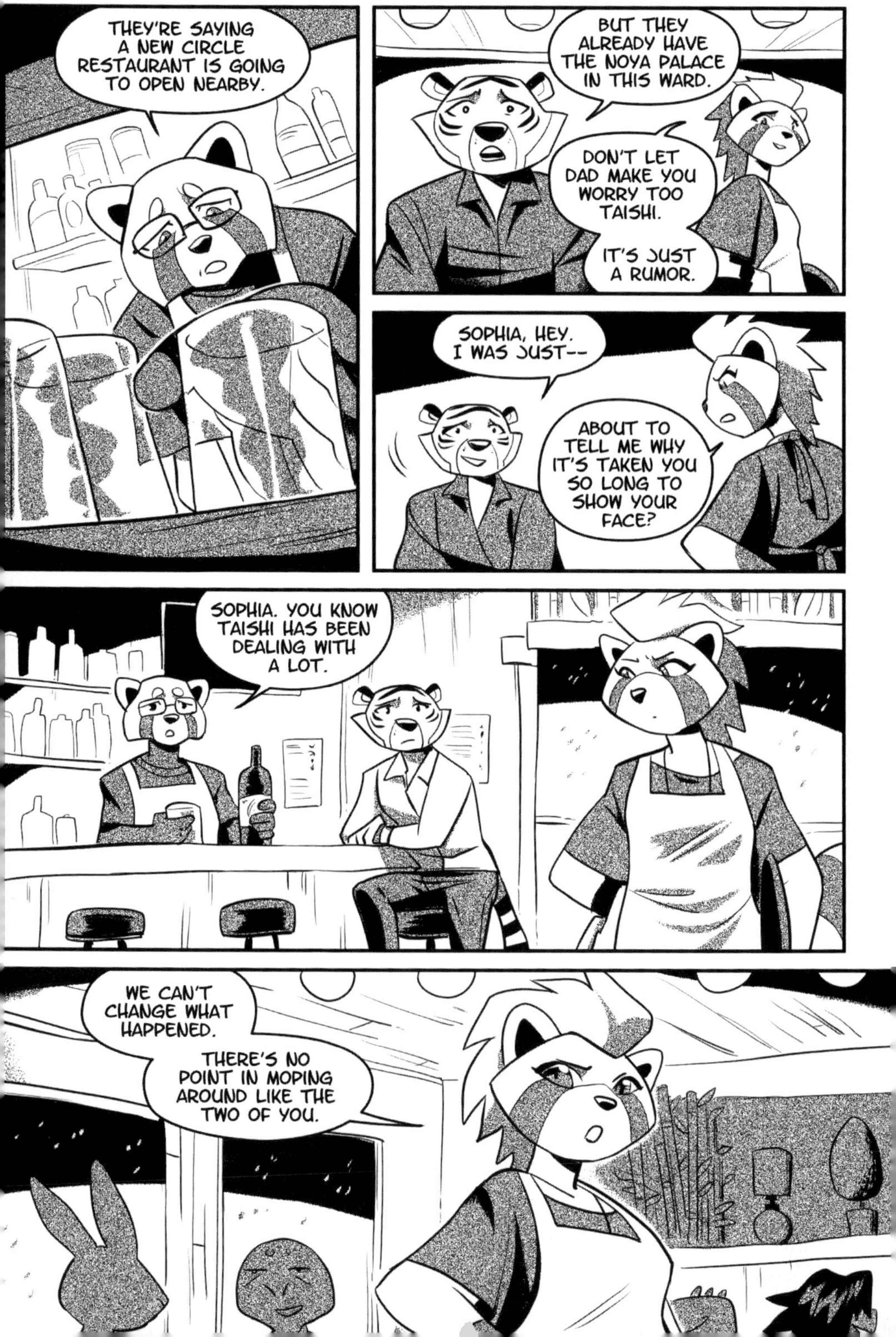
THEY'RE SAYING A NEW CIRCLE RESTAURANT IS GOING TO OPEN NEARBY.
BUT THEY ALREADY HAVE THE NOYA PALACE IN THIS WARD.
DON'T LET DAD MAKE YOU WORRY TOO TAISHI.
IT'S JUST A RUMOR.
SOPHIA, HEY. I WAS JUST--
ABOUT TO TELL ME WHY IT'S TAKEN YOU SO LONG TO SHOW YOUR FACE?
SOPHIA. YOU KNOW TAISHI HAS BEEN DEALING WITH A LOT.
WE CAN'T CHANGE WHAT HAPPENED.
THERE'S NO POINT IN MOPING AROUND LIKE THE TWO OF YOU.

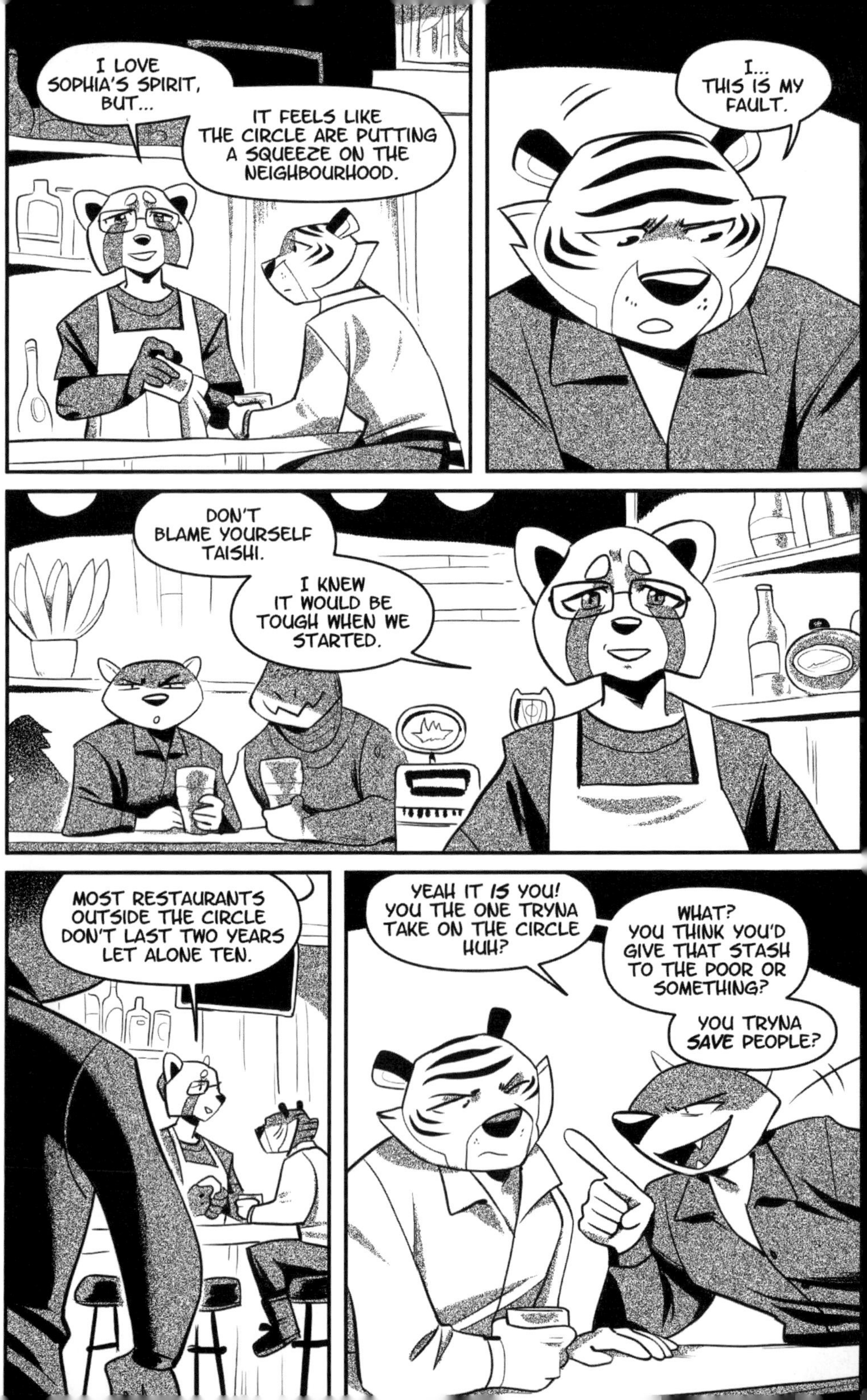
I LOVE SOPHIA'S SPIRIT, BUT...
IT FEELS LIKE THE CIRCLE ARE PUTTING A SQUEEZE ON THE NEIGHBOURHOOD.
I... THIS IS MY FAULT.
DON'T BLAME YOURSELF TAISHI.
I KNEW IT WOULD BE TOUGH WHEN WE STARTED.
MOST RESTAURANTS OUTSIDE THE CIRCLE DON'T LAST TWO YEARS LET ALONE TEN.
YEAH IT *IS* YOU! YOU THE ONE TRYNA TAKE ON THE CIRCLE HUH?
WHAT? YOU THINK YOU'D GIVE THAT STASH TO THE POOR OR SOMETHING?
YOU TRYNA *SAVE* PEOPLE?

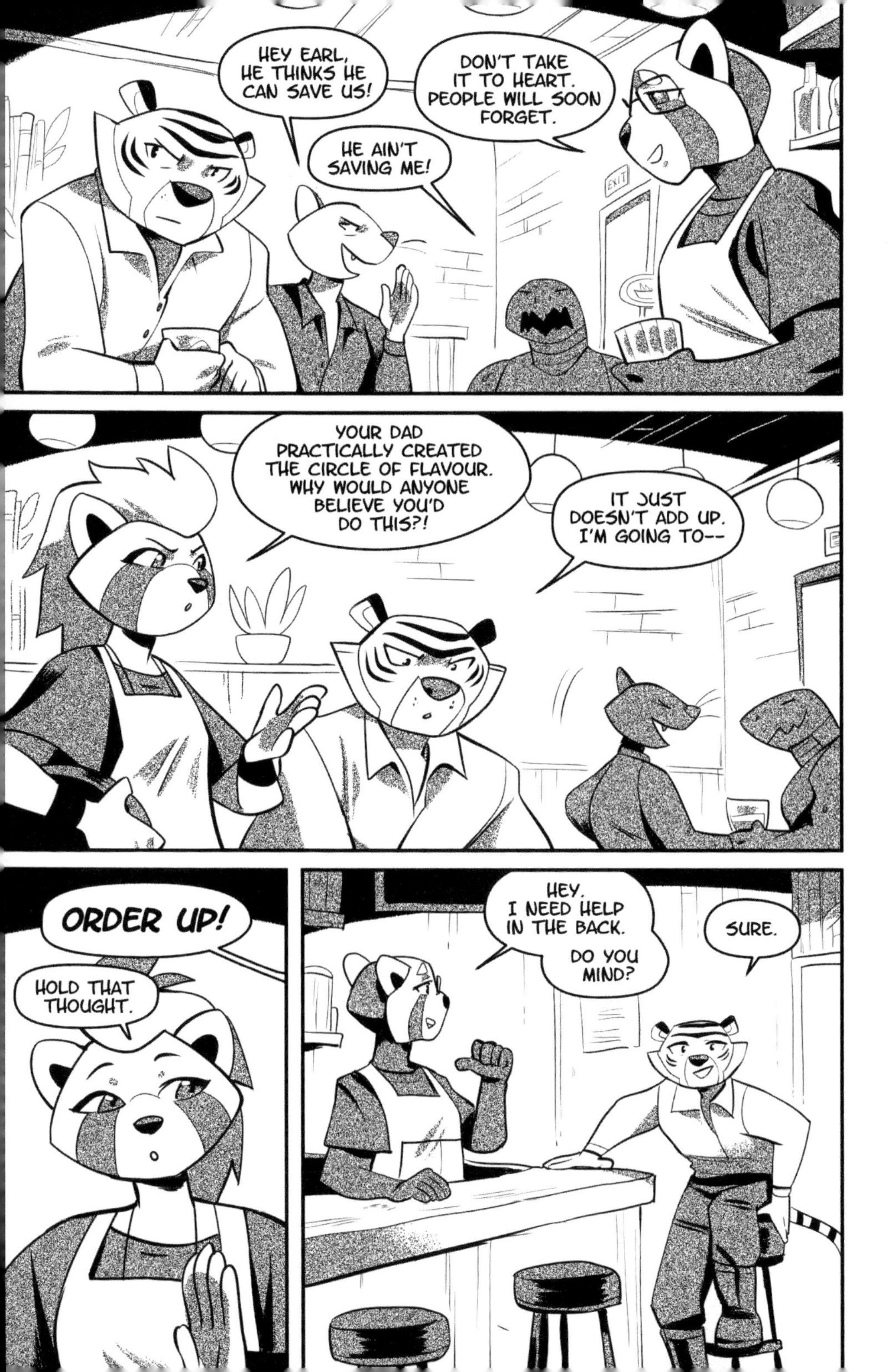
HEY EARL, HE THINKS HE CAN SAVE US!
HE AIN'T SAVING ME!
DON'T TAKE IT TO HEART. PEOPLE WILL SOON FORGET.
EXIT
YOUR DAD PRACTICALLY CREATED THE CIRCLE OF FLAVOUR. WHY WOULD ANYONE BELIEVE YOU'D DO THIS?!
IT JUST DOESN'T ADD UP. I'M GOING TO--
ORDER UP!
HOLD THAT THOUGHT.
HEY. I NEED HELP IN THE BACK.
DO YOU MIND?
SURE.

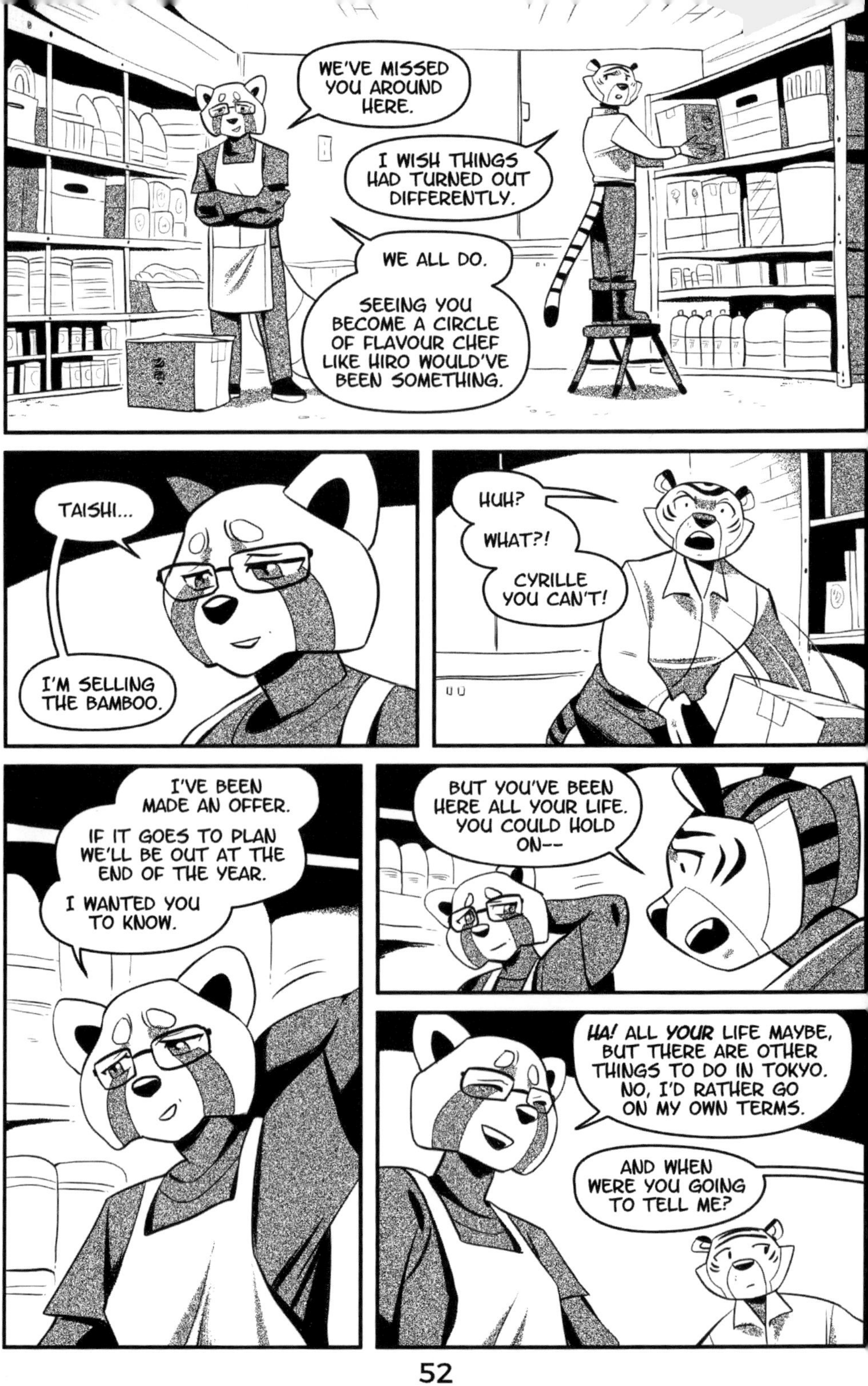
WE'VE MISSED YOU AROUND HERE.
I WISH THINGS HAD TURNED OUT DIFFERENTLY.
WE ALL DO.
SEEING YOU BECOME A CIRCLE OF FLAVOUR CHEF LIKE HIRO WOULD'VE BEEN SOMETHING.
TAISHI...
I'M SELLING THE BAMBOO.
HUH?
WHAT?!
CYRILLE YOU CAN'T!
I'VE BEEN MADE AN OFFER.
IF IT GOES TO PLAN WE'LL BE OUT AT THE END OF THE YEAR.
I WANTED YOU TO KNOW.
BUT YOU'VE BEEN HERE ALL YOUR LIFE. YOU COULD HOLD ON--
HA! ALL *YOUR* LIFE MAYBE, BUT THERE ARE OTHER THINGS TO DO IN TOKYO. NO, I'D RATHER GO ON MY OWN TERMS.
AND WHEN WERE YOU GOING TO TELL ME?

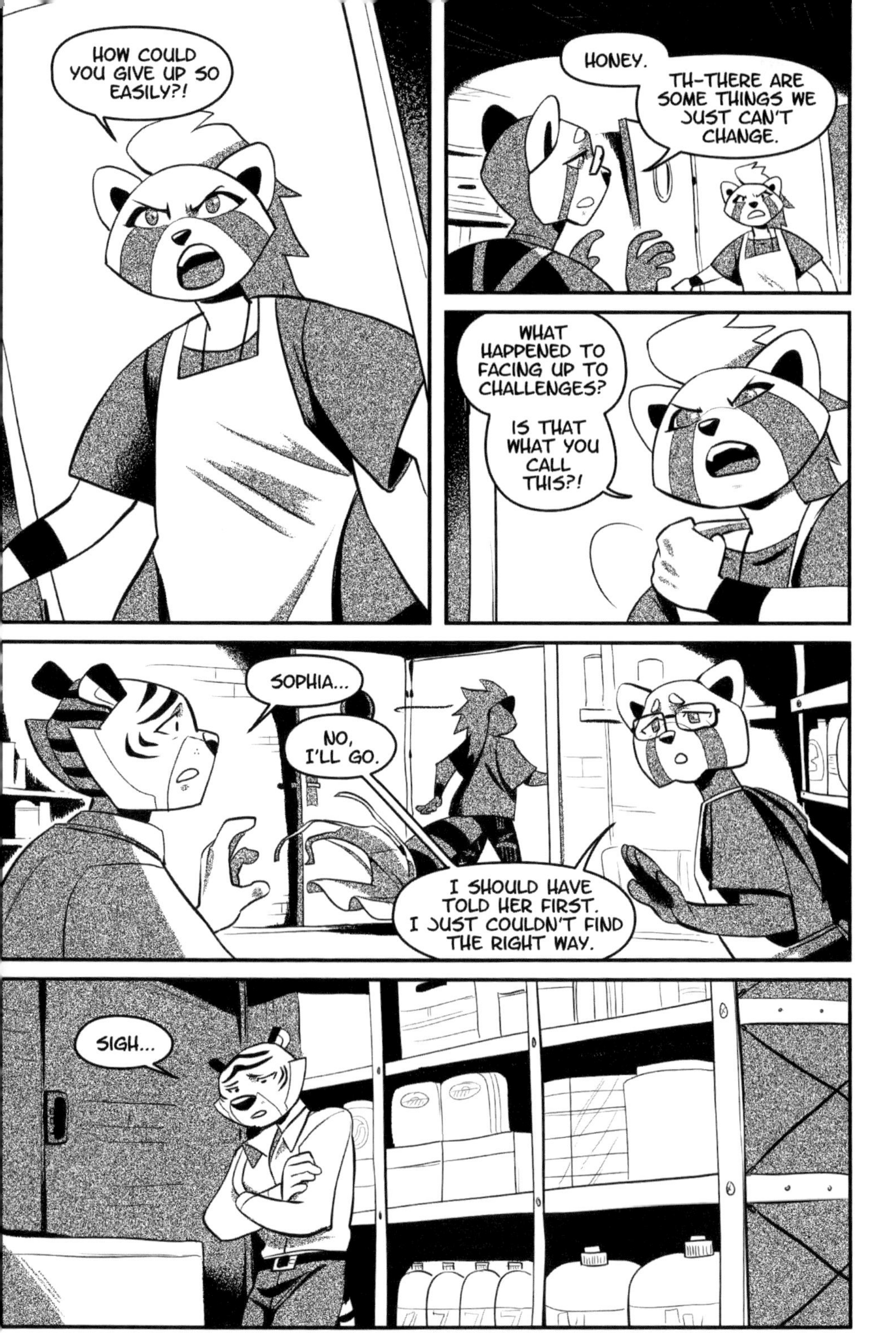
HOW COULD YOU GIVE UP SO EASILY?!
HONEY.
TH-THERE ARE SOME THINGS WE JUST CAN'T CHANGE.
WHAT HAPPENED TO FACING UP TO CHALLENGES?
IS THAT WHAT YOU CALL THIS?!
SOPHIA...
NO, I'LL GO.
I SHOULD HAVE TOLD HER FIRST. I JUST COULDN'T FIND THE RIGHT WAY.
SIGH...

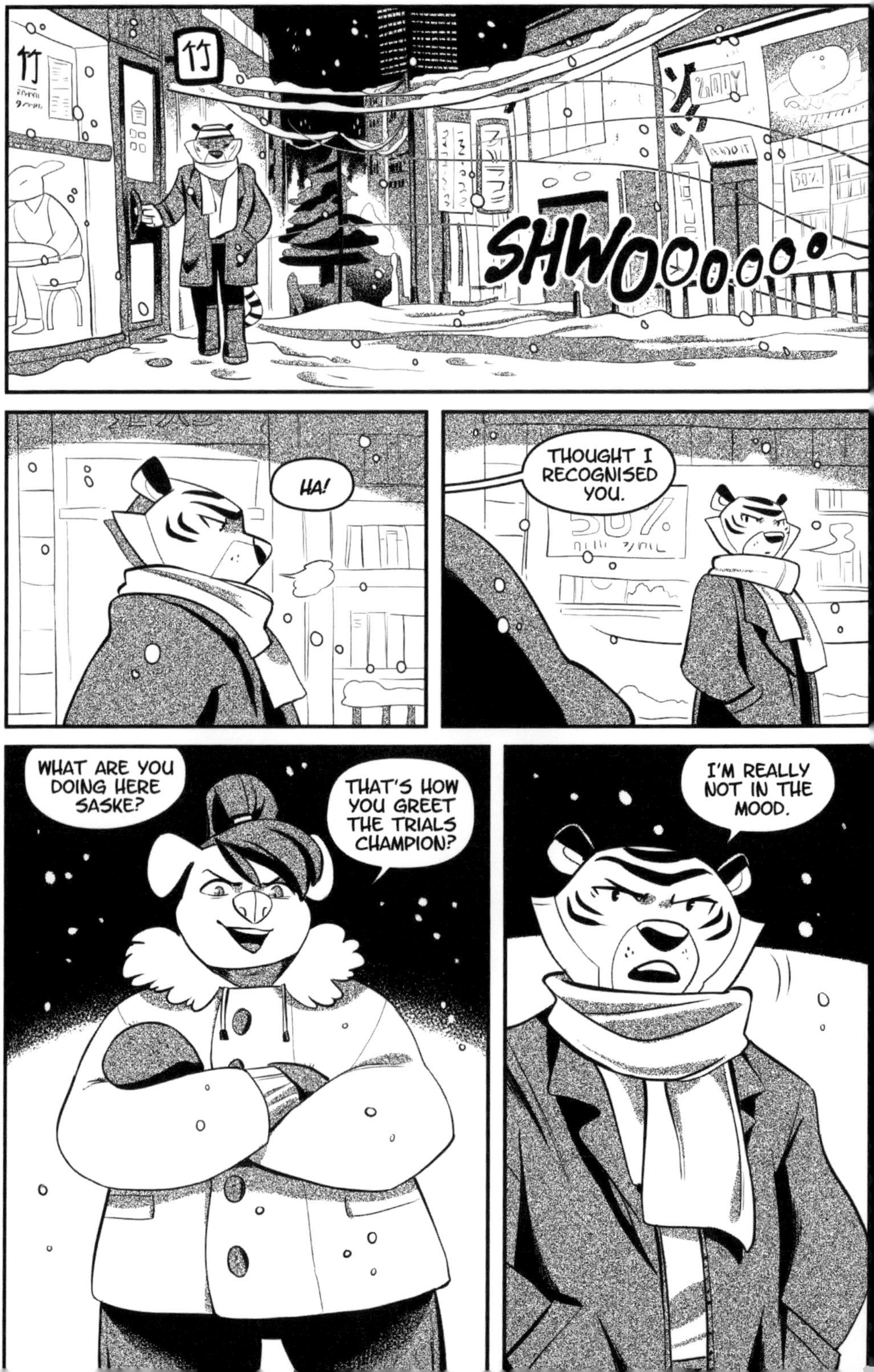
SHWOOOOOO
HA!
THOUGHT I RECOGNISED YOU.
WHAT ARE YOU DOING HERE SASKE?
THAT'S HOW YOU GREET THE TRIALS CHAMPION?
I'M REALLY NOT IN THE MOOD.

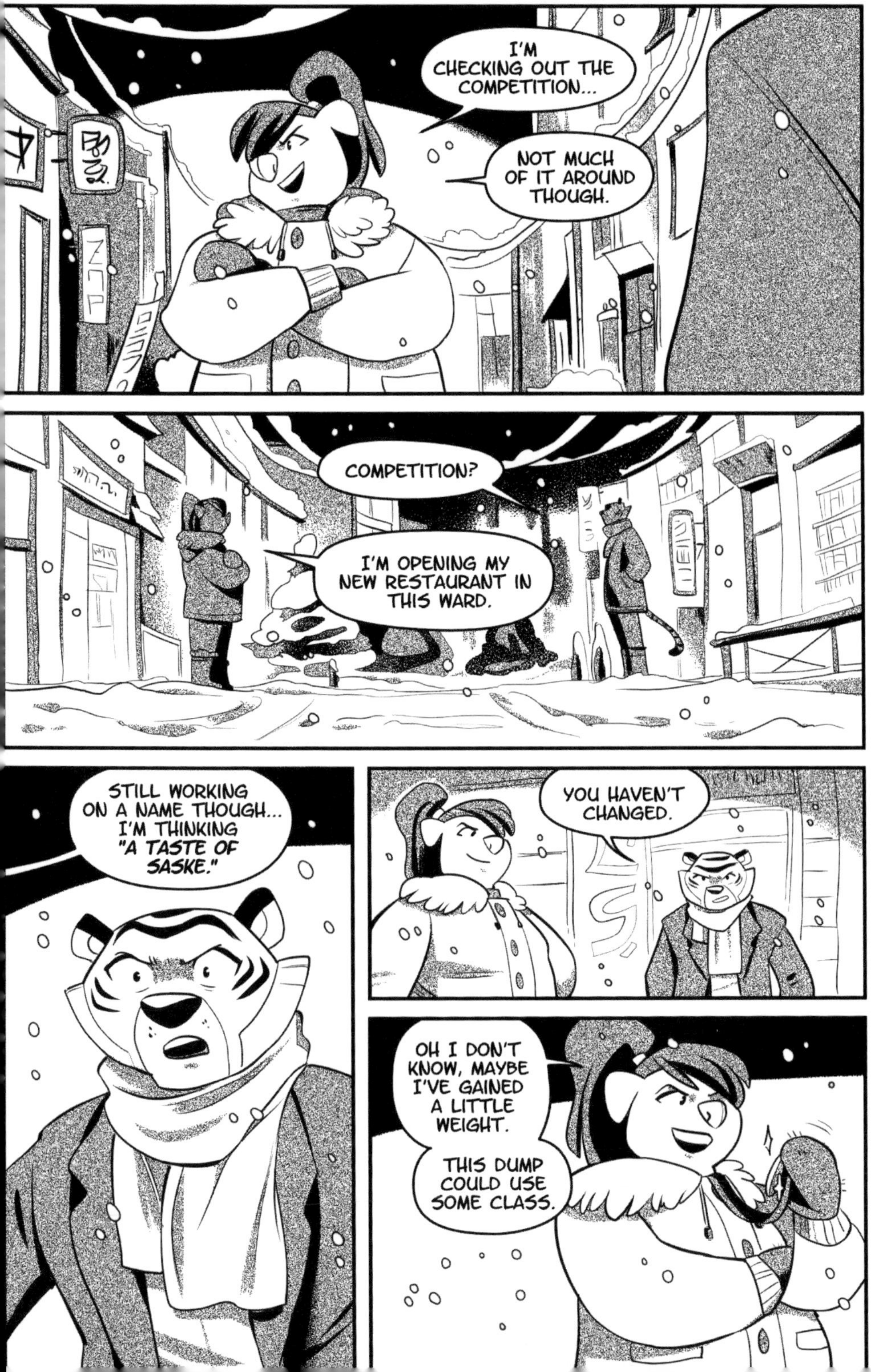
I'M CHECKING OUT THE COMPETITION...
NOT MUCH OF IT AROUND THOUGH.
COMPETITION?
I'M OPENING MY NEW RESTAURANT IN THIS WARD.
STILL WORKING ON A NAME THOUGH... I'M THINKING *"A TASTE OF SASKE."*
YOU HAVEN'T CHANGED.
OH I DON'T KNOW, MAYBE I'VE GAINED A LITTLE WEIGHT.
THIS DUMP COULD USE SOME CLASS.

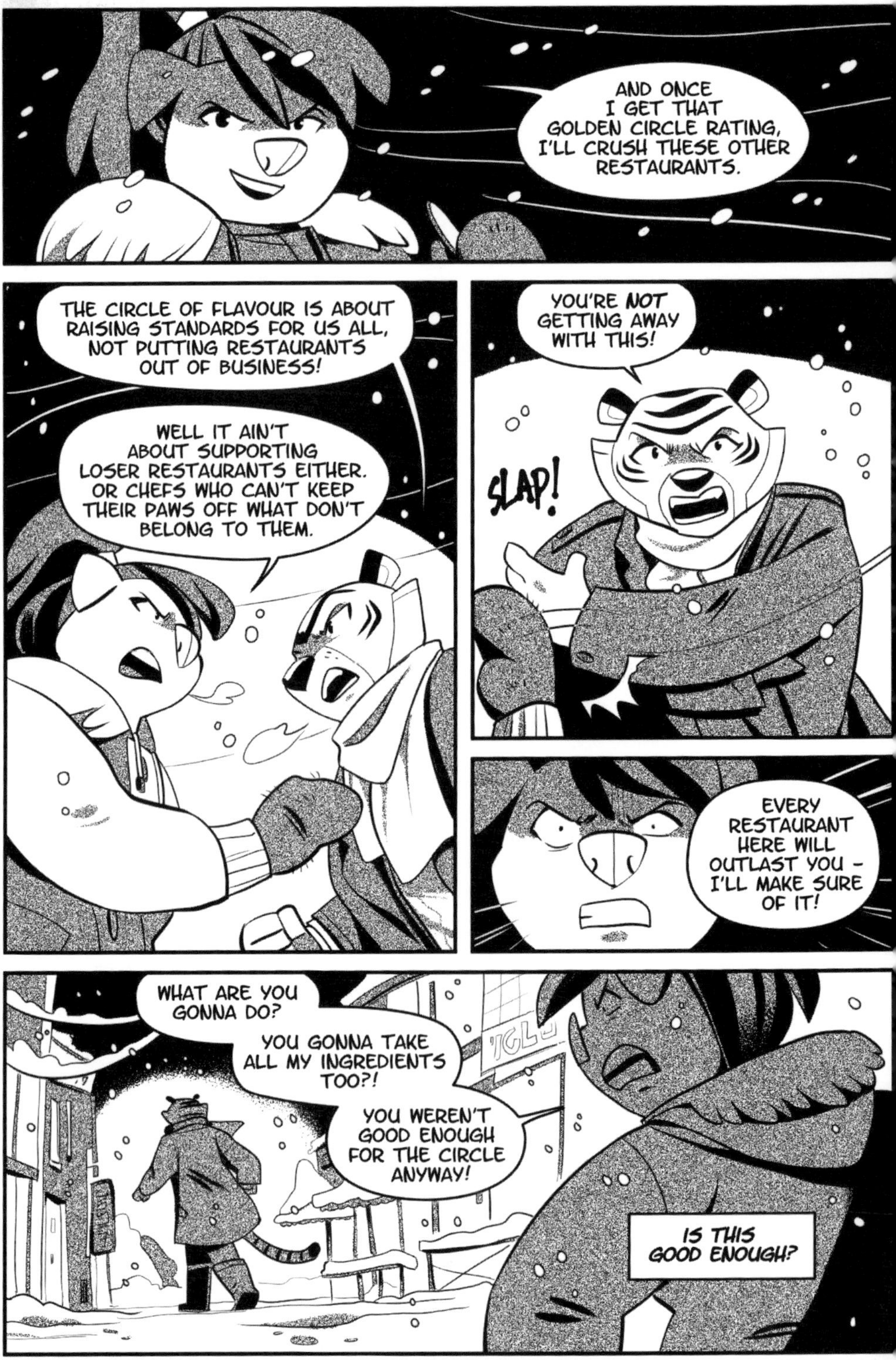
AND ONCE I GET THAT GOLDEN CIRCLE RATING, I'LL CRUSH THESE OTHER RESTAURANTS.
THE CIRCLE OF FLAVOUR IS ABOUT RAISING STANDARDS FOR US ALL, NOT PUTTING RESTAURANTS OUT OF BUSINESS!
WELL IT AIN'T ABOUT SUPPORTING LOSER RESTAURANTS EITHER. OR CHEFS WHO CAN'T KEEP THEIR PAWS OFF WHAT DON'T BELONG TO THEM.
YOU'RE NOT GETTING AWAY WITH THIS!
SLAP!
EVERY RESTAURANT HERE WILL OUTLAST YOU - I'LL MAKE SURE OF IT!
WHAT ARE YOU GONNA DO?
YOU GONNA TAKE ALL MY INGREDIENTS TOO?!
YOU WEREN'T GOOD ENOUGH FOR THE CIRCLE ANYWAY!
IS THIS GOOD ENOUGH?

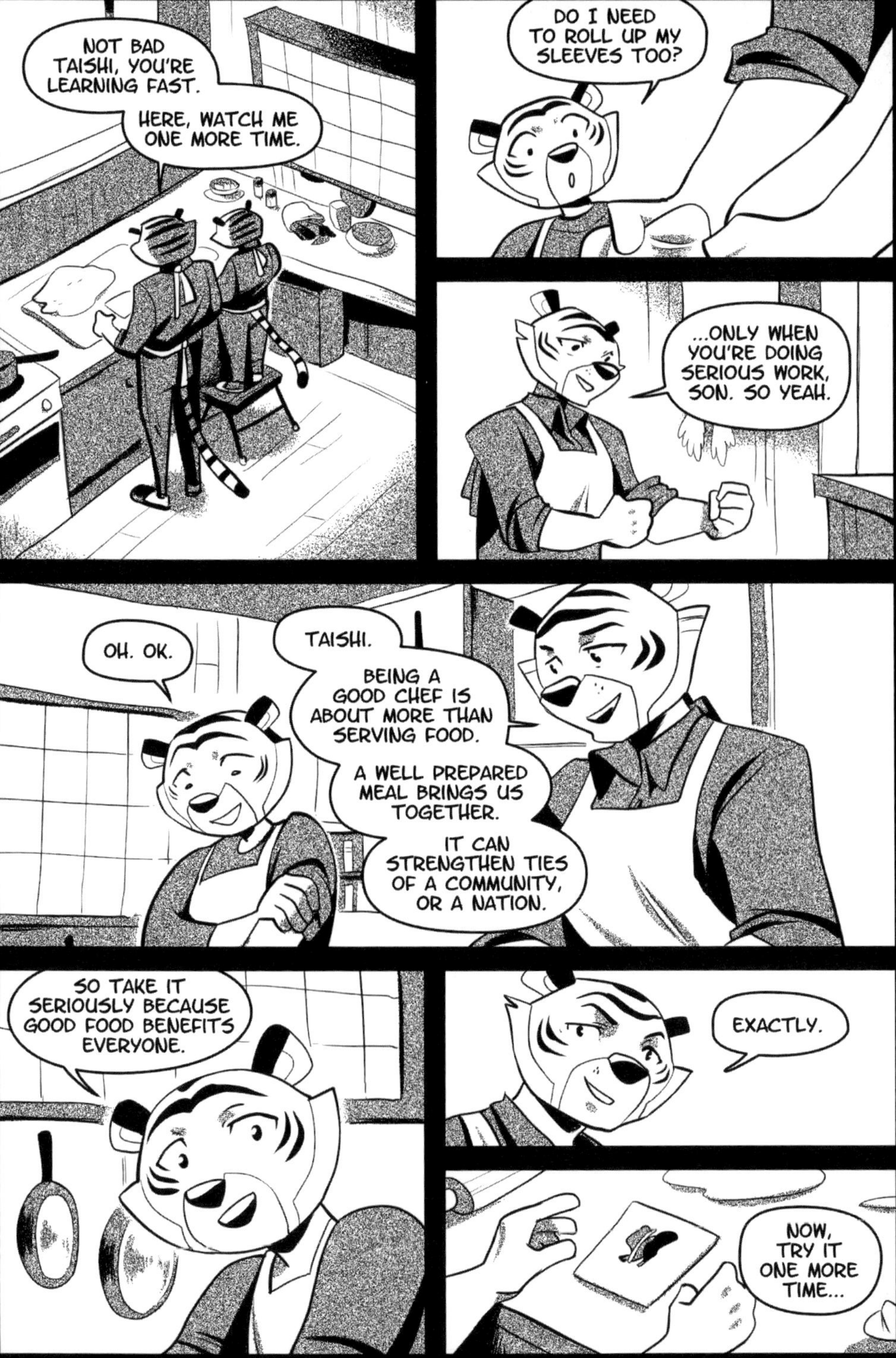
NOT BAD TAISHI, YOU'RE LEARNING FAST.
HERE, WATCH ME ONE MORE TIME.
DO I NEED TO ROLL UP MY SLEEVES TOO?
...ONLY WHEN YOU'RE DOING SERIOUS WORK, SON. SO YEAH.
OH. OK.
TAISHI.
BEING A GOOD CHEF IS ABOUT MORE THAN SERVING FOOD.
A WELL PREPARED MEAL BRINGS US TOGETHER.
IT CAN STRENGTHEN TIES OF A COMMUNITY, OR A NATION.
SO TAKE IT SERIOUSLY BECAUSE GOOD FOOD BENEFITS EVERYONE.
EXACTLY.
NOW, TRY IT ONE MORE TIME...

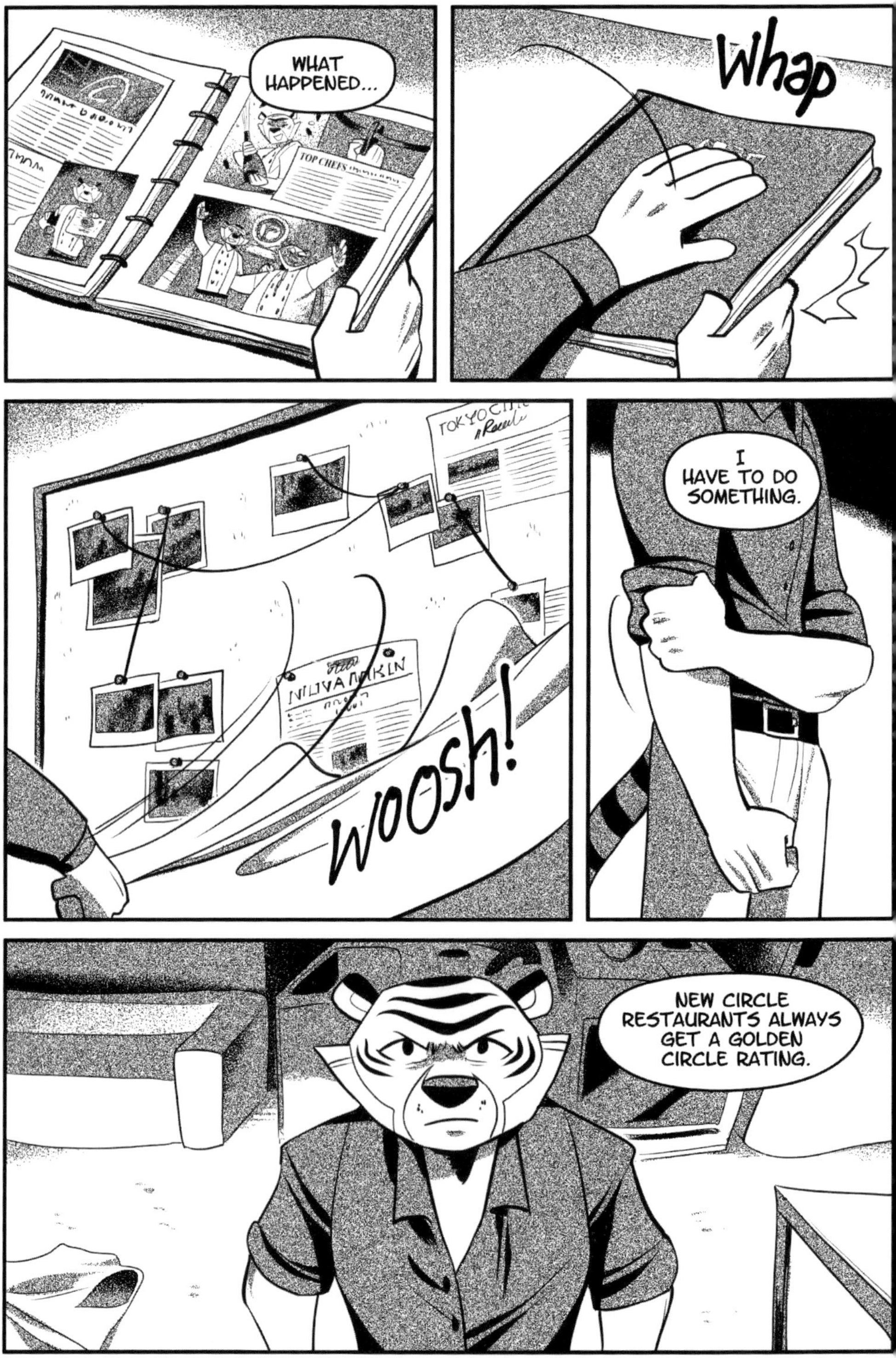
WHAT HAPPENED...
TOP CHEFS
WHAP
TOKYO
WOOSH!
I HAVE TO DO SOMETHING.
NEW CIRCLE RESTAURANTS ALWAYS GET A GOLDEN CIRCLE RATING.

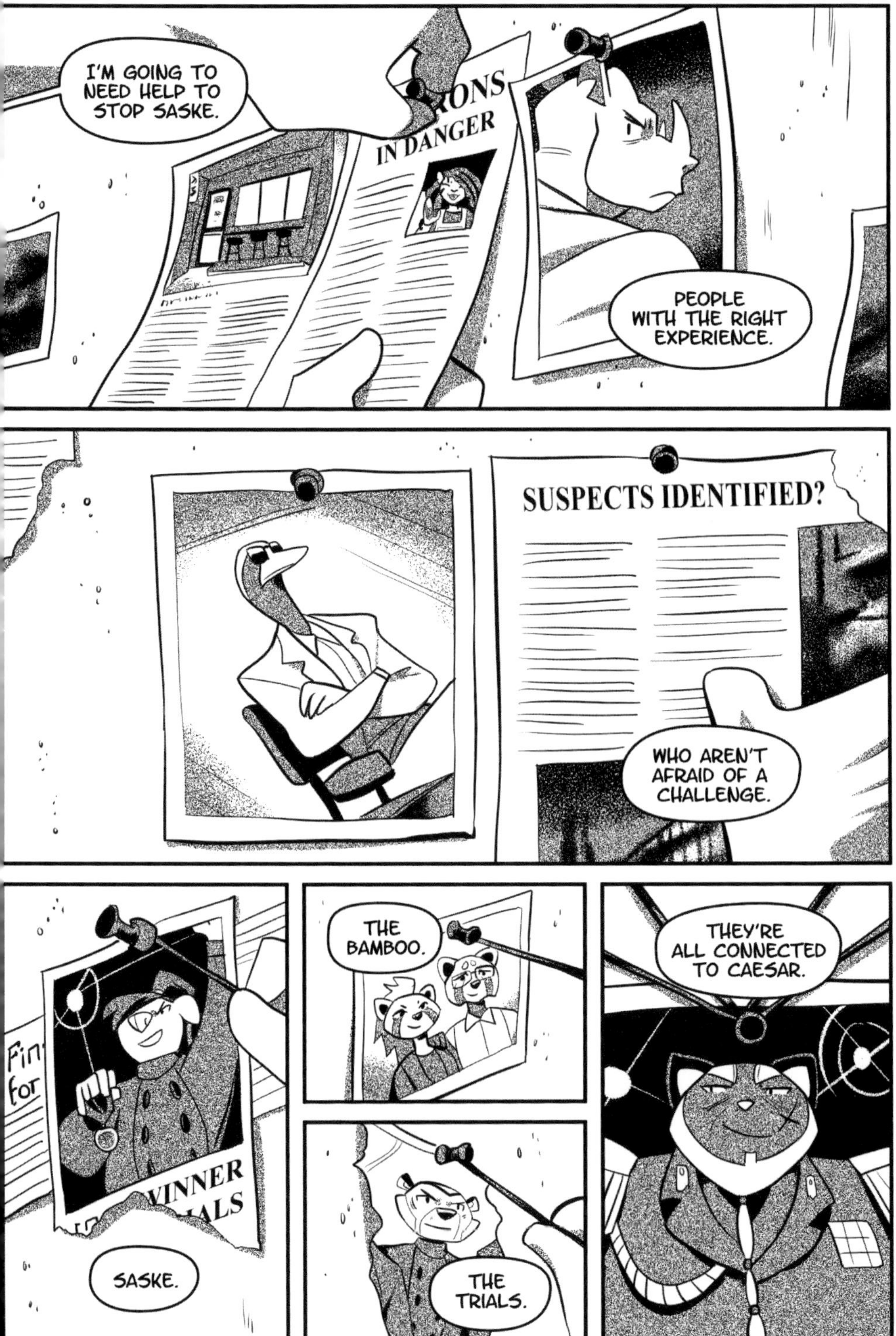
I'M GOING TO NEED HELP TO STOP SASKE.
IN DANGER
PEOPLE WITH THE RIGHT EXPERIENCE.
SUSPECTS IDENTIFIED?
WHO AREN'T AFRAID OF A CHALLENGE.
SASKE.
THE BAMBOO.
THE TRIALS.
THEY'RE ALL CONNECTED TO CAESAR.

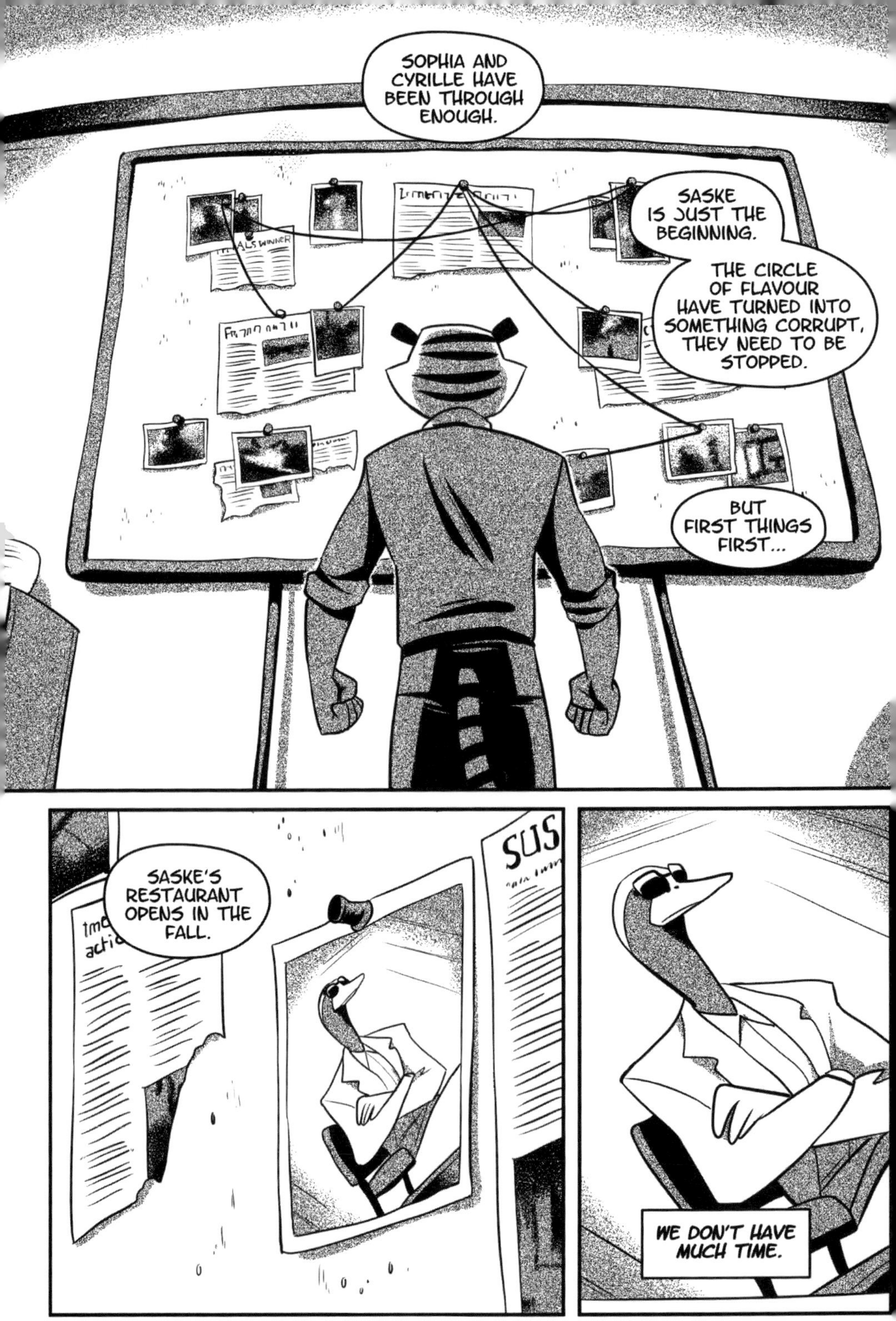
SOPHIA AND CYRILLE HAVE BEEN THROUGH ENOUGH.
SASKE IS JUST THE BEGINNING.
THE CIRCLE OF FLAVOUR HAVE TURNED INTO SOMETHING CORRUPT, THEY NEED TO BE STOPPED.
BUT FIRST THINGS FIRST...
SASKE'S RESTAURANT OPENS IN THE FALL.
SUS
WE DON'T HAVE MUCH TIME.

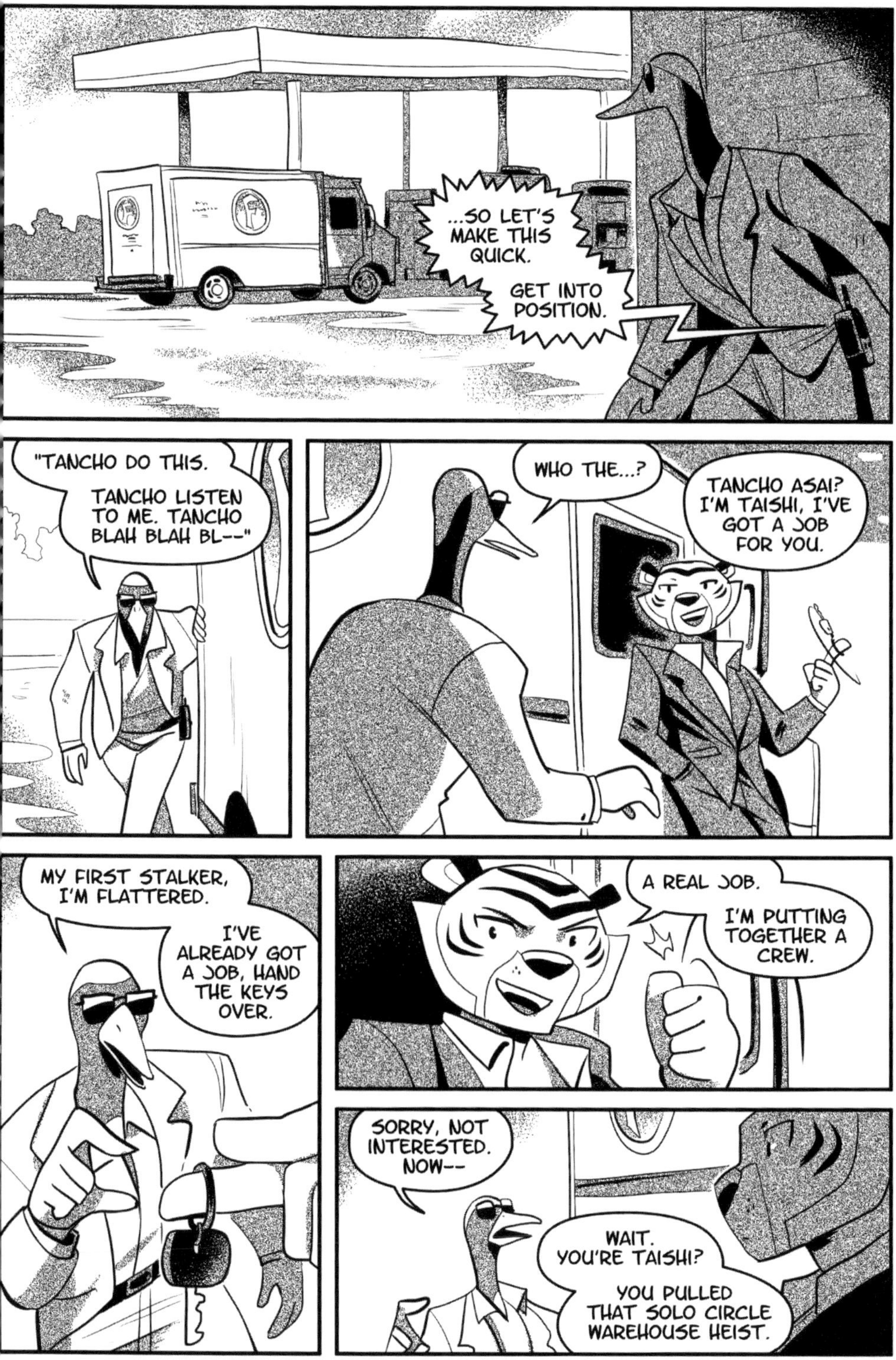
...SO LET'S MAKE THIS QUICK.
GET INTO POSITION.
"TANCHO DO THIS.
TANCHO LISTEN TO ME. TANCHO BLAH BLAH BL--"
WHO THE...?
TANCHO ASAI? I'M TAISHI, I'VE GOT A JOB FOR YOU.
MY FIRST STALKER, I'M FLATTERED.
I'VE ALREADY GOT A JOB, HAND THE KEYS OVER.
A REAL JOB.
I'M PUTTING TOGETHER A CREW.
SORRY, NOT INTERESTED. NOW--
WAIT. YOU'RE TAISHI?
YOU PULLED THAT SOLO CIRCLE WAREHOUSE HEIST.

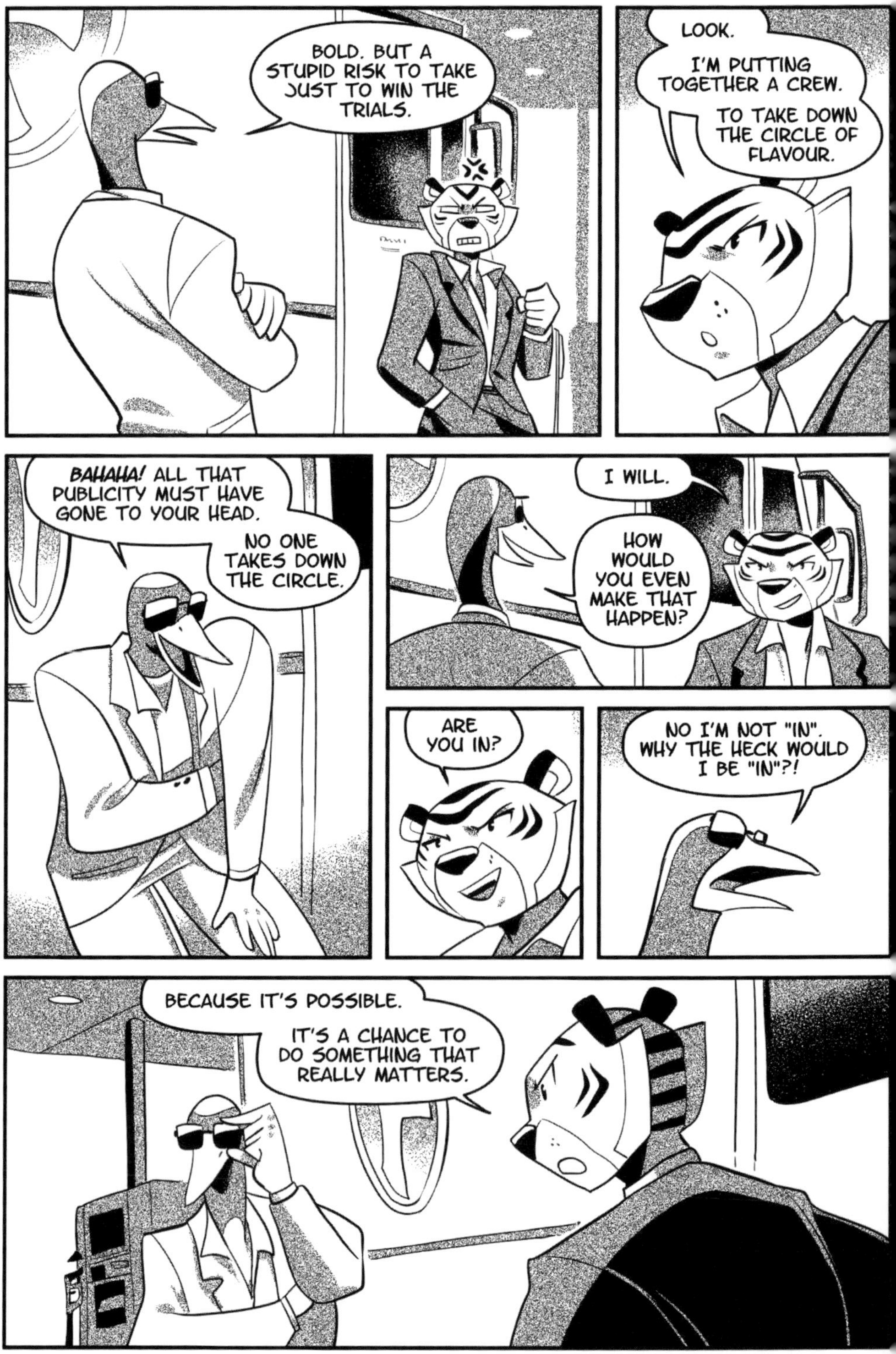
BOLD, BUT A STUPID RISK TO TAKE JUST TO WIN THE TRIALS.
LOOK.
I'M PUTTING TOGETHER A CREW.
TO TAKE DOWN THE CIRCLE OF FLAVOUR.
BAHAHA! ALL THAT PUBLICITY MUST HAVE GONE TO YOUR HEAD.
NO ONE TAKES DOWN THE CIRCLE.
I WILL.
HOW WOULD YOU EVEN MAKE THAT HAPPEN?
ARE YOU IN?
NO I'M NOT "IN". WHY THE HECK WOULD I BE "IN"?!
BECAUSE IT'S POSSIBLE.
IT'S A CHANCE TO DO SOMETHING THAT REALLY MATTERS.

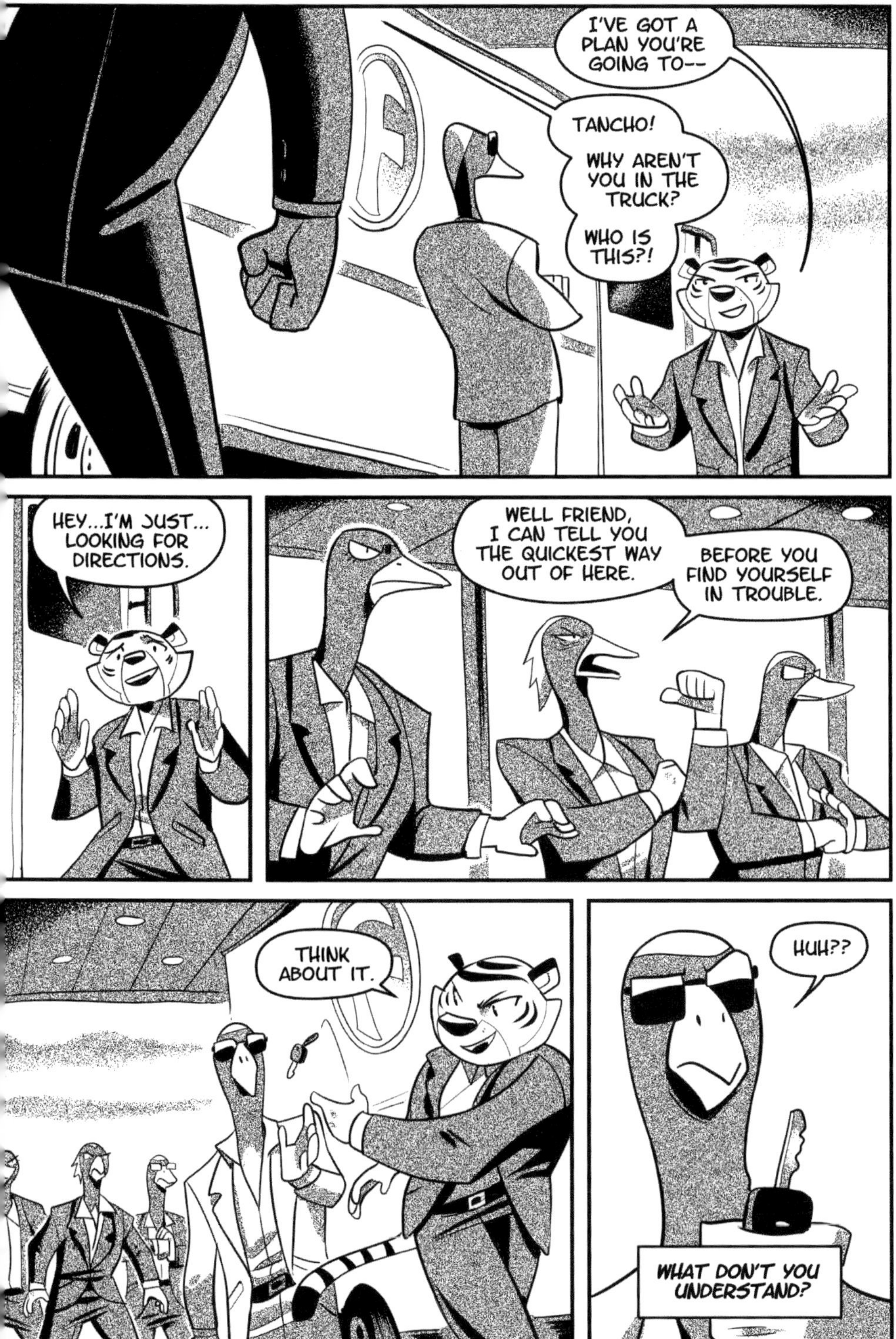
I'VE GOT A PLAN YOU'RE GOING TO--
TANCHO!
WHY AREN'T YOU IN THE TRUCK?
WHO IS THIS?!
HEY...I'M JUST... LOOKING FOR DIRECTIONS.
WELL FRIEND, I CAN TELL YOU THE QUICKEST WAY OUT OF HERE.
BEFORE YOU FIND YOURSELF IN TROUBLE.
THINK ABOUT IT.
HUH??
WHAT DON'T YOU UNDERSTAND?

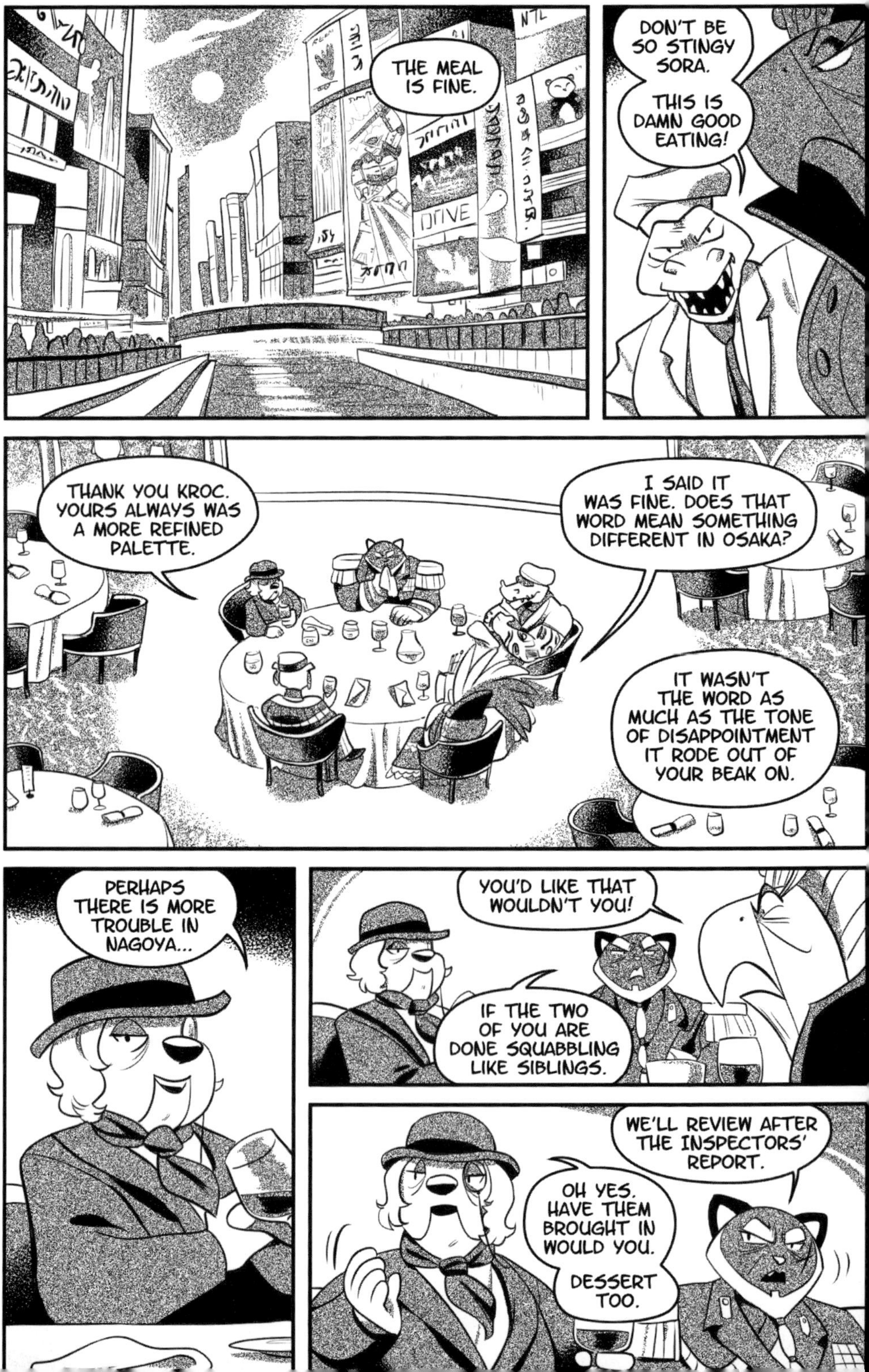
THE MEAL IS FINE.
DON'T BE SO STINGY SORA.
THIS IS DAMN GOOD EATING!
THANK YOU KROC. YOURS ALWAYS WAS A MORE REFINED PALETTE.
I SAID IT WAS FINE. DOES THAT WORD MEAN SOMETHING DIFFERENT IN OSAKA?
IT WASN'T THE WORD AS MUCH AS THE TONE OF DISAPPOINTMENT IT RODE OUT OF YOUR BEAK ON.
PERHAPS THERE IS MORE TROUBLE IN NAGOYA...
YOU'D LIKE THAT WOULDN'T YOU!
IF THE TWO OF YOU ARE DONE SQUABBLING LIKE SIBLINGS.
WE'LL REVIEW AFTER THE INSPECTORS' REPORT.
OH YES. HAVE THEM BROUGHT IN WOULD YOU.
DESSERT TOO.

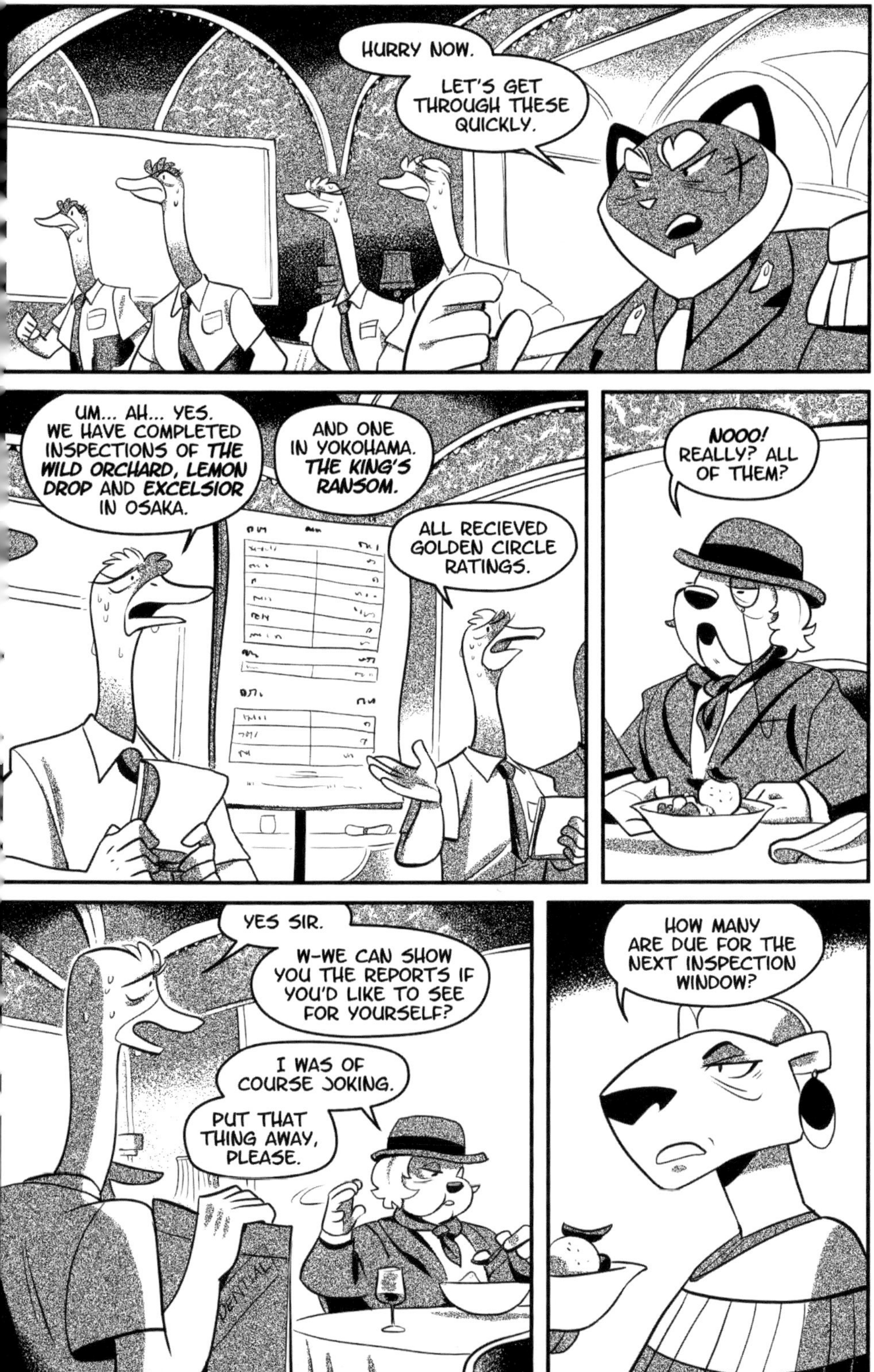
HURRY NOW.
LET'S GET THROUGH THESE QUICKLY.
UM... AH... YES. WE HAVE COMPLETED INSPECTIONS OF THE WILD ORCHARD, LEMON DROP AND EXCELSIOR IN OSAKA.
AND ONE IN YOKOHAMA. THE KING'S RANSOM.
ALL RECIEVED GOLDEN CIRCLE RATINGS.
NOOO! REALLY? ALL OF THEM?
YES SIR.
W-WE CAN SHOW YOU THE REPORTS IF YOU'D LIKE TO SEE FOR YOURSELF?
I WAS OF COURSE JOKING.
PUT THAT THING AWAY, PLEASE.
HOW MANY ARE DUE FOR THE NEXT INSPECTION WINDOW?

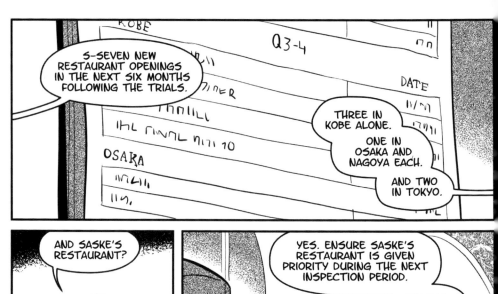

S-SEVEN NEW RESTAURANT OPENINGS IN THE NEXT SIX MONTHS FOLLOWING THE TRIALS.

THREE IN KOBE ALONE.

ONE IN OSAKA AND NAGOYA EACH.

AND TWO IN TOKYO.

AND SASKE'S RESTAURANT?

YES. ENSURE SASKE'S RESTAURANT IS GIVEN PRIORITY DURING THE NEXT INSPECTION PERIOD.

THAT IS ALL.

SPEAKING OF TOKYO.

WHAT HAPPENED TO THAT KID STEALING OUR SUPPLIES?

ROTTING IN SOME BACKWATER DIVE.

WHAT WOULD POSSESS HIM TO STEAL INGREDIENTS FROM THE CIRCLE OF FLAVOUR...

HIS DADDY WOULDA BEEN SO DISAPPOINTED, HAHA!

INDEED.

HIRO ALWAYS LIKED TO DO THE RIGHT THING.

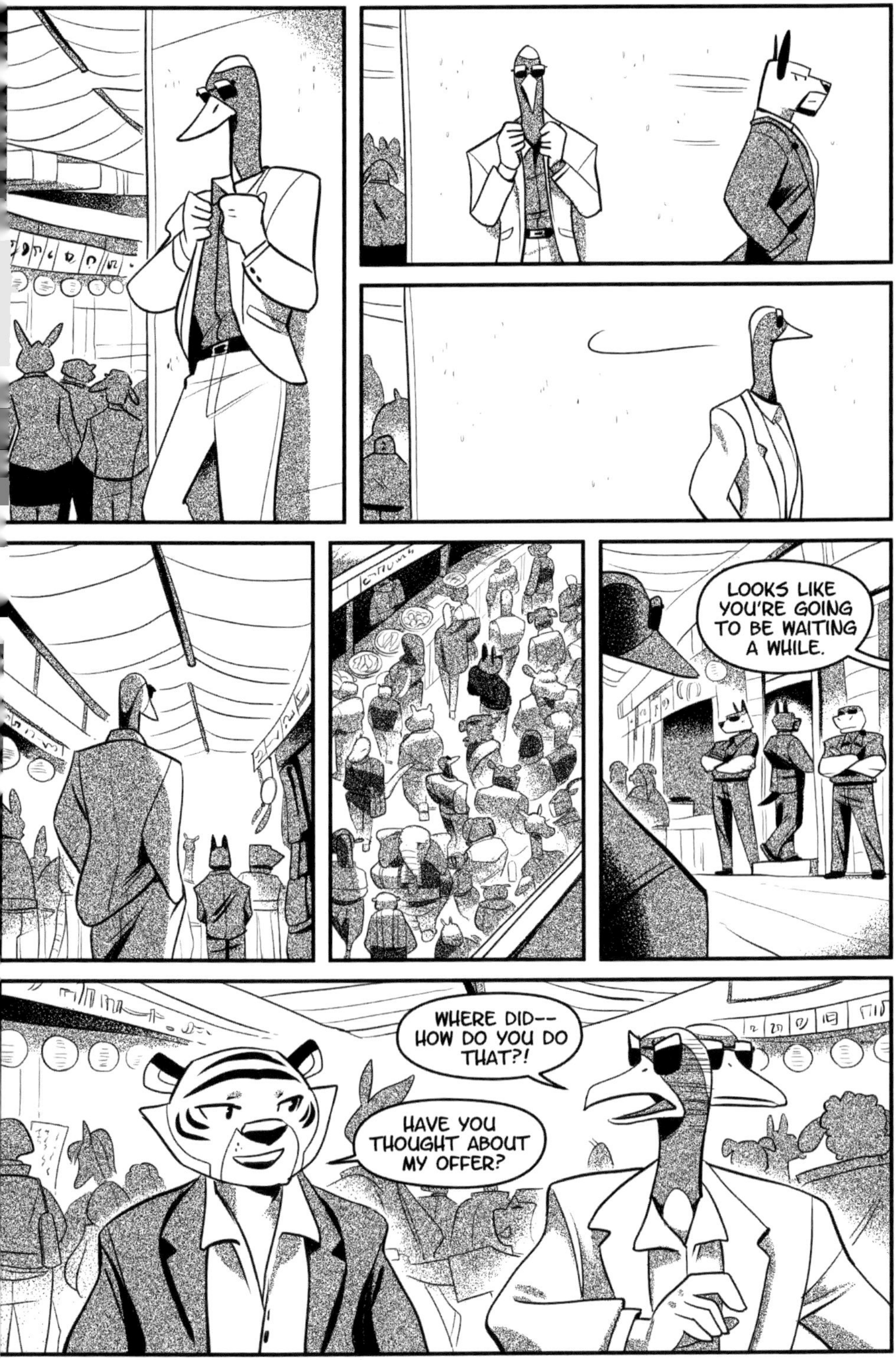
LOOKS LIKE YOU'RE GOING TO BE WAITING A WHILE.
WHERE DID-- HOW DO YOU DO THAT?!
HAVE YOU THOUGHT ABOUT MY OFFER?

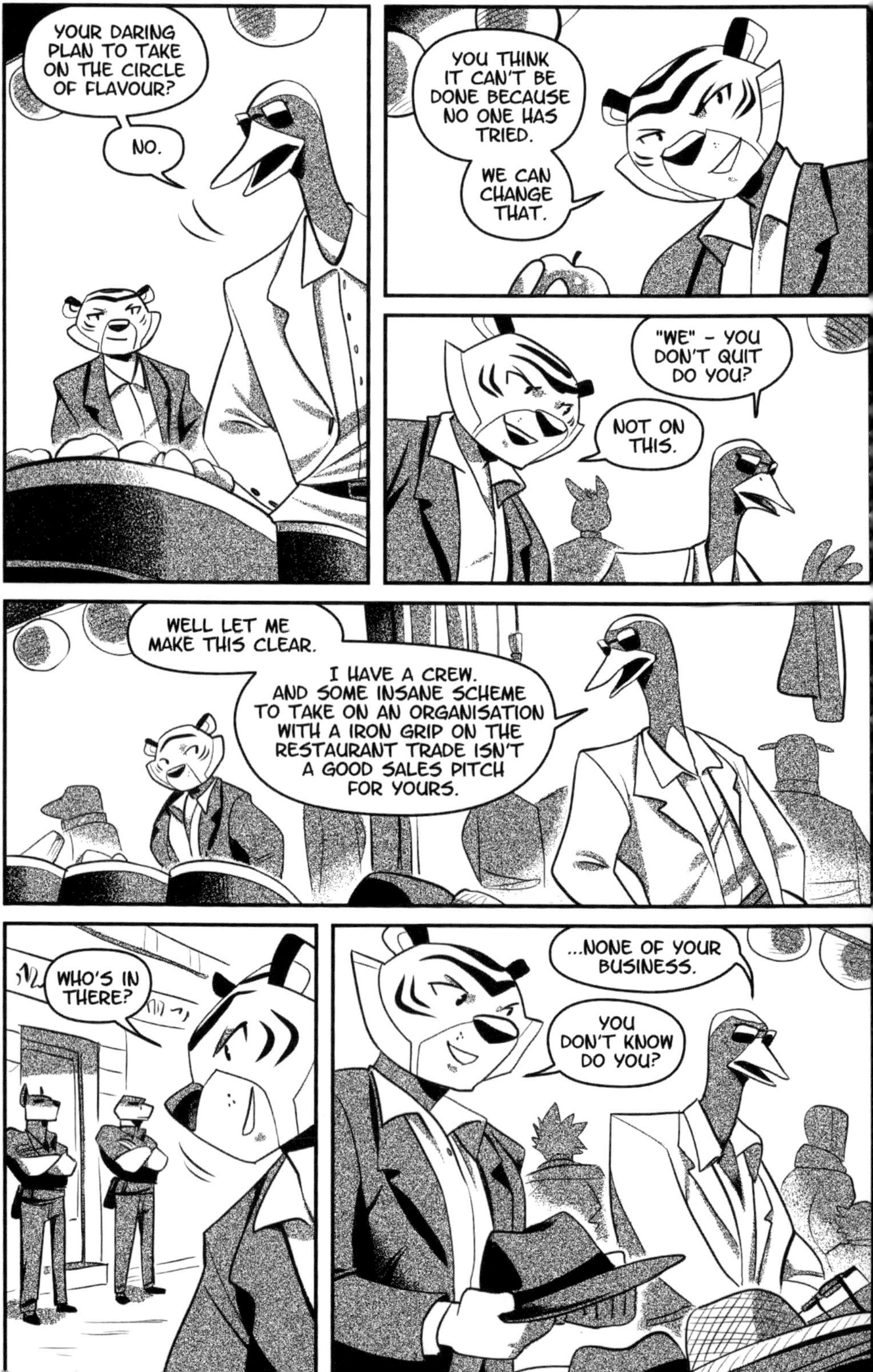
YOUR DARING PLAN TO TAKE ON THE CIRCLE OF FLAVOUR?
NO.
YOU THINK IT CAN'T BE DONE BECAUSE NO ONE HAS TRIED.
WE CAN CHANGE THAT.
"WE" - YOU DON'T QUIT DO YOU?
NOT ON THIS.
WELL LET ME MAKE THIS CLEAR.
I HAVE A CREW. AND SOME INSANE SCHEME TO TAKE ON AN ORGANISATION WITH A IRON GRIP ON THE RESTAURANT TRADE ISN'T A GOOD SALES PITCH FOR YOURS.
WHO'S IN THERE?
...NONE OF YOUR BUSINESS.
YOU DON'T KNOW DO YOU?

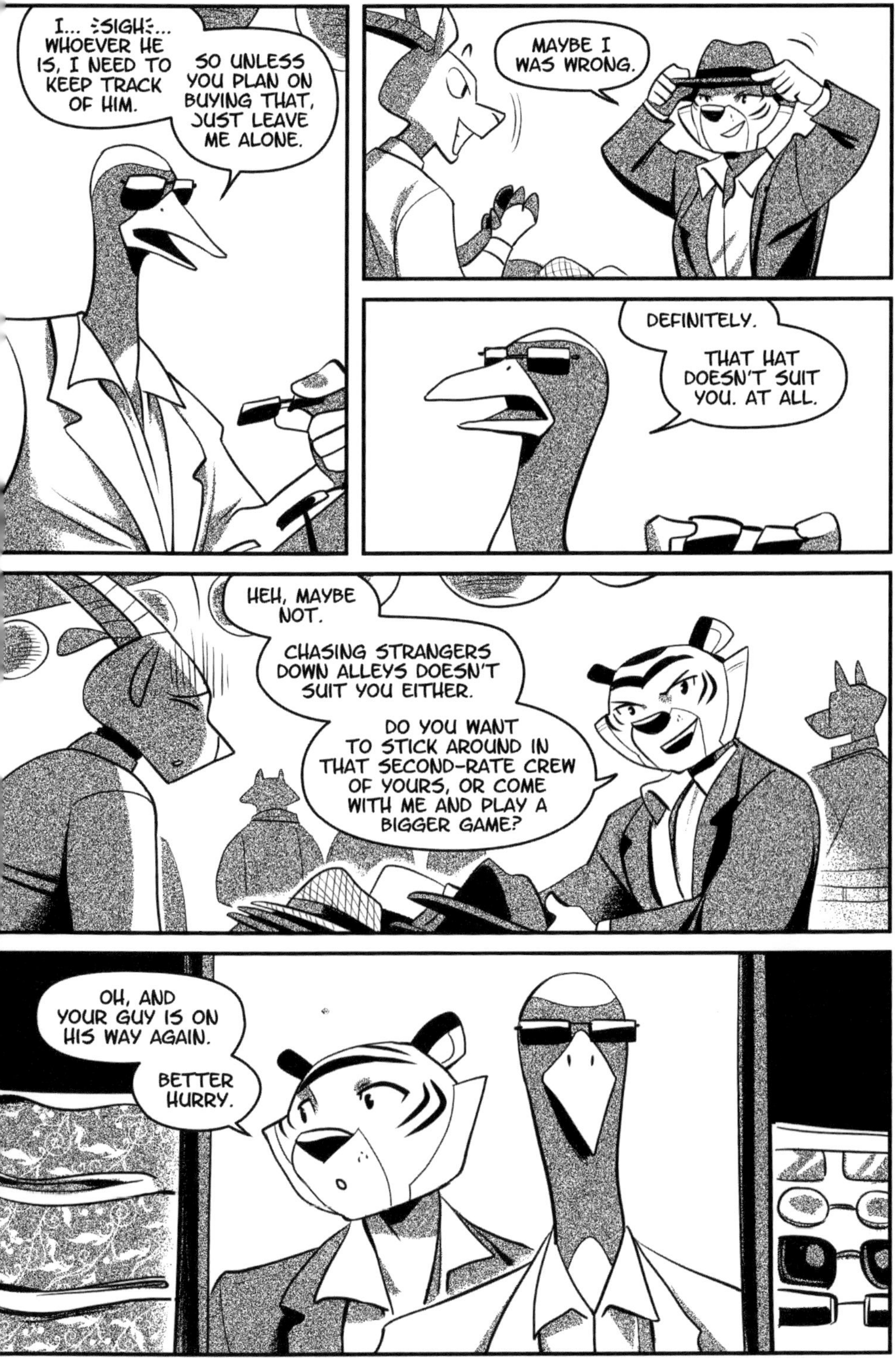
I... ⁝SIGH⁝... WHOEVER HE IS, I NEED TO KEEP TRACK OF HIM.
SO UNLESS YOU PLAN ON BUYING THAT, JUST LEAVE ME ALONE.
MAYBE I WAS WRONG.
DEFINITELY.
THAT HAT DOESN'T SUIT YOU. AT ALL.
HEH, MAYBE NOT.
CHASING STRANGERS DOWN ALLEYS DOESN'T SUIT YOU EITHER.
DO YOU WANT TO STICK AROUND IN THAT SECOND-RATE CREW OF YOURS, OR COME WITH ME AND PLAY A BIGGER GAME?
OH, AND YOUR GUY IS ON HIS WAY AGAIN.
BETTER HURRY.

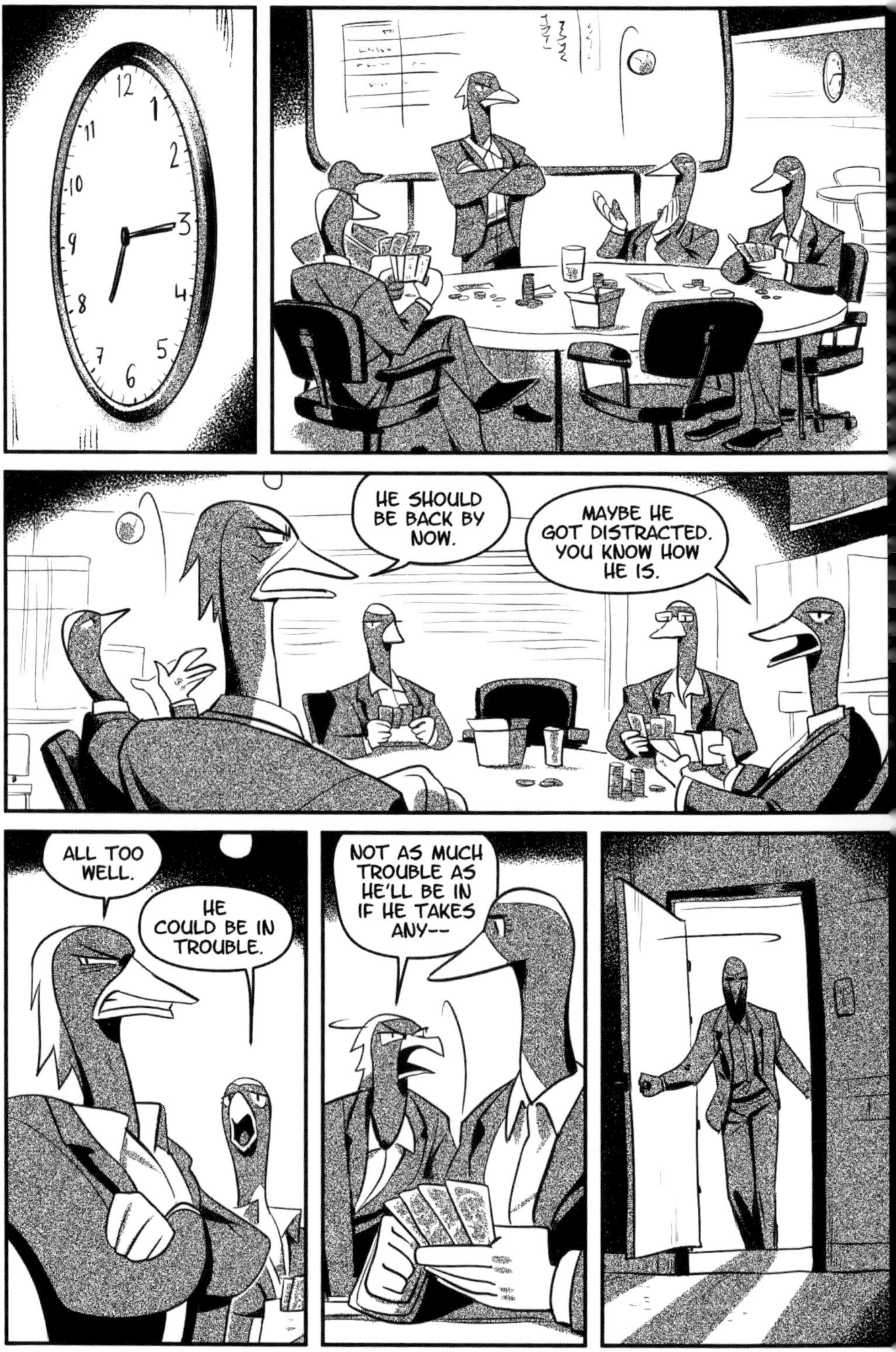
HE SHOULD BE BACK BY NOW.
MAYBE HE GOT DISTRACTED. YOU KNOW HOW HE IS.
ALL TOO WELL.
HE COULD BE IN TROUBLE.
NOT AS MUCH TROUBLE AS HE'LL BE IN IF HE TAKES ANY--

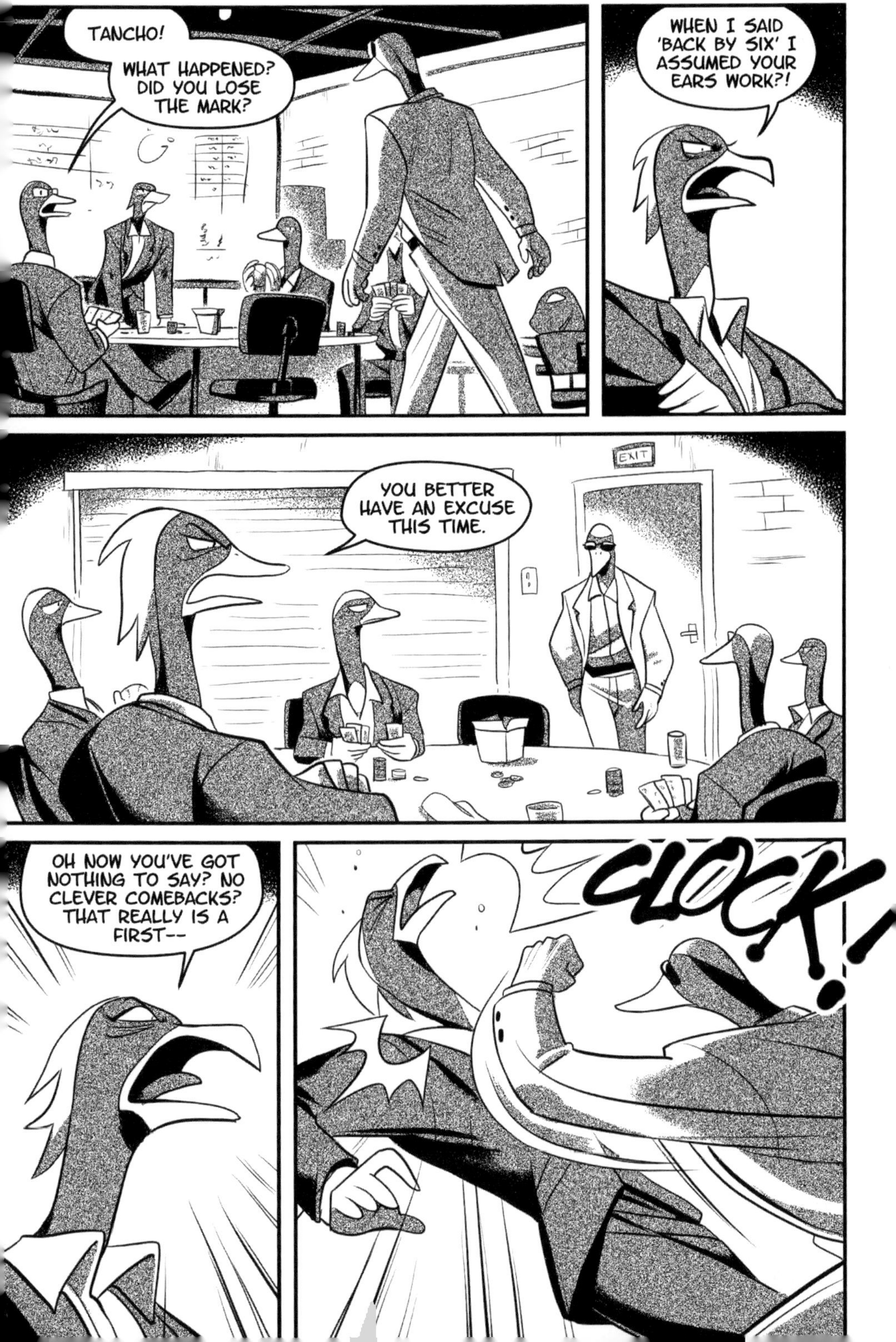

TANCHO!
WHAT HAPPENED? DID YOU LOSE THE MARK?
WHEN I SAID 'BACK BY SIX' I ASSUMED YOUR EARS WORK?!
EXIT
YOU BETTER HAVE AN EXCUSE THIS TIME.
OH NOW YOU'VE GOT NOTHING TO SAY? NO CLEVER COMEBACKS? THAT REALLY IS A FIRST--
CLOCK!!

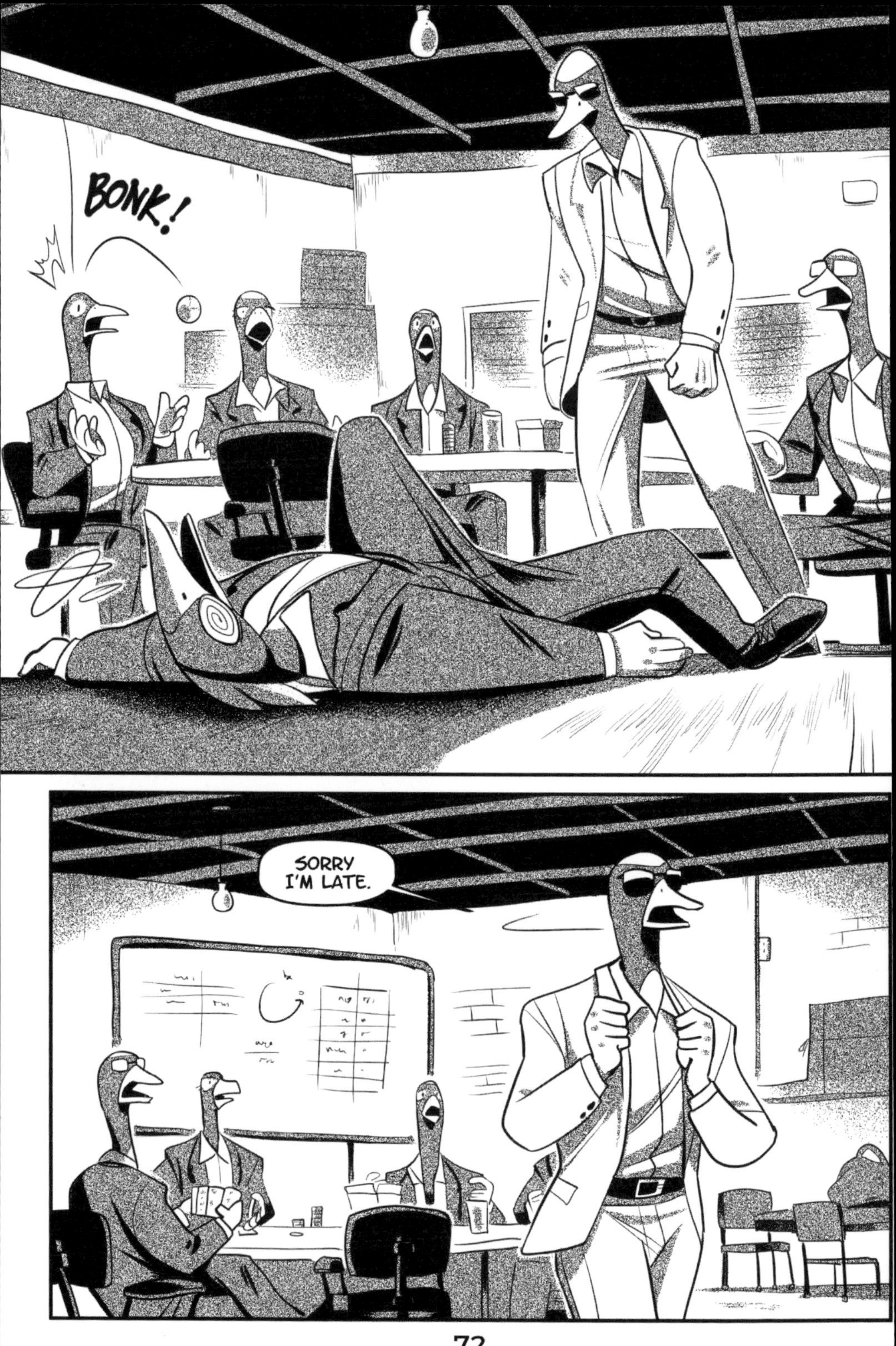
BONK!
SORRY I'M LATE.

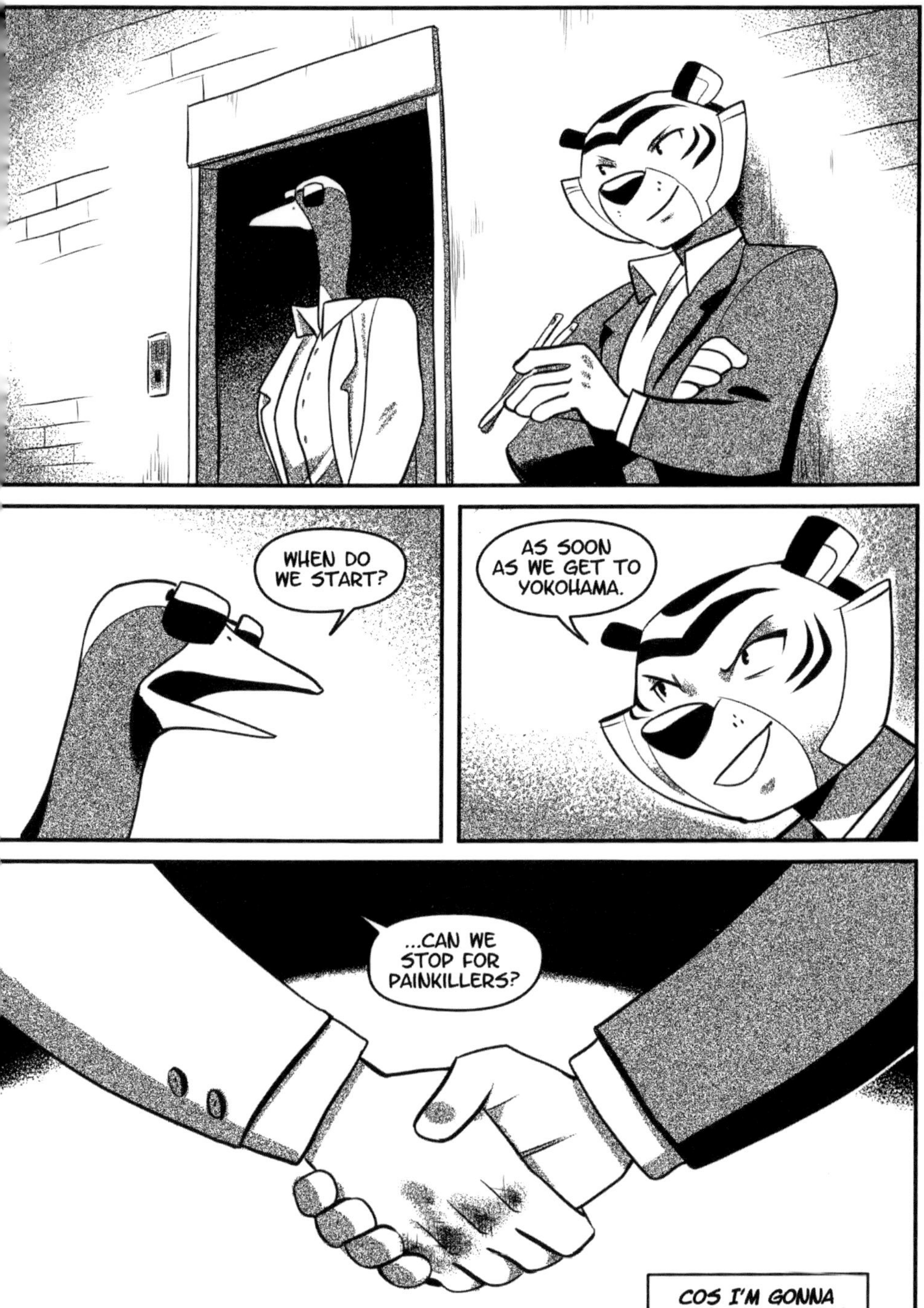
WHEN DO WE START?
AS SOON AS WE GET TO YOKOHAMA.
...CAN WE STOP FOR PAINKILLERS?
COS I'M GONNA PUT YOU A WORLD OF HURT!

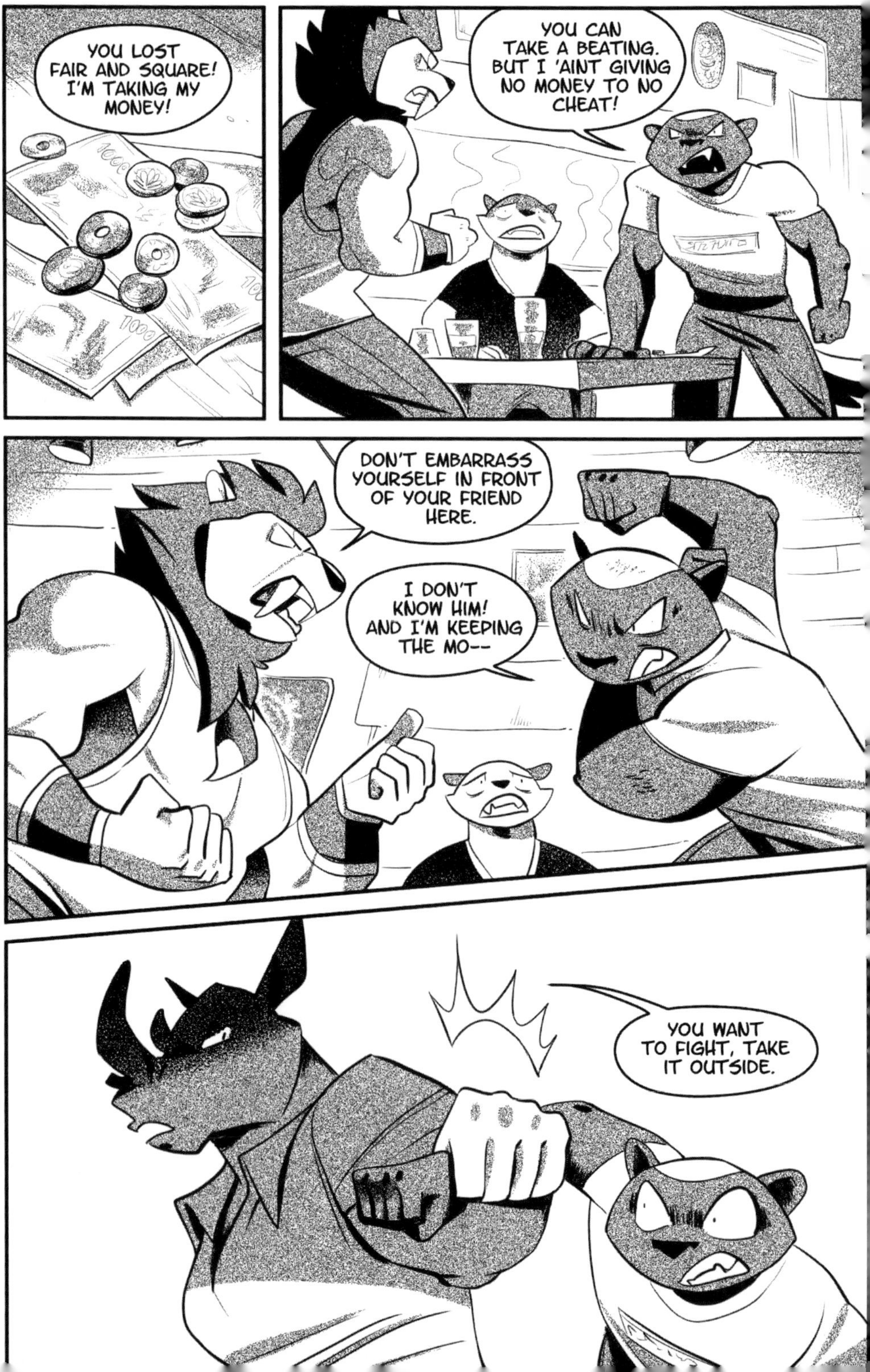
YOU LOST FAIR AND SQUARE! I'M TAKING MY MONEY!
YOU CAN TAKE A BEATING. BUT I 'AINT GIVING NO MONEY TO NO CHEAT!
DON'T EMBARRASS YOURSELF IN FRONT OF YOUR FRIEND HERE.
I DON'T KNOW HIM! AND I'M KEEPING THE MO--
YOU WANT TO FIGHT, TAKE IT OUTSIDE.

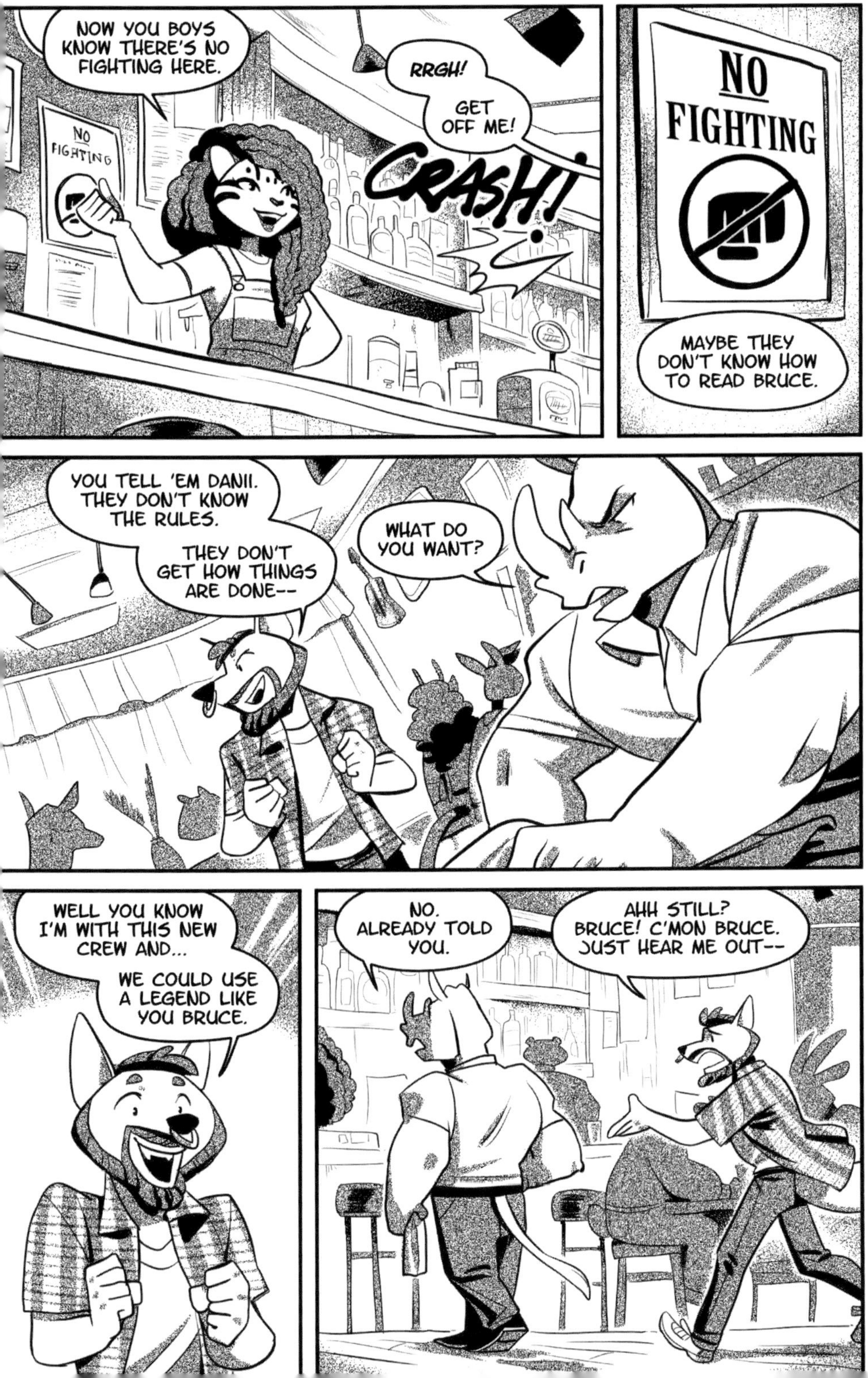
NOW YOU BOYS KNOW THERE'S NO FIGHTING HERE.
NO FIGHTING
RRGH!
GET OFF ME!
CRASH!
NO FIGHTING
MAYBE THEY DON'T KNOW HOW TO READ BRUCE.
YOU TELL 'EM DANII. THEY DON'T KNOW THE RULES.
THEY DON'T GET HOW THINGS ARE DONE--
WHAT DO YOU WANT?
WELL YOU KNOW I'M WITH THIS NEW CREW AND...
WE COULD USE A LEGEND LIKE YOU BRUCE.
NO. ALREADY TOLD YOU.
AHH STILL? BRUCE! C'MON BRUCE. JUST HEAR ME OUT--

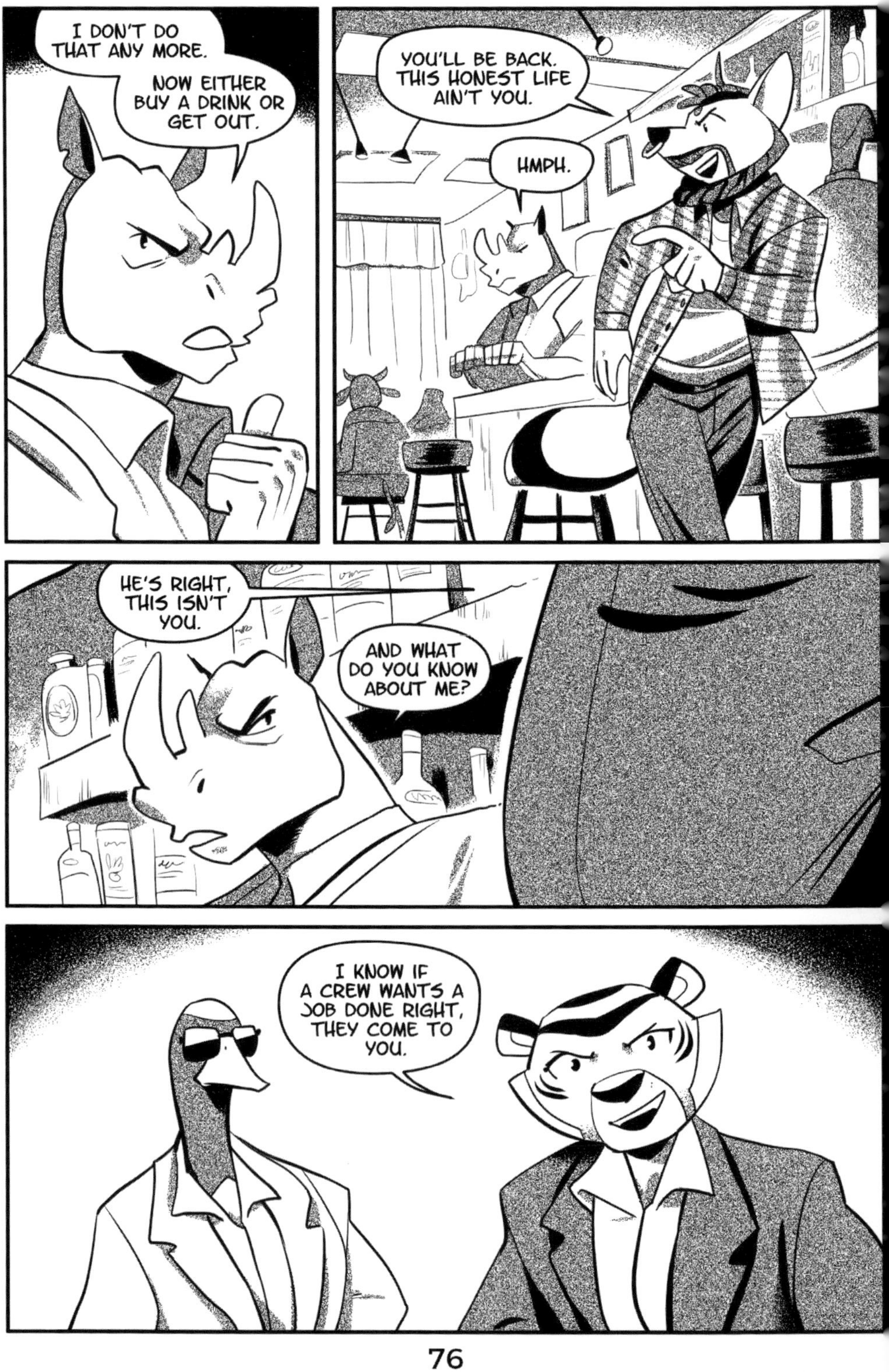
I DON'T DO THAT ANY MORE.
NOW EITHER BUY A DRINK OR GET OUT.
YOU'LL BE BACK. THIS HONEST LIFE AIN'T YOU.
HMPH.
HE'S RIGHT, THIS ISN'T YOU.
AND WHAT DO YOU KNOW ABOUT ME?
I KNOW IF A CREW WANTS A JOB DONE RIGHT, THEY COME TO YOU.

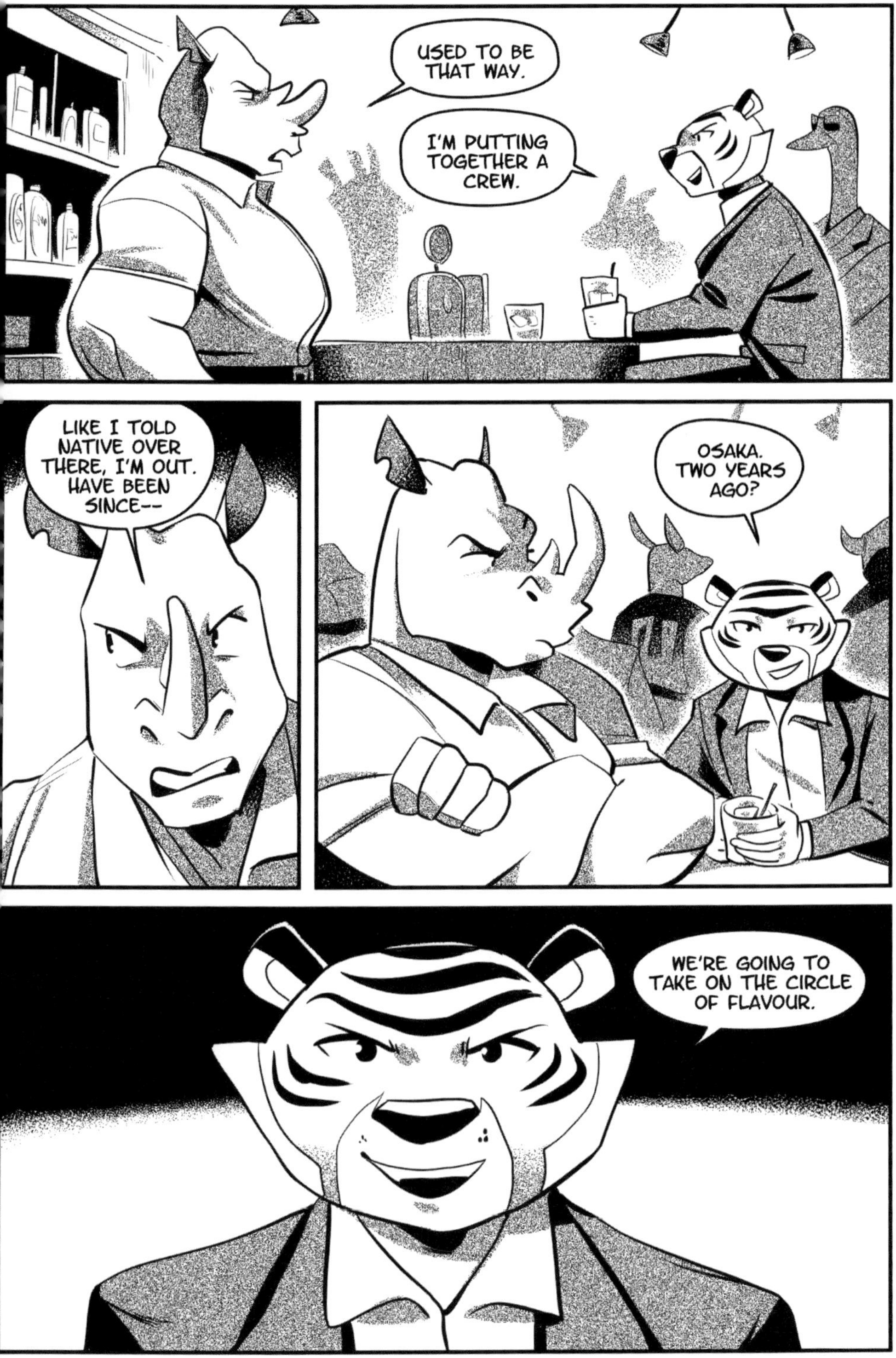
USED TO BE THAT WAY.
I'M PUTTING TOGETHER A CREW.
LIKE I TOLD NATIVE OVER THERE, I'M OUT. HAVE BEEN SINCE--
OSAKA. TWO YEARS AGO?
WE'RE GOING TO TAKE ON THE CIRCLE OF FLAVOUR.

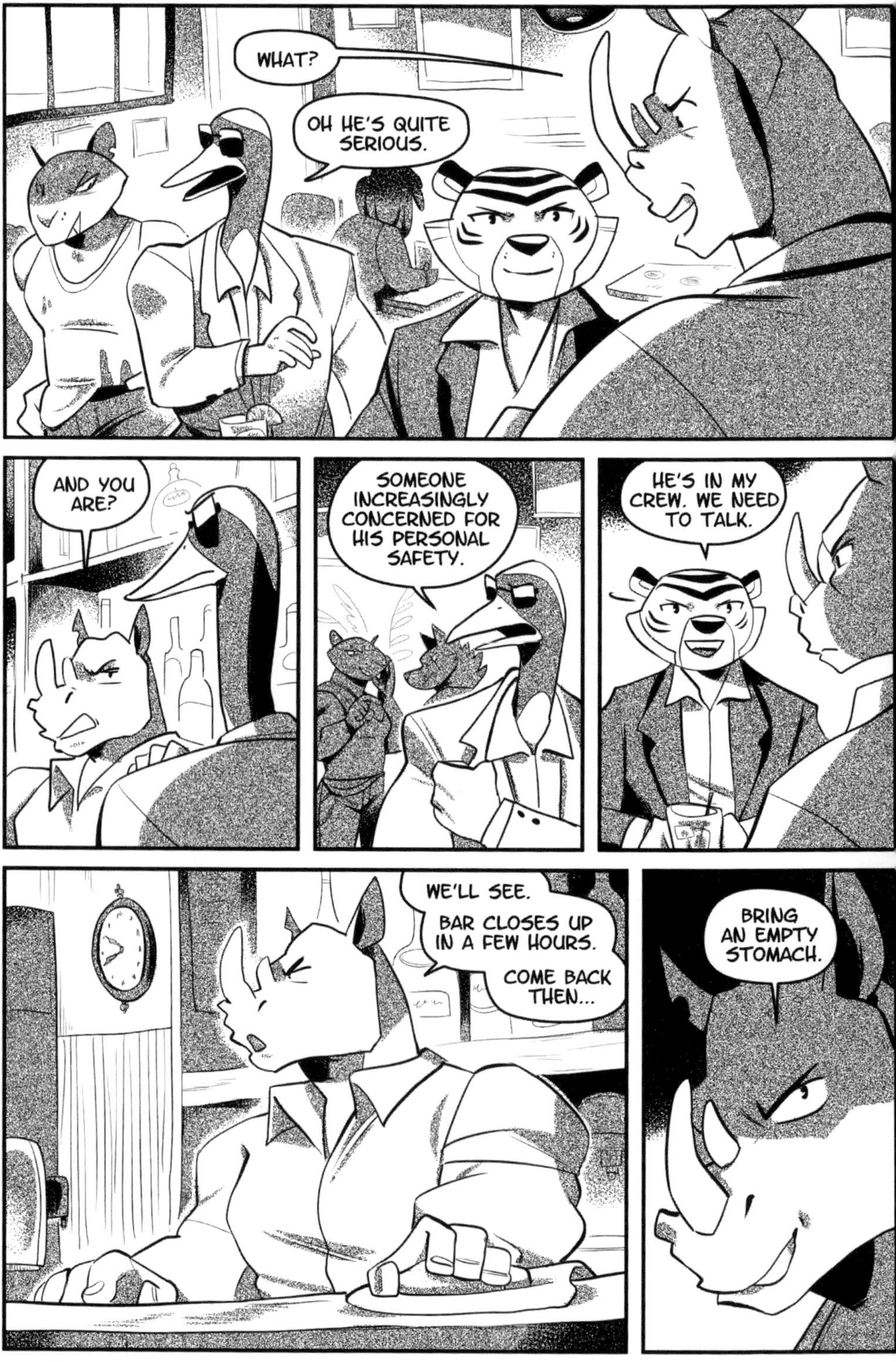

WHAT?
OH HE'S QUITE SERIOUS.
AND YOU ARE?
SOMEONE INCREASINGLY CONCERNED FOR HIS PERSONAL SAFETY.
HE'S IN MY CREW. WE NEED TO TALK.
WE'LL SEE.
BAR CLOSES UP IN A FEW HOURS.
COME BACK THEN...
BRING AN EMPTY STOMACH.

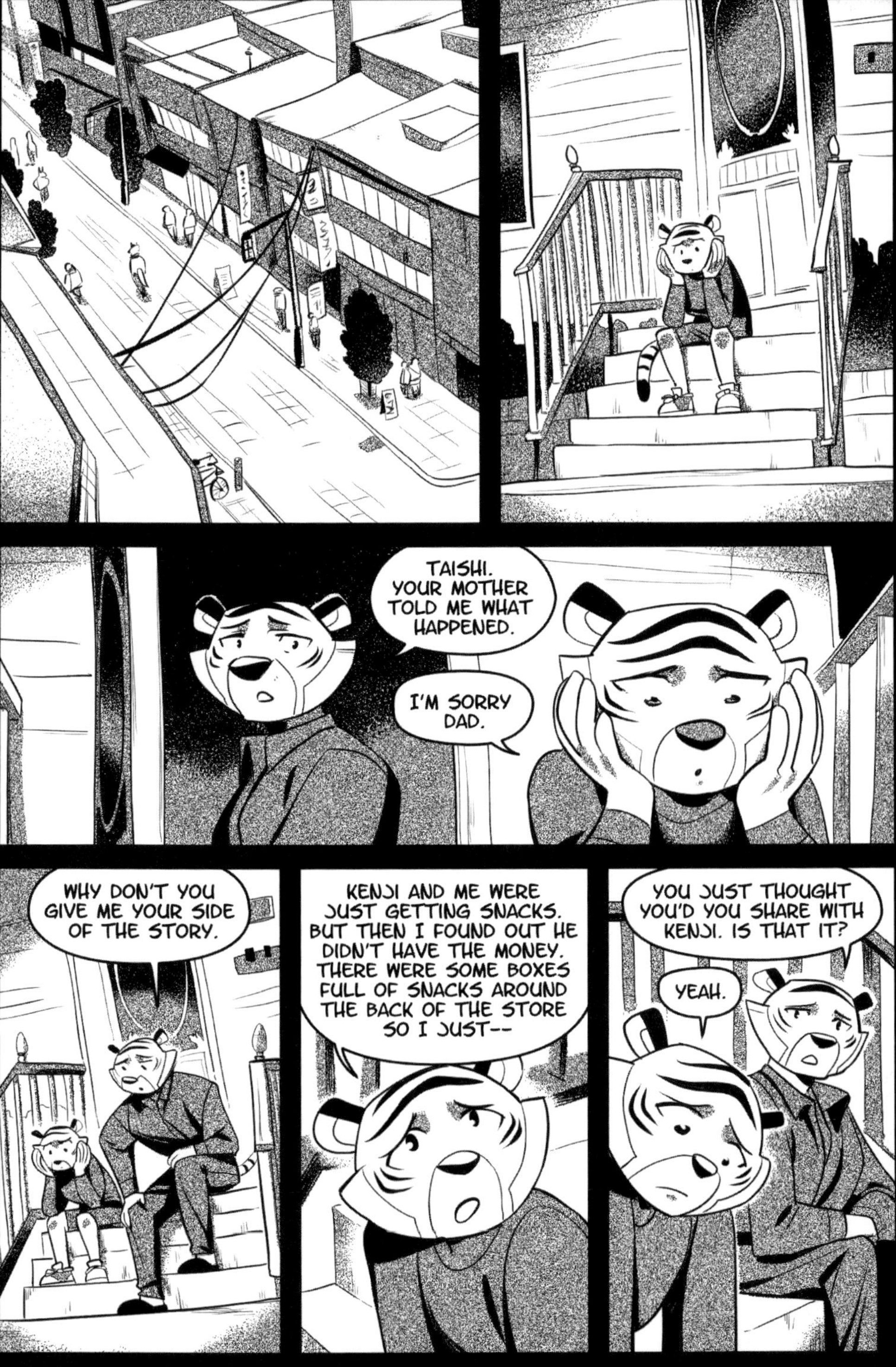
TAISHI. YOUR MOTHER TOLD ME WHAT HAPPENED.
I'M SORRY DAD.
WHY DON'T YOU GIVE ME YOUR SIDE OF THE STORY.
KENJI AND ME WERE JUST GETTING SNACKS. BUT THEN I FOUND OUT HE DIDN'T HAVE THE MONEY. THERE WERE SOME BOXES FULL OF SNACKS AROUND THE BACK OF THE STORE SO I JUST--
YOU JUST THOUGHT YOU'D YOU SHARE WITH KENJI. IS THAT IT?
YEAH.

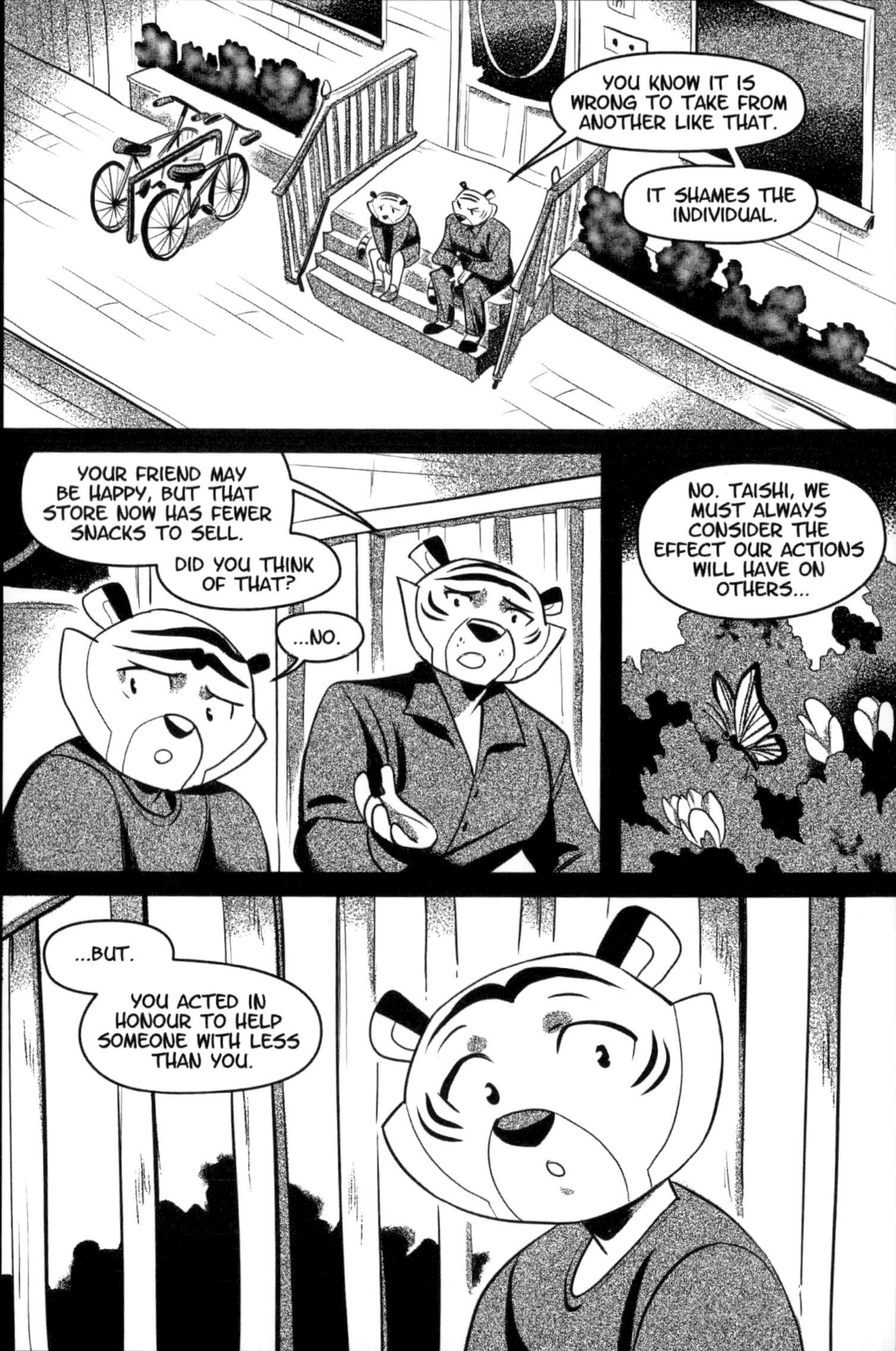
YOU KNOW IT IS WRONG TO TAKE FROM ANOTHER LIKE THAT.
IT SHAMES THE INDIVIDUAL.
YOUR FRIEND MAY BE HAPPY, BUT THAT STORE NOW HAS FEWER SNACKS TO SELL.
DID YOU THINK OF THAT?
...NO.
NO. TAISHI, WE MUST ALWAYS CONSIDER THE EFFECT OUR ACTIONS WILL HAVE ON OTHERS...
...BUT.
YOU ACTED IN HONOUR TO HELP SOMEONE WITH LESS THAN YOU.

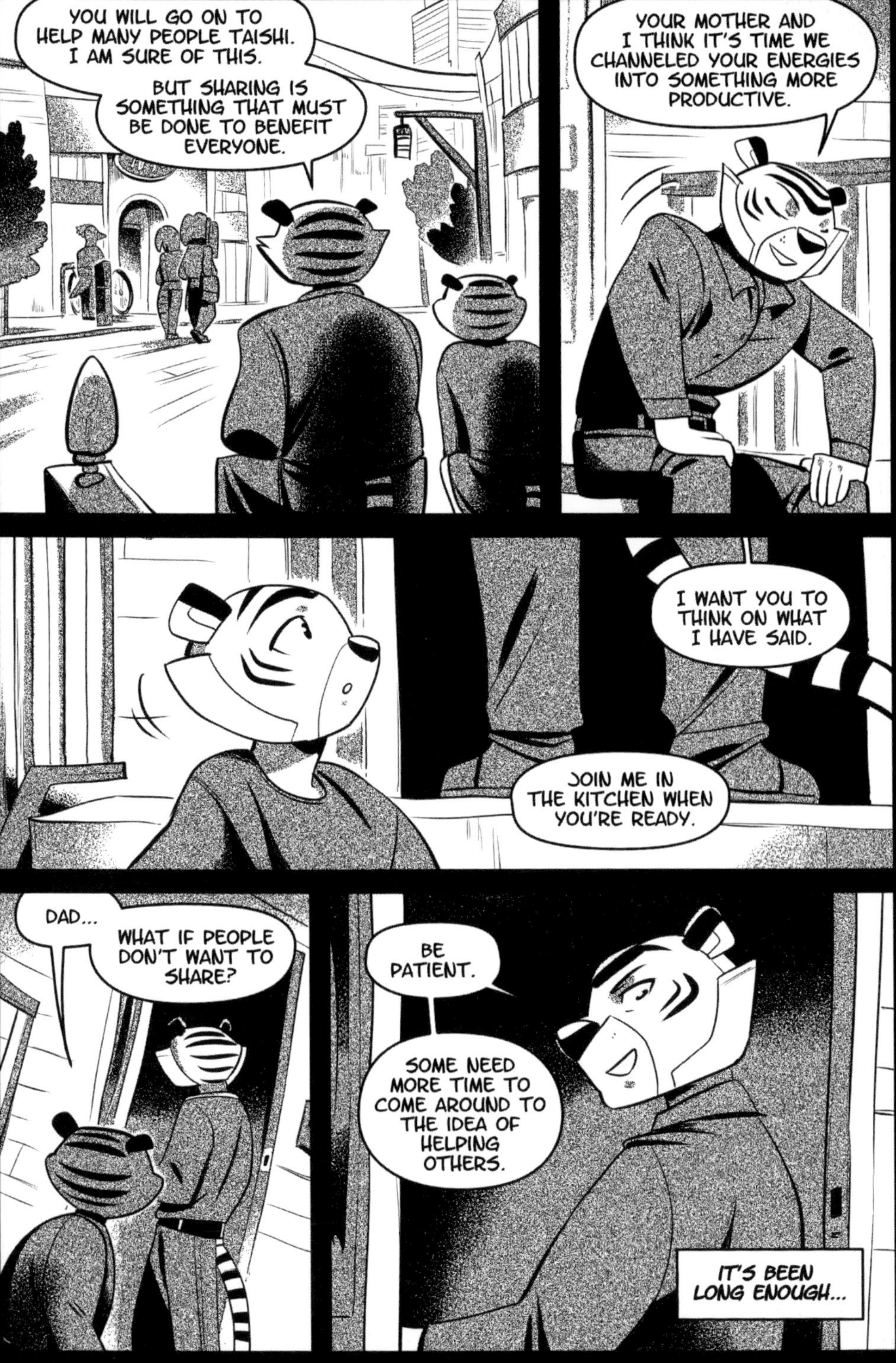
YOU WILL GO ON TO HELP MANY PEOPLE TAISHI. I AM SURE OF THIS.
BUT SHARING IS SOMETHING THAT MUST BE DONE TO BENEFIT EVERYONE.
YOUR MOTHER AND I THINK IT'S TIME WE CHANNELED YOUR ENERGIES INTO SOMETHING MORE PRODUCTIVE.
I WANT YOU TO THINK ON WHAT I HAVE SAID.
JOIN ME IN THE KITCHEN WHEN YOU'RE READY.
DAD...
WHAT IF PEOPLE DON'T WANT TO SHARE?
BE PATIENT.
SOME NEED MORE TIME TO COME AROUND TO THE IDEA OF HELPING OTHERS.
IT'S BEEN LONG ENOUGH...

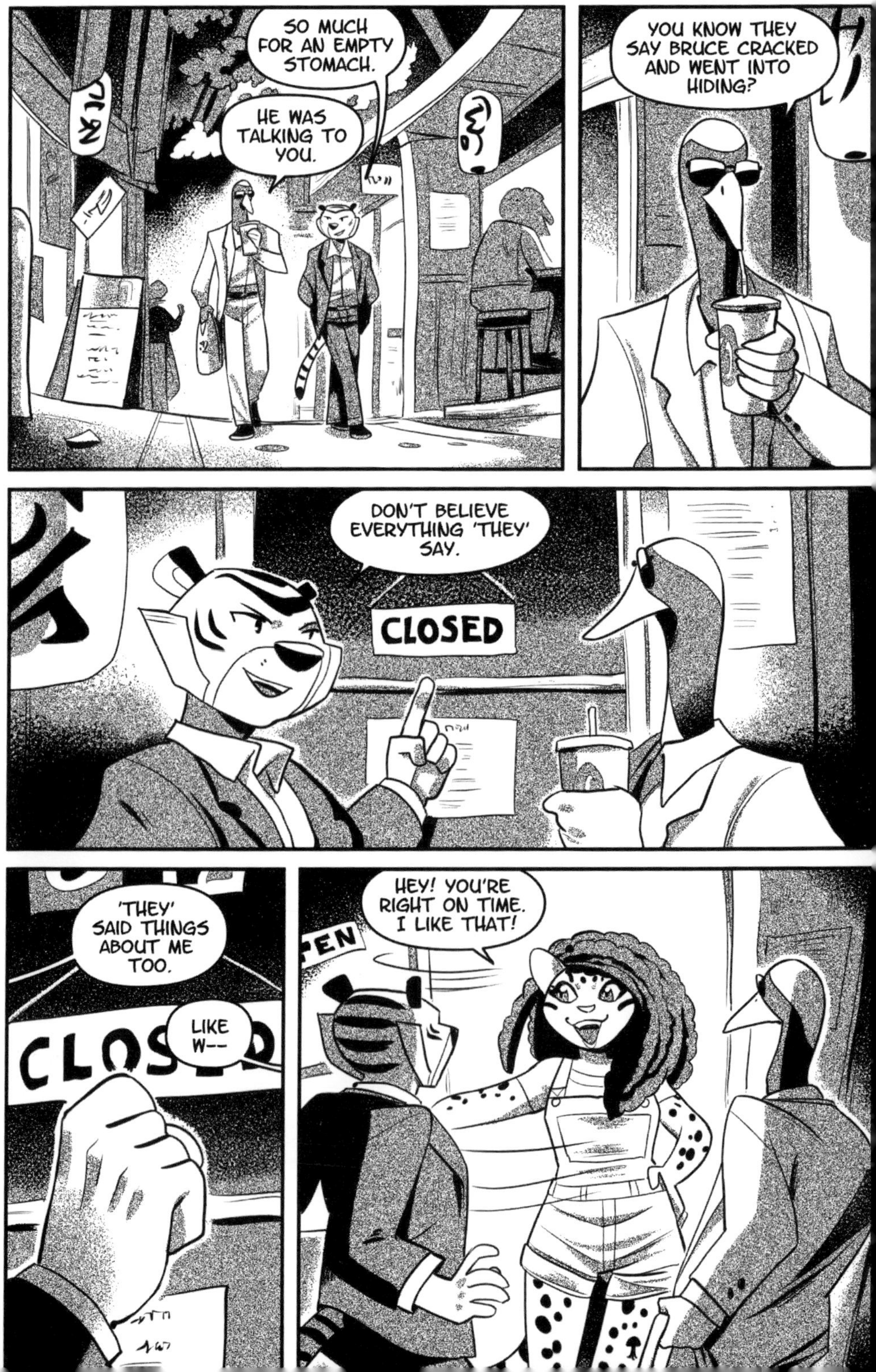
SO MUCH FOR AN EMPTY STOMACH.
HE WAS TALKING TO YOU.
YOU KNOW THEY SAY BRUCE CRACKED AND WENT INTO HIDING?
DON'T BELIEVE EVERYTHING 'THEY' SAY.
CLOSED
'THEY' SAID THINGS ABOUT ME TOO.
LIKE W--
HEY! YOU'RE RIGHT ON TIME. I LIKE THAT!

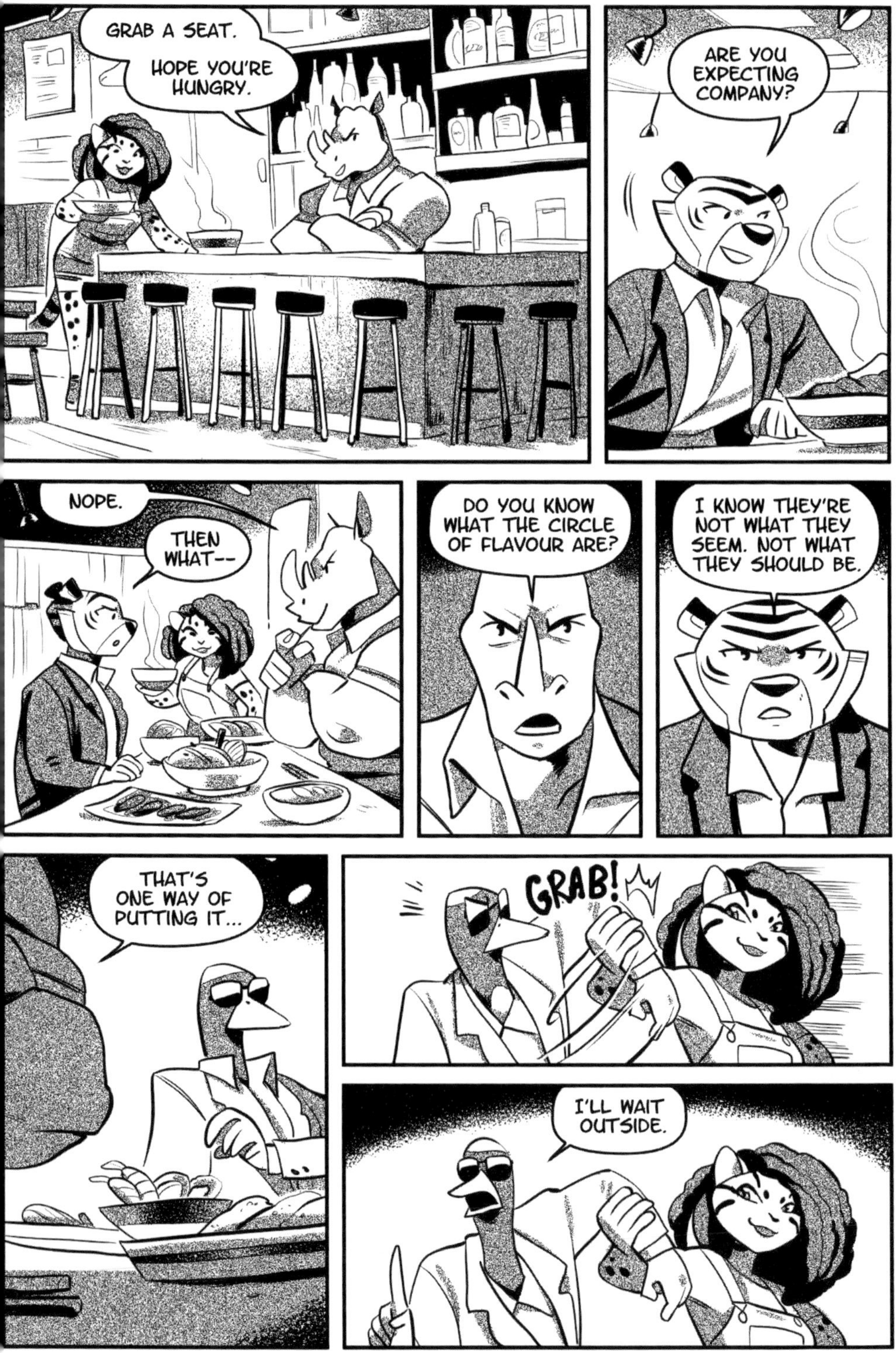
GRAB A SEAT.
HOPE YOU'RE HUNGRY.
ARE YOU EXPECTING COMPANY?
NOPE.
THEN WHAT--
DO YOU KNOW WHAT THE CIRCLE OF FLAVOUR ARE?
I KNOW THEY'RE NOT WHAT THEY SEEM. NOT WHAT THEY SHOULD BE.
THAT'S ONE WAY OF PUTTING IT...
GRAB!
I'LL WAIT OUTSIDE.

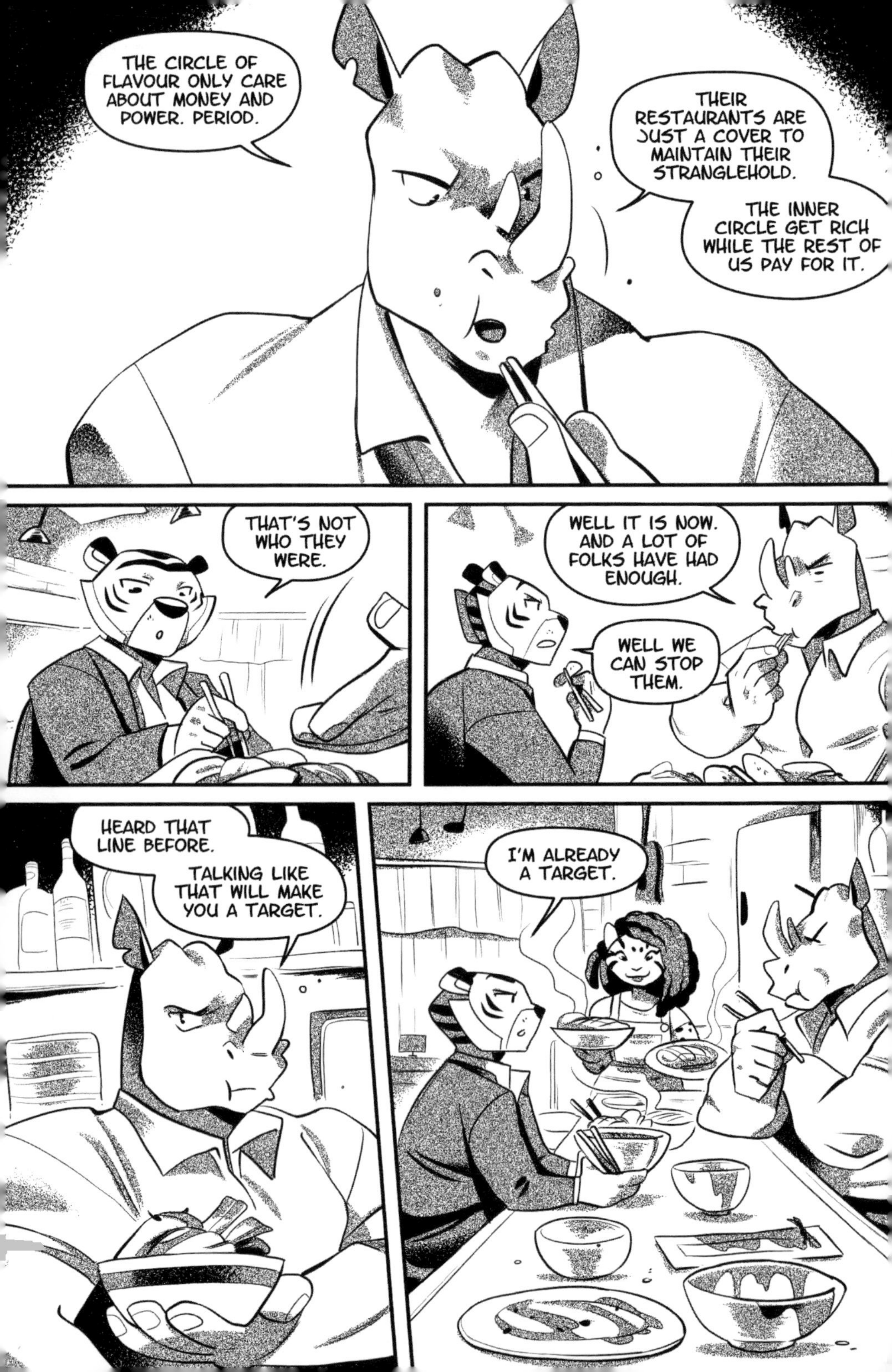
THE CIRCLE OF FLAVOUR ONLY CARE ABOUT MONEY AND POWER. PERIOD.
THEIR RESTAURANTS ARE JUST A COVER TO MAINTAIN THEIR STRANGLEHOLD.
THE INNER CIRCLE GET RICH WHILE THE REST OF US PAY FOR IT.
THAT'S NOT WHO THEY WERE.
WELL IT IS NOW. AND A LOT OF FOLKS HAVE HAD ENOUGH.
WELL WE CAN STOP THEM.
HEARD THAT LINE BEFORE.
TALKING LIKE THAT WILL MAKE YOU A TARGET.
I'M ALREADY A TARGET.

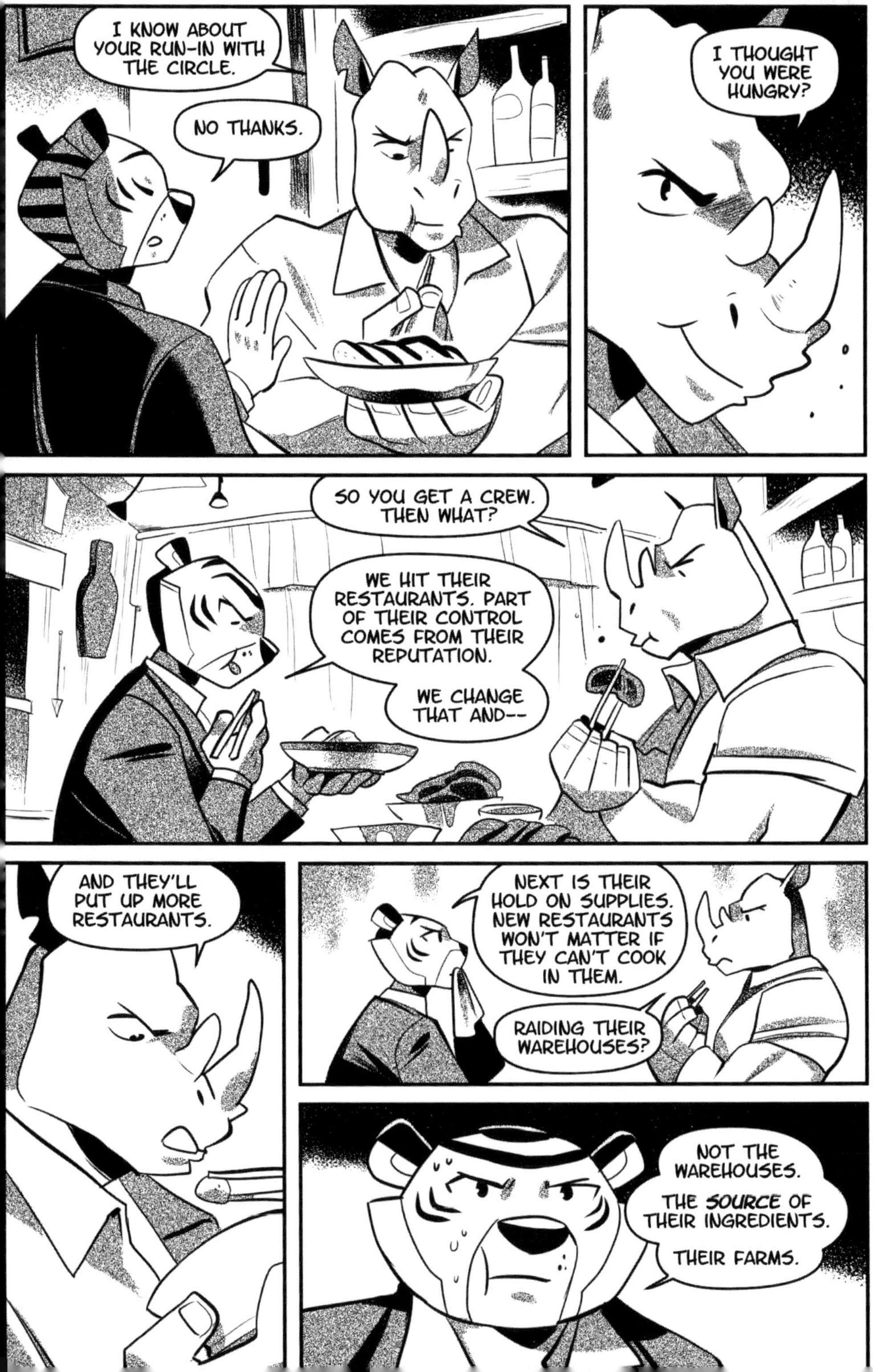
I KNOW ABOUT YOUR RUN-IN WITH THE CIRCLE.
NO THANKS.
I THOUGHT YOU WERE HUNGRY?
SO YOU GET A CREW. THEN WHAT?
WE HIT THEIR RESTAURANTS. PART OF THEIR CONTROL COMES FROM THEIR REPUTATION.
WE CHANGE THAT AND--
AND THEY'LL PUT UP MORE RESTAURANTS.
NEXT IS THEIR HOLD ON SUPPLIES. NEW RESTAURANTS WON'T MATTER IF THEY CAN'T COOK IN THEM.
RAIDING THEIR WAREHOUSES?
NOT THE WAREHOUSES.
THE *SOURCE* OF THEIR INGREDIENTS.
THEIR FARMS.

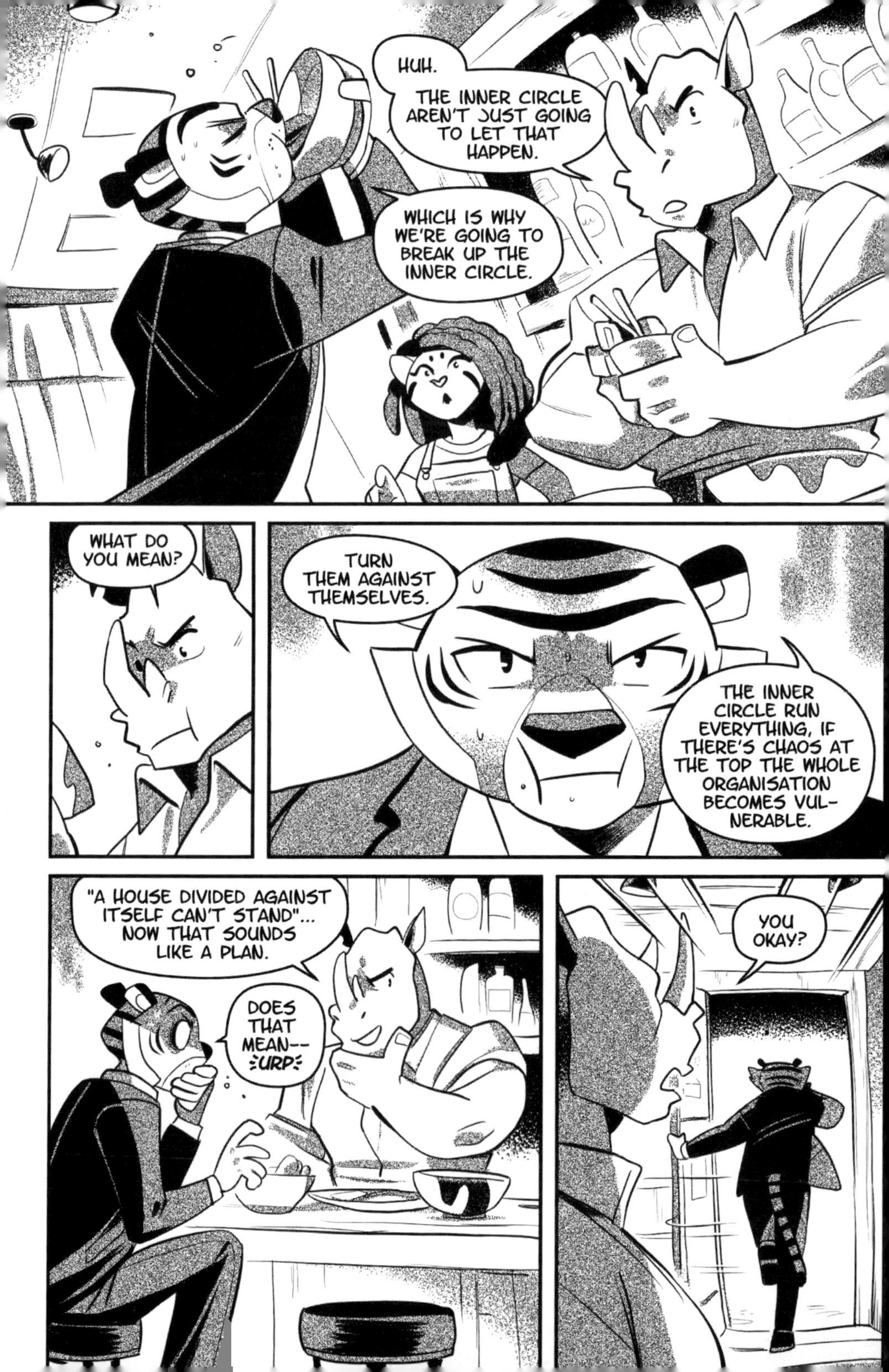
HUH.
THE INNER CIRCLE AREN'T JUST GOING TO LET THAT HAPPEN.
WHICH IS WHY WE'RE GOING TO BREAK UP THE INNER CIRCLE.
WHAT DO YOU MEAN?
TURN THEM AGAINST THEMSELVES.
THE INNER CIRCLE RUN EVERYTHING, IF THERE'S CHAOS AT THE TOP THE WHOLE ORGANISATION BECOMES VUL-NERABLE.
"A HOUSE DIVIDED AGAINST ITSELF CAN'T STAND"... NOW THAT SOUNDS LIKE A PLAN.
DOES THAT MEAN-- URP
YOU OKAY?

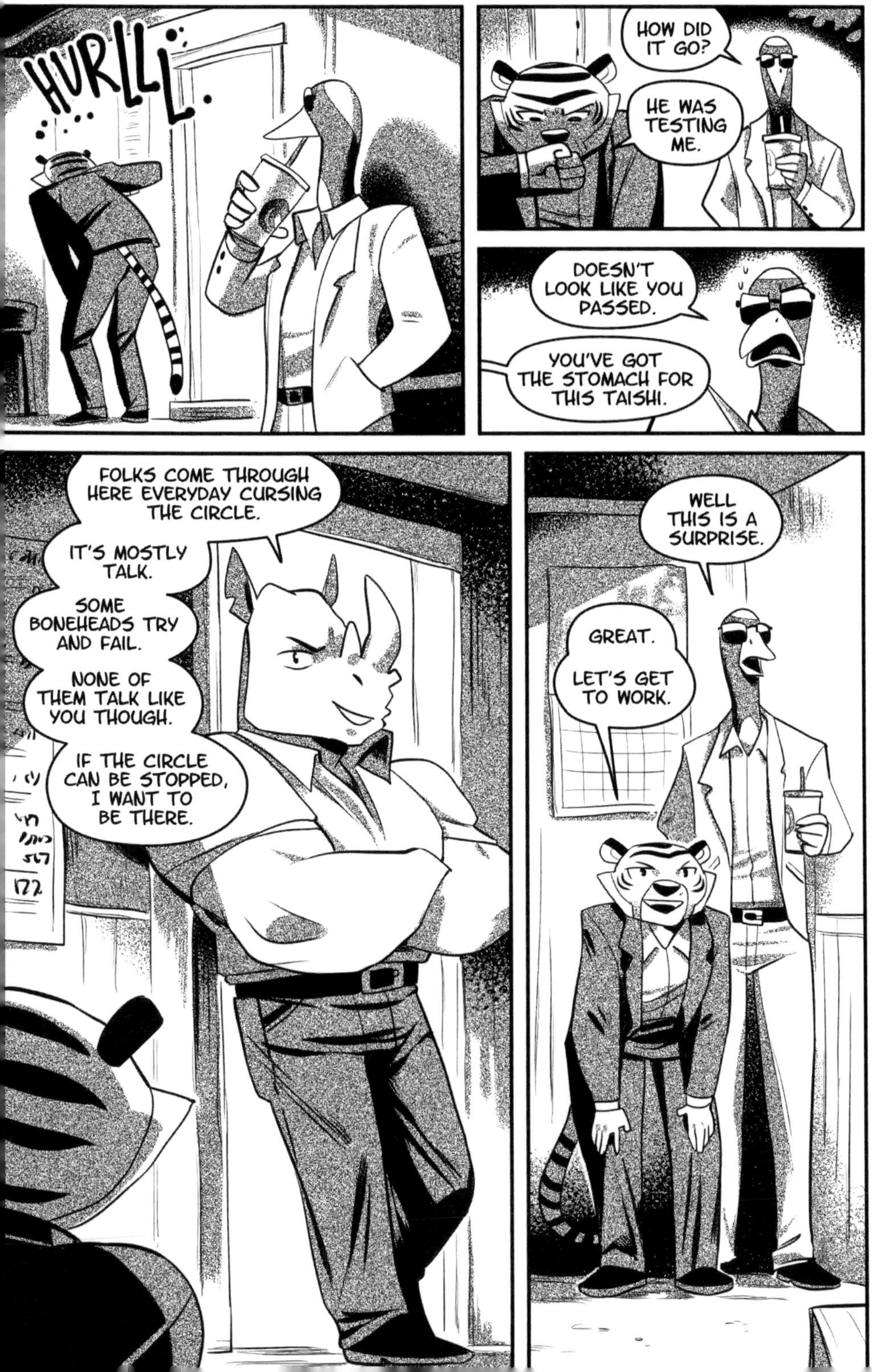
HURLLL
HOW DID IT GO?
HE WAS TESTING ME.
DOESN'T LOOK LIKE YOU PASSED.
YOU'VE GOT THE STOMACH FOR THIS TAISHI.
FOLKS COME THROUGH HERE EVERYDAY CURSING THE CIRCLE.
IT'S MOSTLY TALK.
SOME BONEHEADS TRY AND FAIL.
NONE OF THEM TALK LIKE YOU THOUGH.
IF THE CIRCLE CAN BE STOPPED, I WANT TO BE THERE.
WELL THIS IS A SURPRISE.
GREAT.
LET'S GET TO WORK.

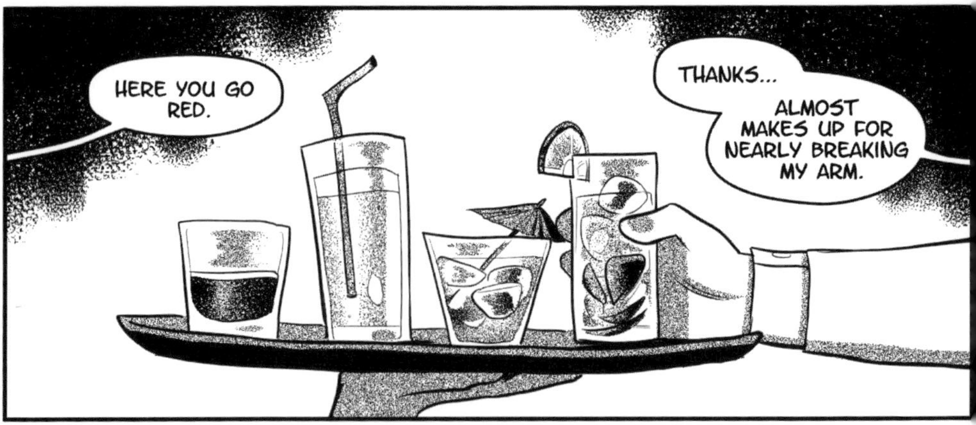
HERE YOU GO RED.
THANKS...
ALMOST MAKES UP FOR NEARLY BREAKING MY ARM.

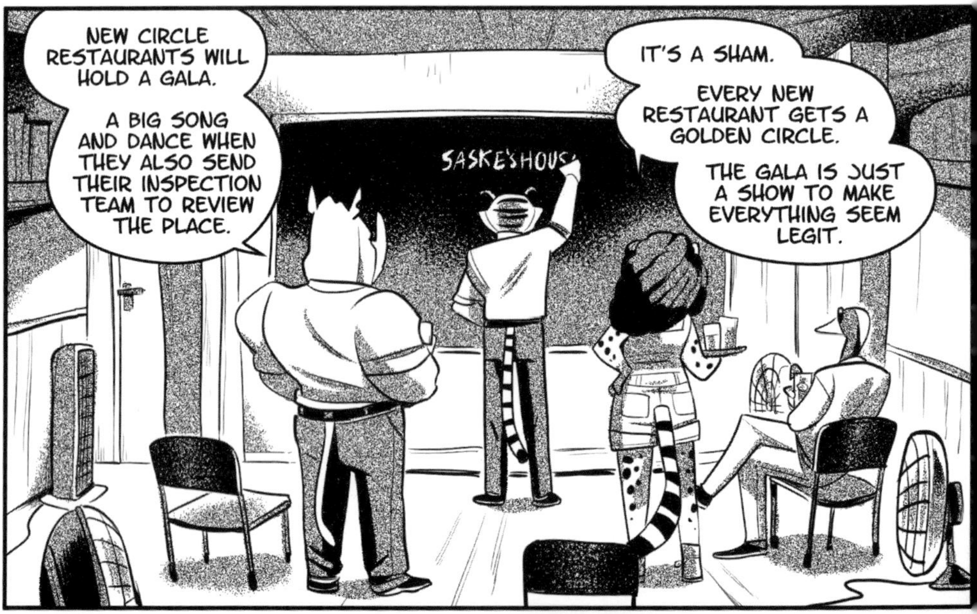
NEW CIRCLE RESTAURANTS WILL HOLD A GALA.
A BIG SONG AND DANCE WHEN THEY ALSO SEND THEIR INSPECTION TEAM TO REVIEW THE PLACE.
SASKE'S HOUS
IT'S A SHAM.
EVERY NEW RESTAURANT GETS A GOLDEN CIRCLE.
THE GALA IS JUST A SHOW TO MAKE EVERYTHING SEEM LEGIT.

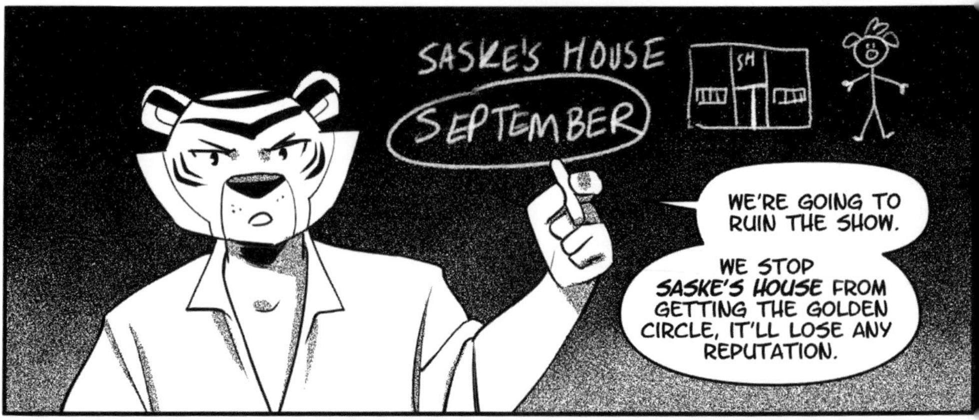
SASKE'S HOUSE
SEPTEMBER
SH
WE'RE GOING TO RUIN THE SHOW.
WE STOP ***SASKE'S HOUSE*** FROM GETTING THE GOLDEN CIRCLE, IT'LL LOSE ANY REPUTATION.

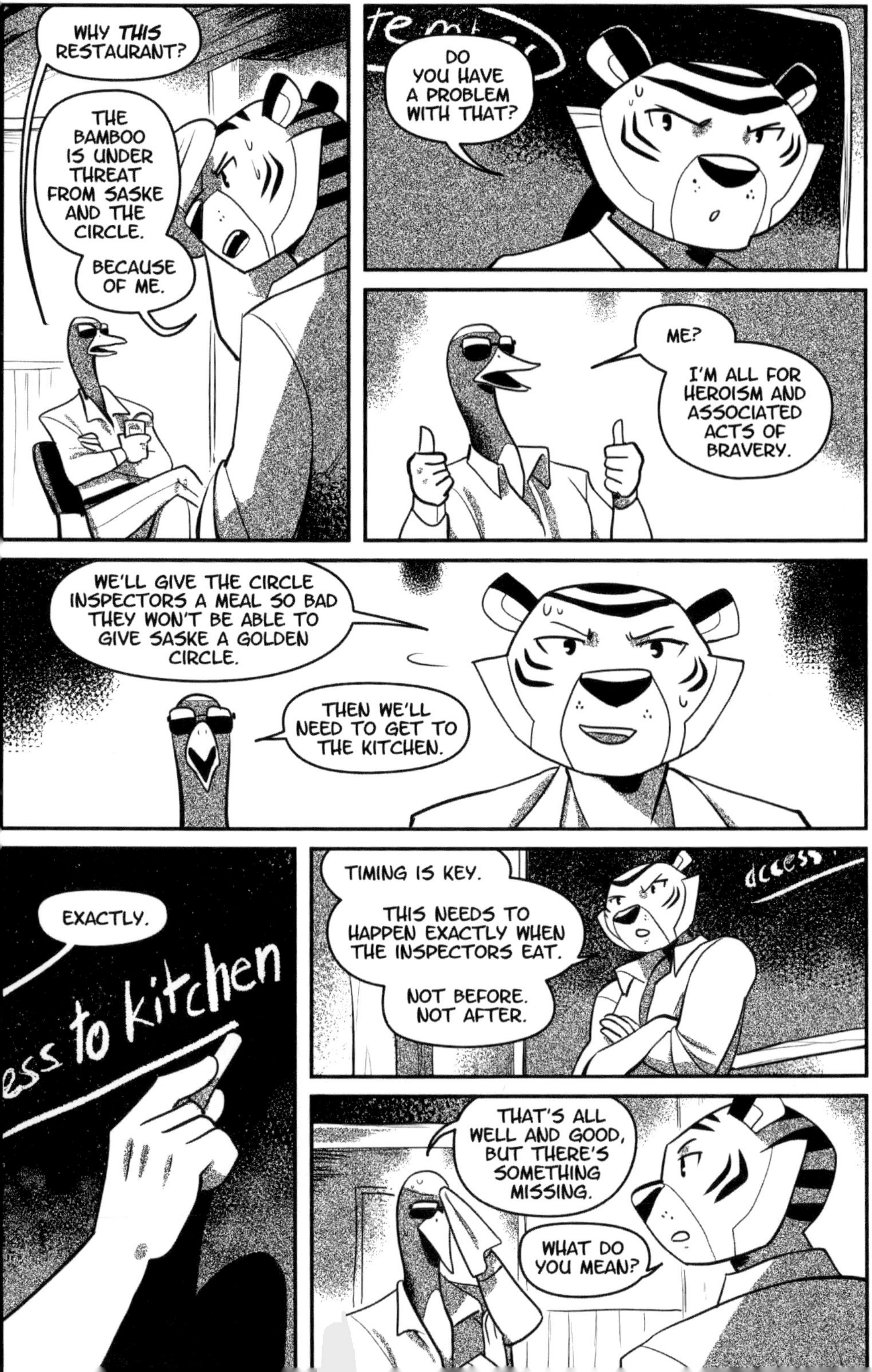
WHY THIS RESTAURANT?
THE BAMBOO IS UNDER THREAT FROM SASKE AND THE CIRCLE.
BECAUSE OF ME.
DO YOU HAVE A PROBLEM WITH THAT?
ME?
I'M ALL FOR HEROISM AND ASSOCIATED ACTS OF BRAVERY.
WE'LL GIVE THE CIRCLE INSPECTORS A MEAL SO BAD THEY WON'T BE ABLE TO GIVE SASKE A GOLDEN CIRCLE.
THEN WE'LL NEED TO GET TO THE KITCHEN.
EXACTLY.
ess to kitchen
TIMING IS KEY.
THIS NEEDS TO HAPPEN EXACTLY WHEN THE INSPECTORS EAT.
NOT BEFORE. NOT AFTER.
THAT'S ALL WELL AND GOOD, BUT THERE'S SOMETHING MISSING.
WHAT DO YOU MEAN?

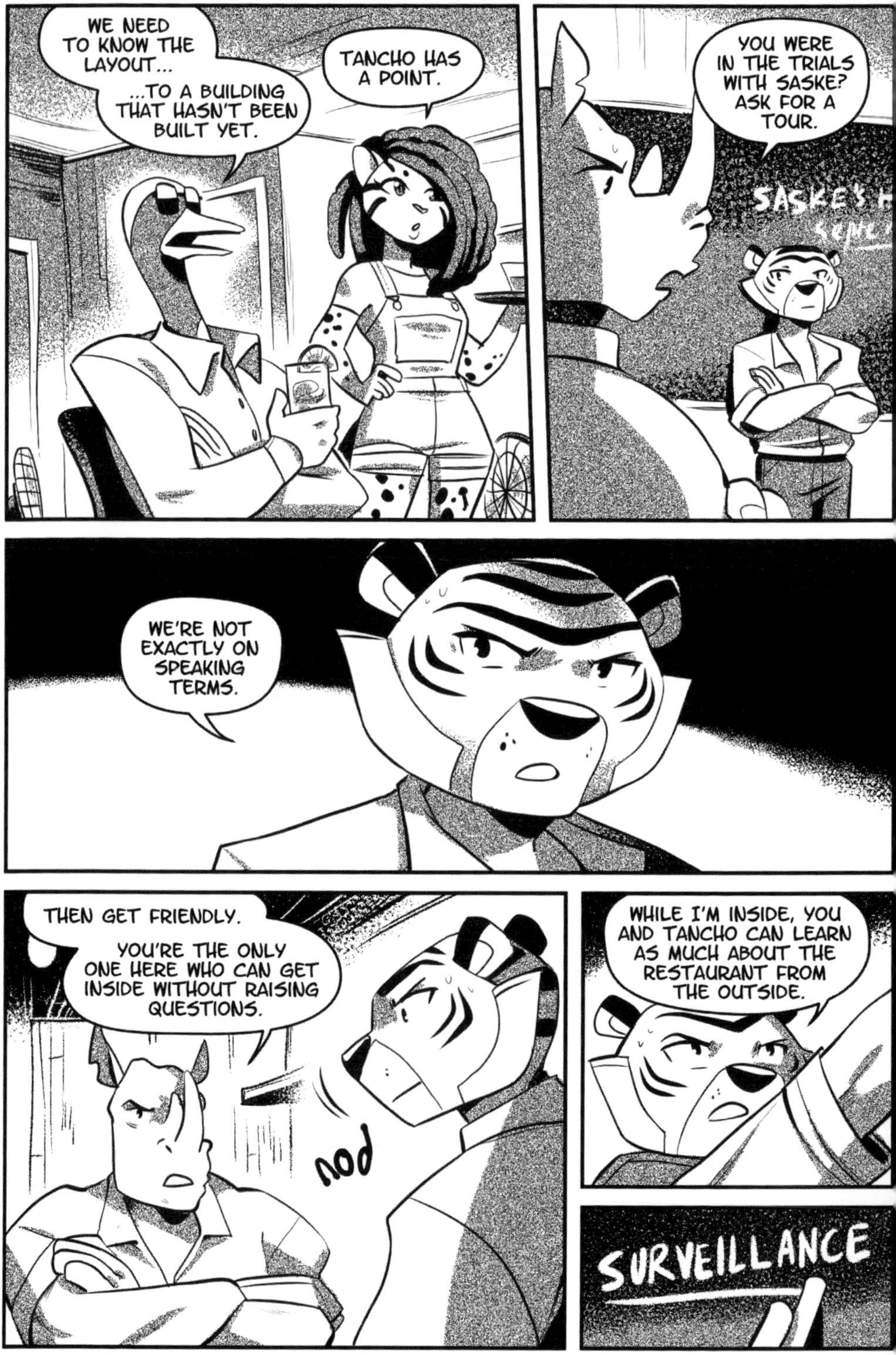
WE NEED TO KNOW THE LAYOUT...
...TO A BUILDING THAT HASN'T BEEN BUILT YET.
TANCHO HAS A POINT.
YOU WERE IN THE TRIALS WITH SASKE? ASK FOR A TOUR.
SASKE'S
WE'RE NOT EXACTLY ON SPEAKING TERMS.
THEN GET FRIENDLY.
YOU'RE THE ONLY ONE HERE WHO CAN GET INSIDE WITHOUT RAISING QUESTIONS.
nod
WHILE I'M INSIDE, YOU AND TANCHO CAN LEARN AS MUCH ABOUT THE RESTAURANT FROM THE OUTSIDE.
SURVEILLANCE

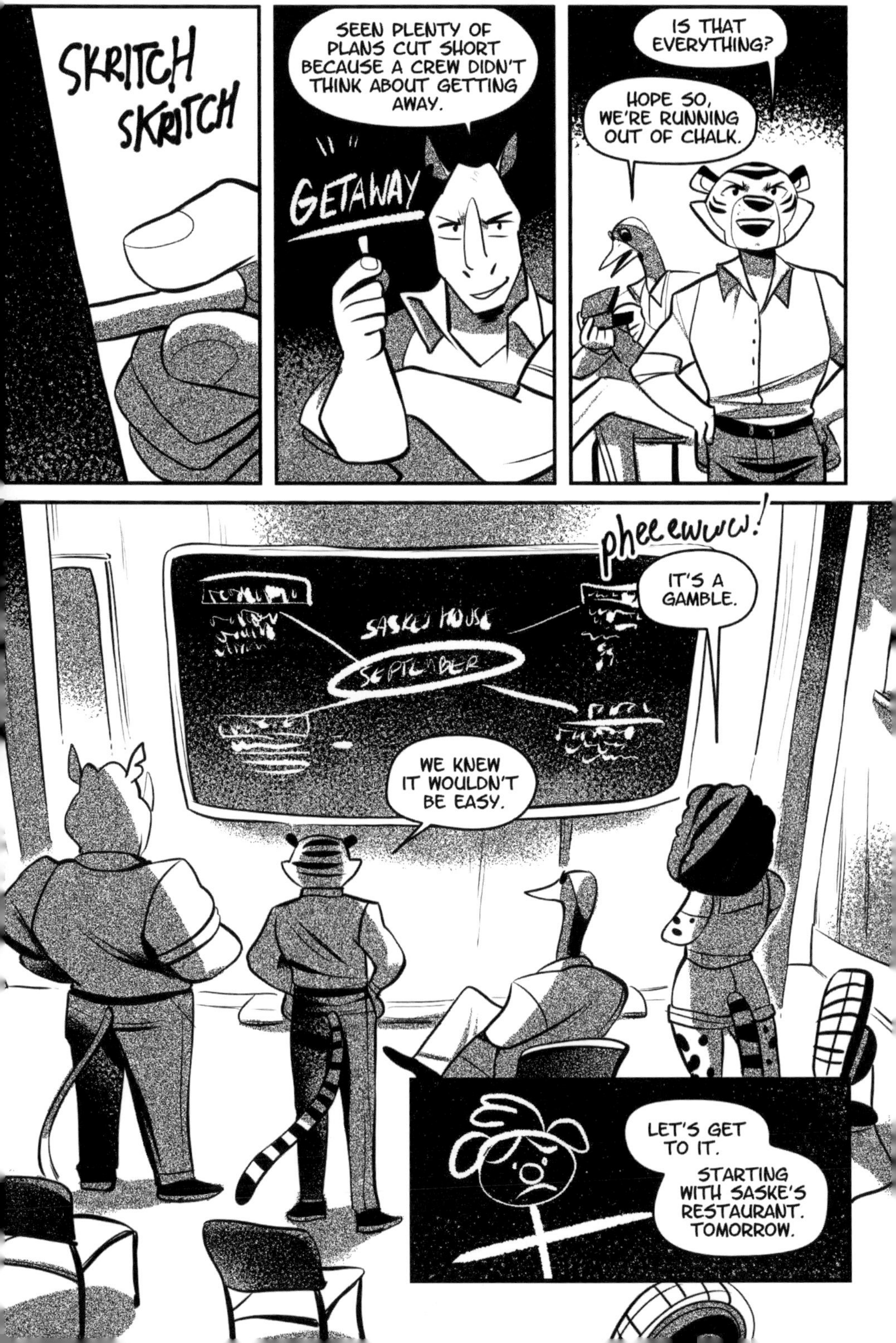
SKRITCH
SKRITCH
SEEN PLENTY OF PLANS CUT SHORT BECAUSE A CREW DIDN'T THINK ABOUT GETTING AWAY.
GETAWAY
IS THAT EVERYTHING?
HOPE SO, WE'RE RUNNING OUT OF CHALK.
pheeewww!
IT'S A GAMBLE.
WE KNEW IT WOULDN'T BE EASY.
LET'S GET TO IT.
STARTING WITH SASKE'S RESTAURANT. TOMORROW.

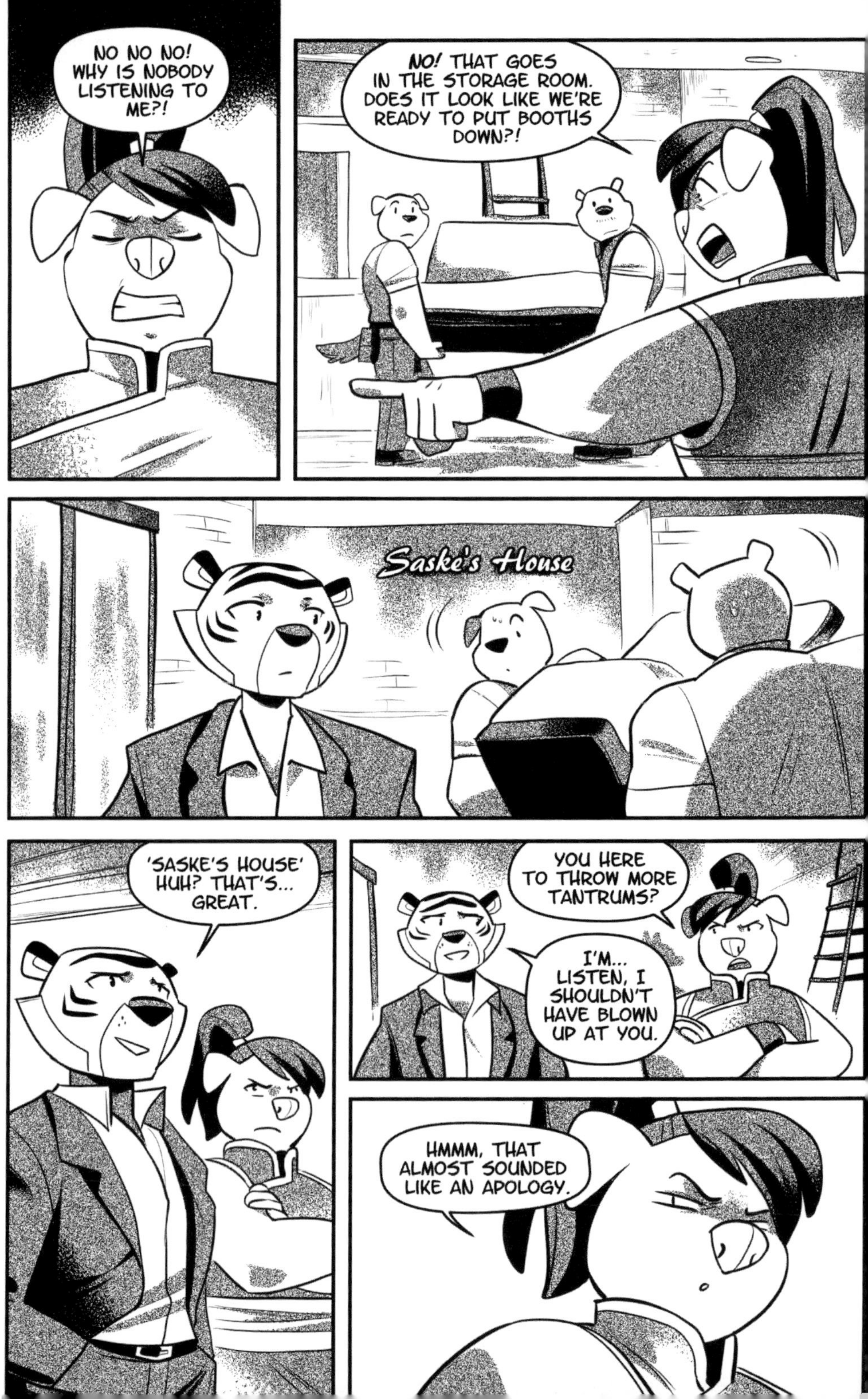
NO NO NO! WHY IS NOBODY LISTENING TO ME?!
NO! THAT GOES IN THE STORAGE ROOM. DOES IT LOOK LIKE WE'RE READY TO PUT BOOTHS DOWN?!
Saske's House
'SASKE'S HOUSE' HUH? THAT'S... GREAT.
YOU HERE TO THROW MORE TANTRUMS?
I'M... LISTEN, I SHOULDN'T HAVE BLOWN UP AT YOU.
HMMM, THAT ALMOST SOUNDED LIKE AN APOLOGY.

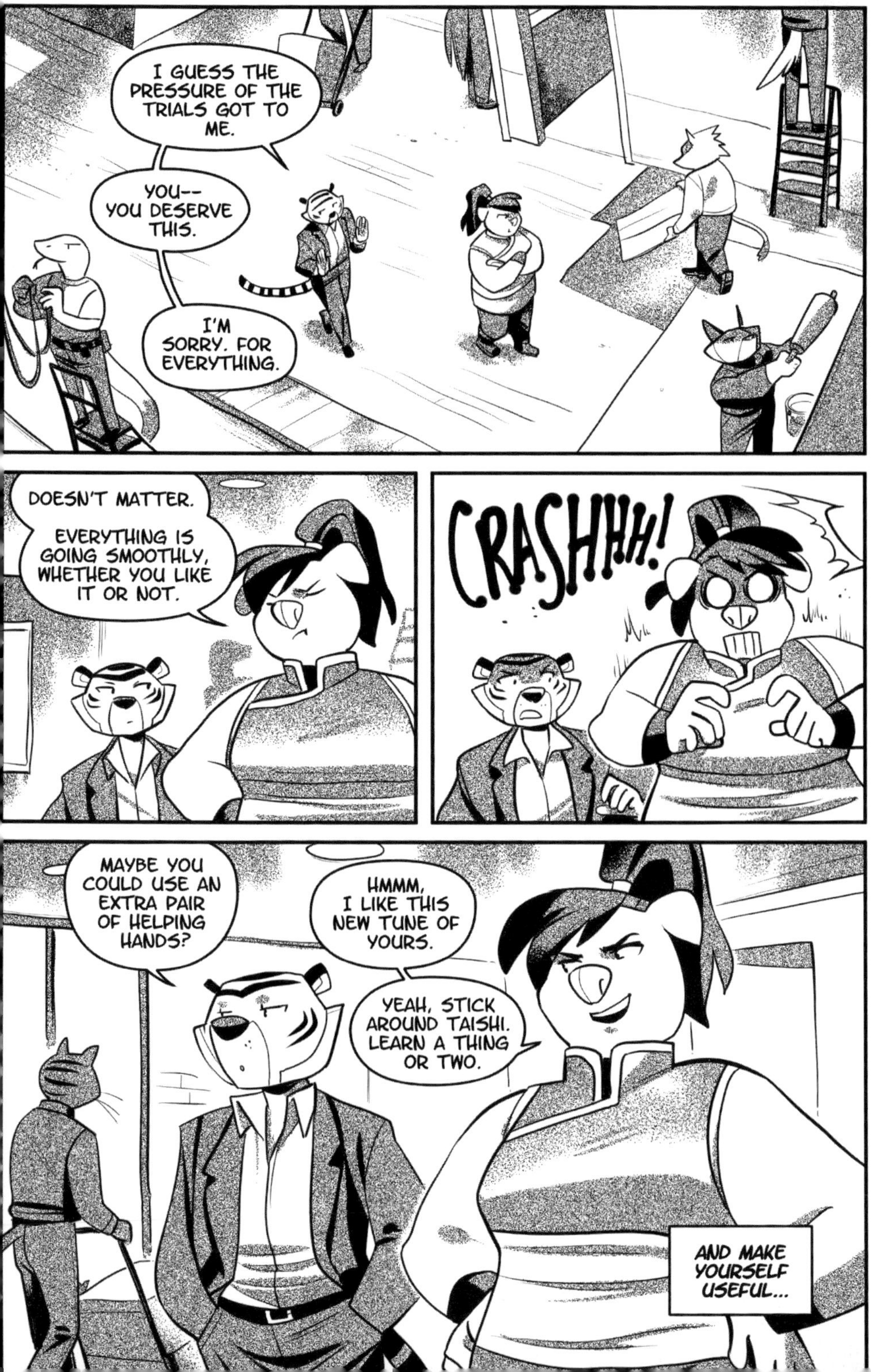
I GUESS THE PRESSURE OF THE TRIALS GOT TO ME.
YOU-- YOU DESERVE THIS.
I'M SORRY. FOR EVERYTHING.
DOESN'T MATTER.
EVERYTHING IS GOING SMOOTHLY, WHETHER YOU LIKE IT OR NOT.
CRASHHH!
MAYBE YOU COULD USE AN EXTRA PAIR OF HELPING HANDS?
HMMM, I LIKE THIS NEW TUNE OF YOURS.
YEAH, STICK AROUND TAISHI. LEARN A THING OR TWO.
AND MAKE YOURSELF USEFUL...

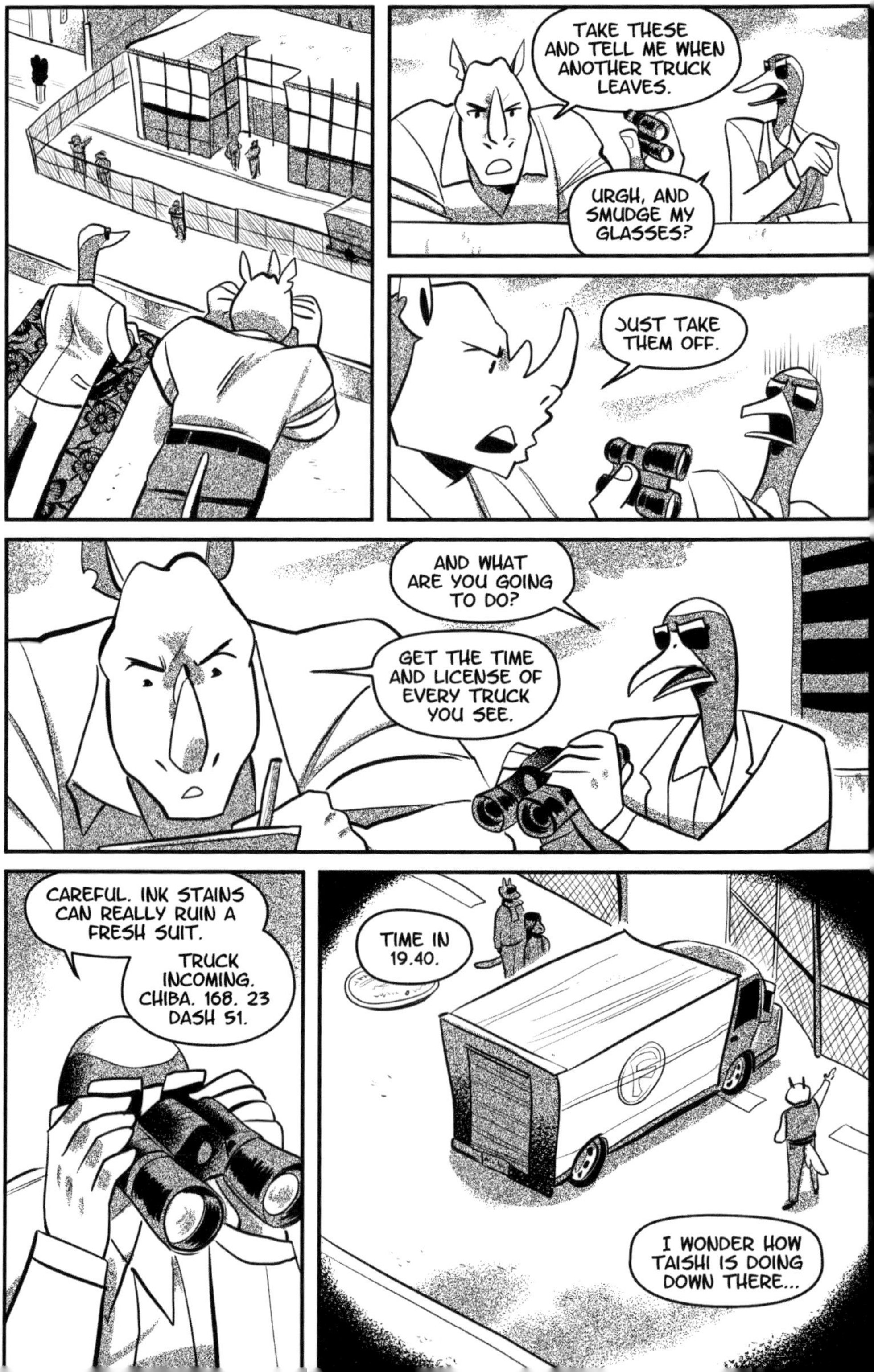
TAKE THESE AND TELL ME WHEN ANOTHER TRUCK LEAVES.
URGH, AND SMUDGE MY GLASSES?
JUST TAKE THEM OFF.
AND WHAT ARE YOU GOING TO DO?
GET THE TIME AND LICENSE OF EVERY TRUCK YOU SEE.
CAREFUL. INK STAINS CAN REALLY RUIN A FRESH SUIT.
TRUCK INCOMING. CHIBA. 168. 23 DASH 51.
TIME IN 19.40.
I WONDER HOW TAISHI IS DOING DOWN THERE...

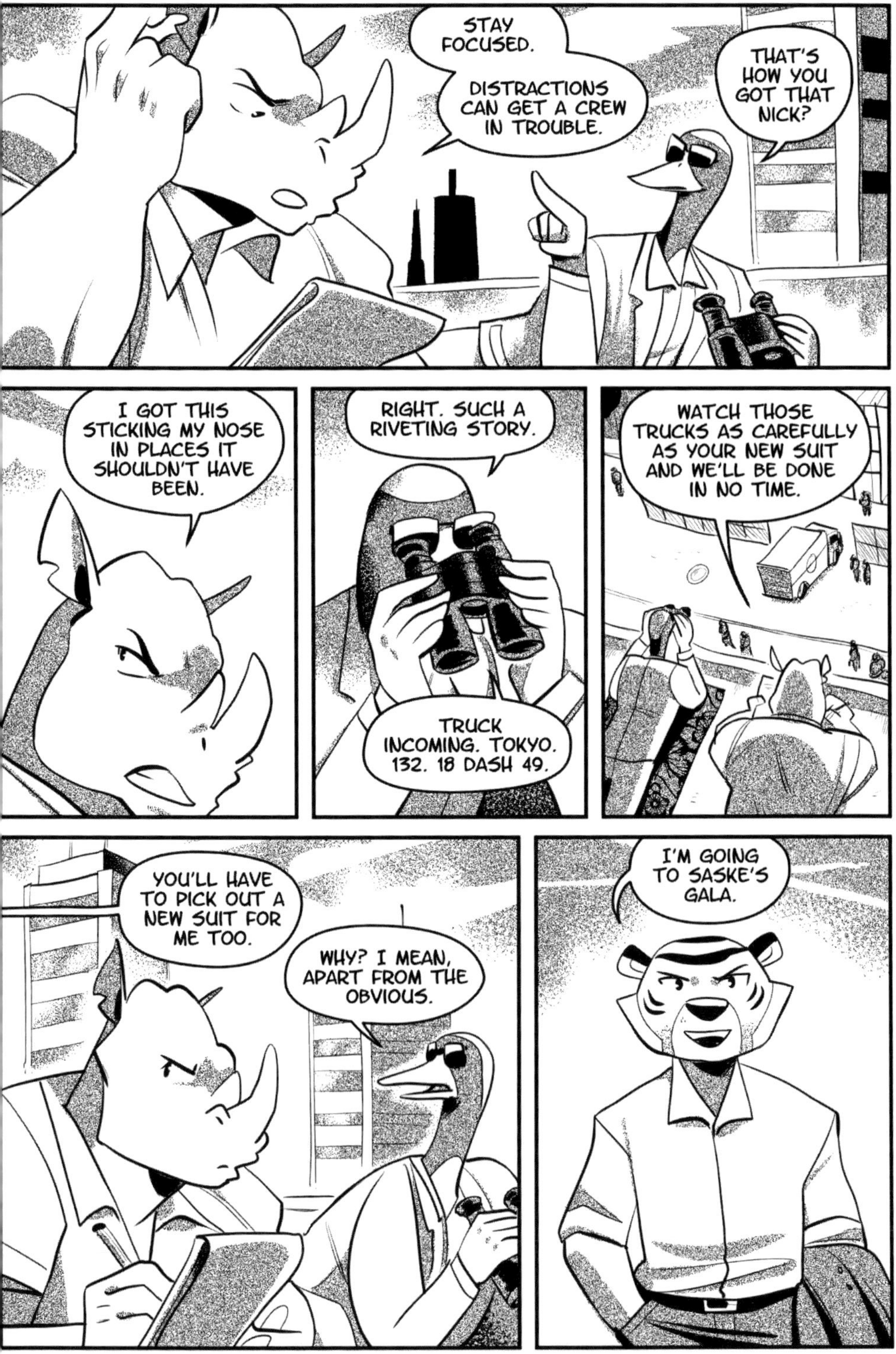
STAY FOCUSED.
DISTRACTIONS CAN GET A CREW IN TROUBLE.
THAT'S HOW YOU GOT THAT NICK?
I GOT THIS STICKING MY NOSE IN PLACES IT SHOULDN'T HAVE BEEN.
RIGHT. SUCH A RIVETING STORY.
TRUCK INCOMING. TOKYO. 132. 18 DASH 49.
WATCH THOSE TRUCKS AS CAREFULLY AS YOUR NEW SUIT AND WE'LL BE DONE IN NO TIME.
YOU'LL HAVE TO PICK OUT A NEW SUIT FOR ME TOO.
WHY? I MEAN, APART FROM THE OBVIOUS.
I'M GOING TO SASKE'S GALA.

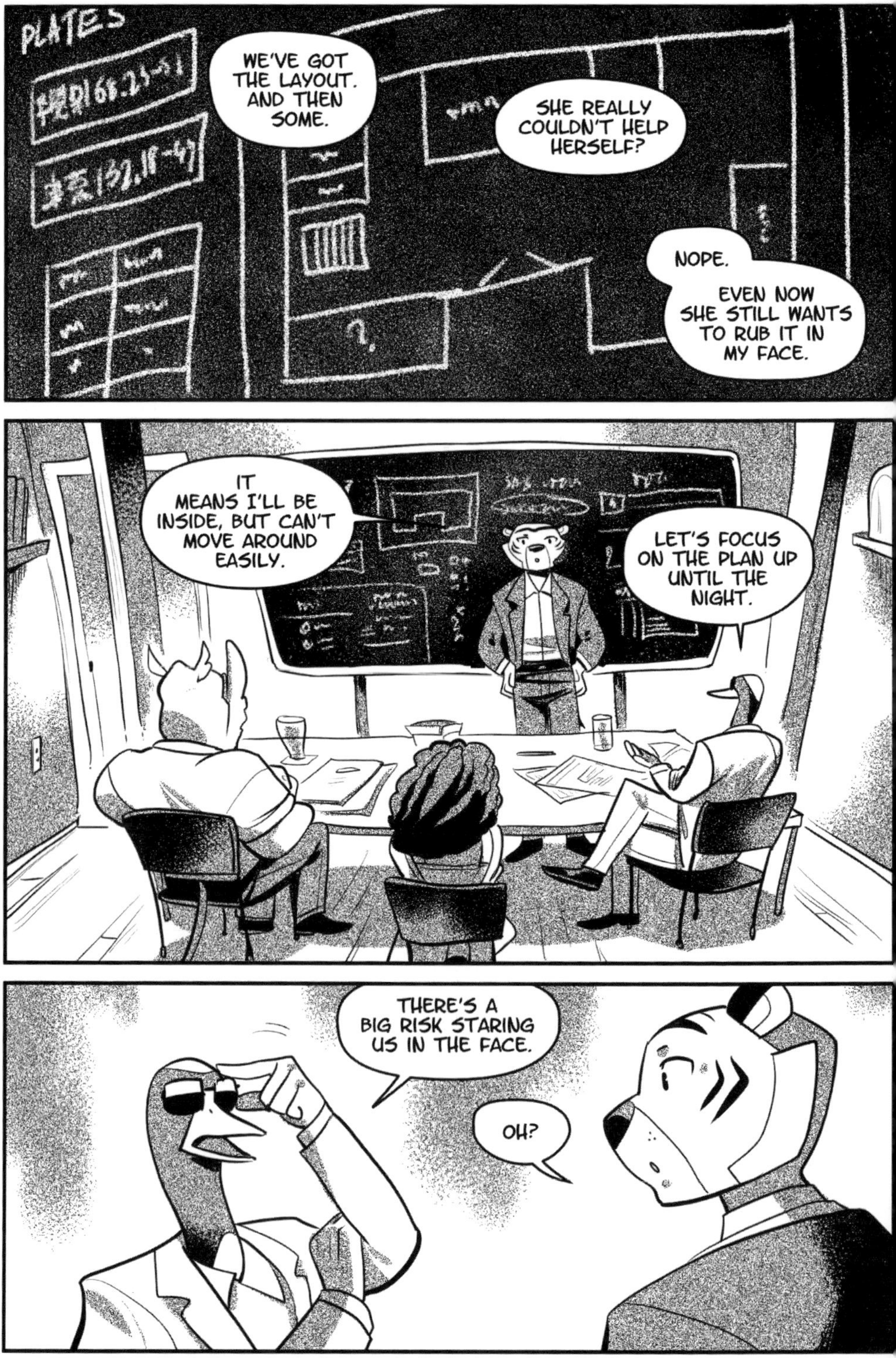
PLATES
WE'VE GOT THE LAYOUT. AND THEN SOME.
SHE REALLY COULDN'T HELP HERSELF?
NOPE.
EVEN NOW SHE STILL WANTS TO RUB IT IN MY FACE.
IT MEANS I'LL BE INSIDE, BUT CAN'T MOVE AROUND EASILY.
LET'S FOCUS ON THE PLAN UP UNTIL THE NIGHT.
THERE'S A BIG RISK STARING US IN THE FACE.
OH?

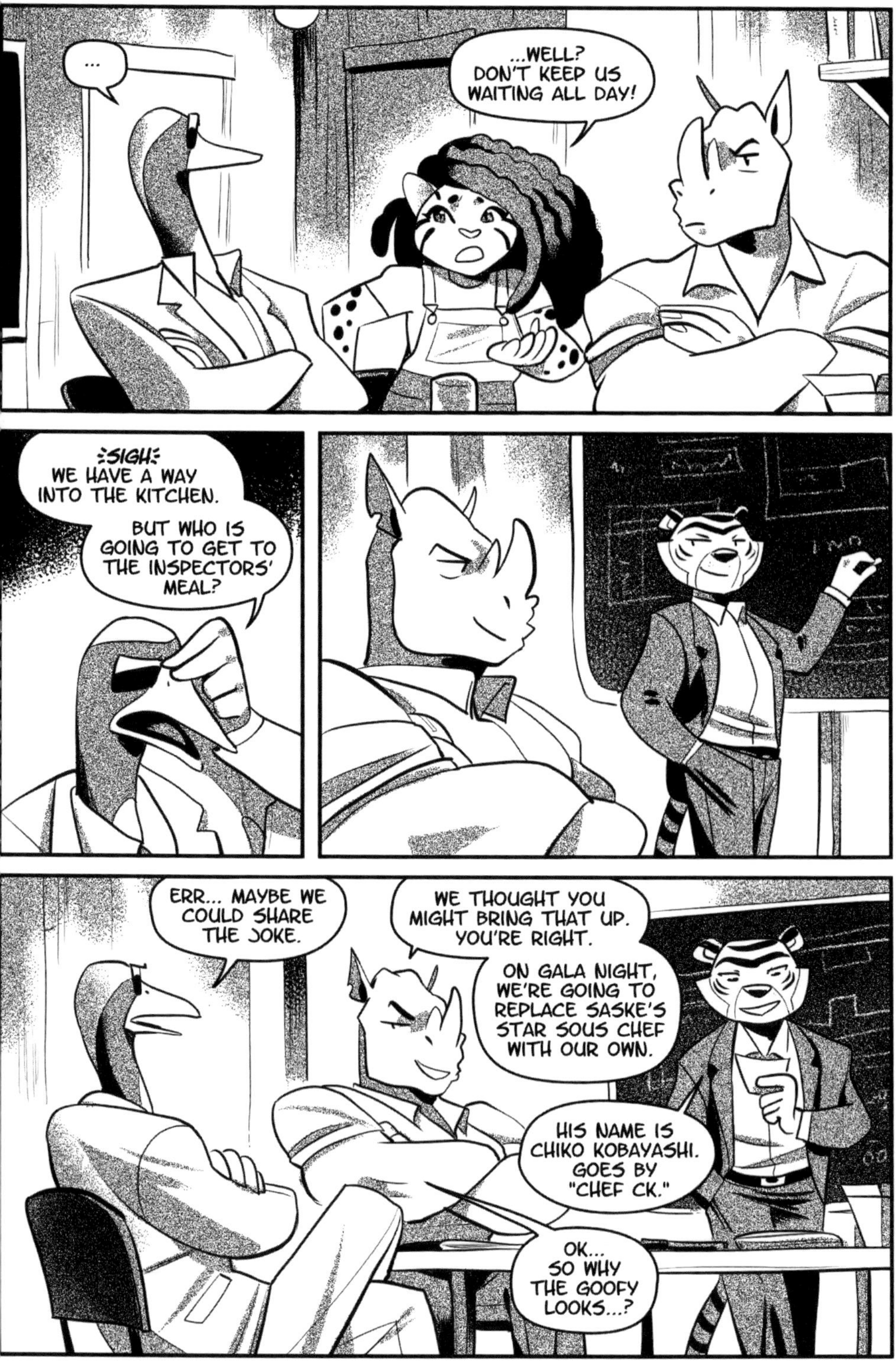
...
...WELL? DON'T KEEP US WAITING ALL DAY!
SIGH
WE HAVE A WAY INTO THE KITCHEN.
BUT WHO IS GOING TO GET TO THE INSPECTORS' MEAL?
ERR... MAYBE WE COULD SHARE THE JOKE.
WE THOUGHT YOU MIGHT BRING THAT UP. YOU'RE RIGHT.
ON GALA NIGHT, WE'RE GOING TO REPLACE SASKE'S STAR SOUS CHEF WITH OUR OWN.
HIS NAME IS CHIKO KOBAYASHI. GOES BY "CHEF CK."
OK... SO WHY THE GOOFY LOOKS...?

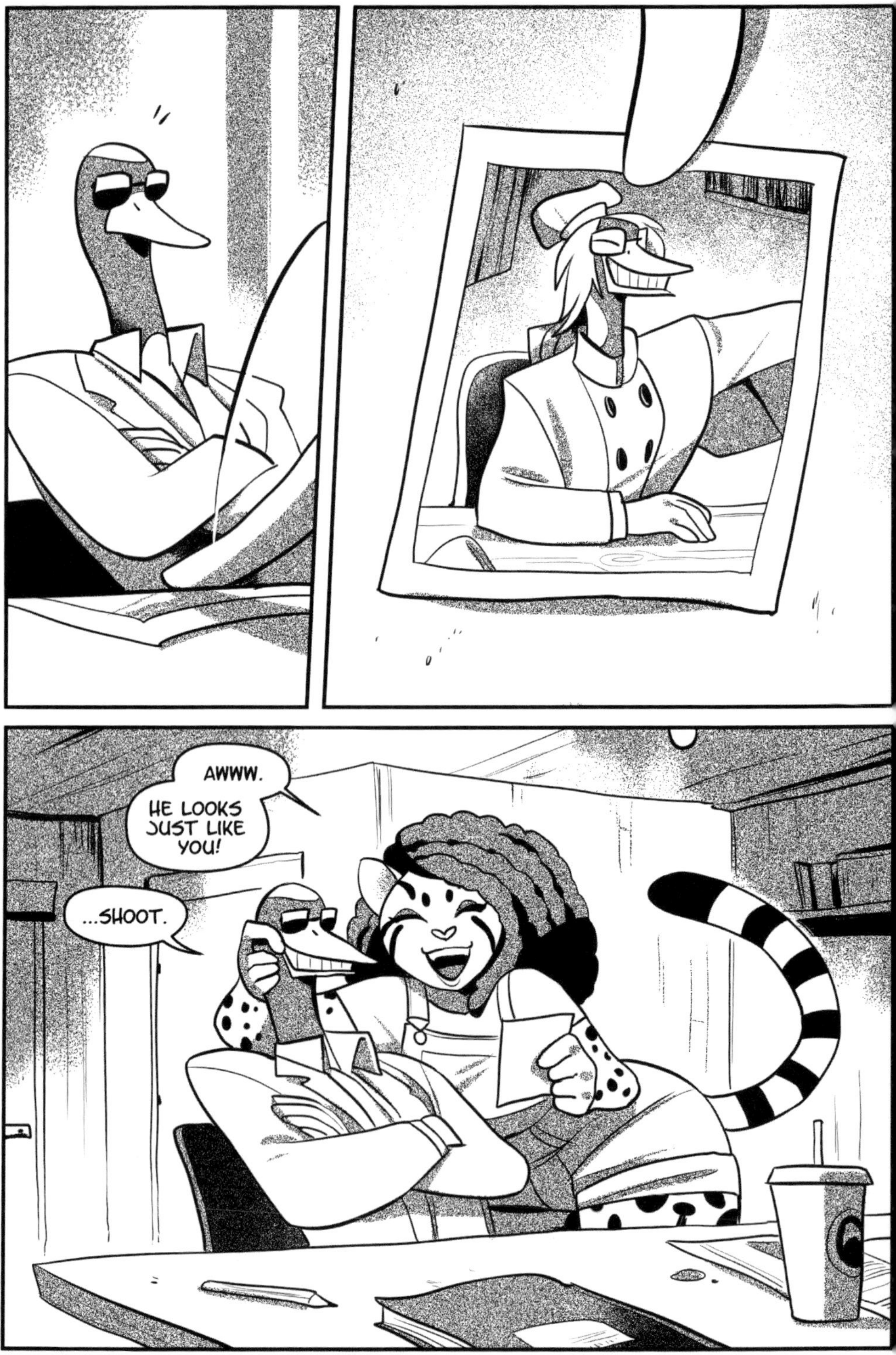
AWWW.
HE LOOKS JUST LIKE YOU!
...SHOOT.

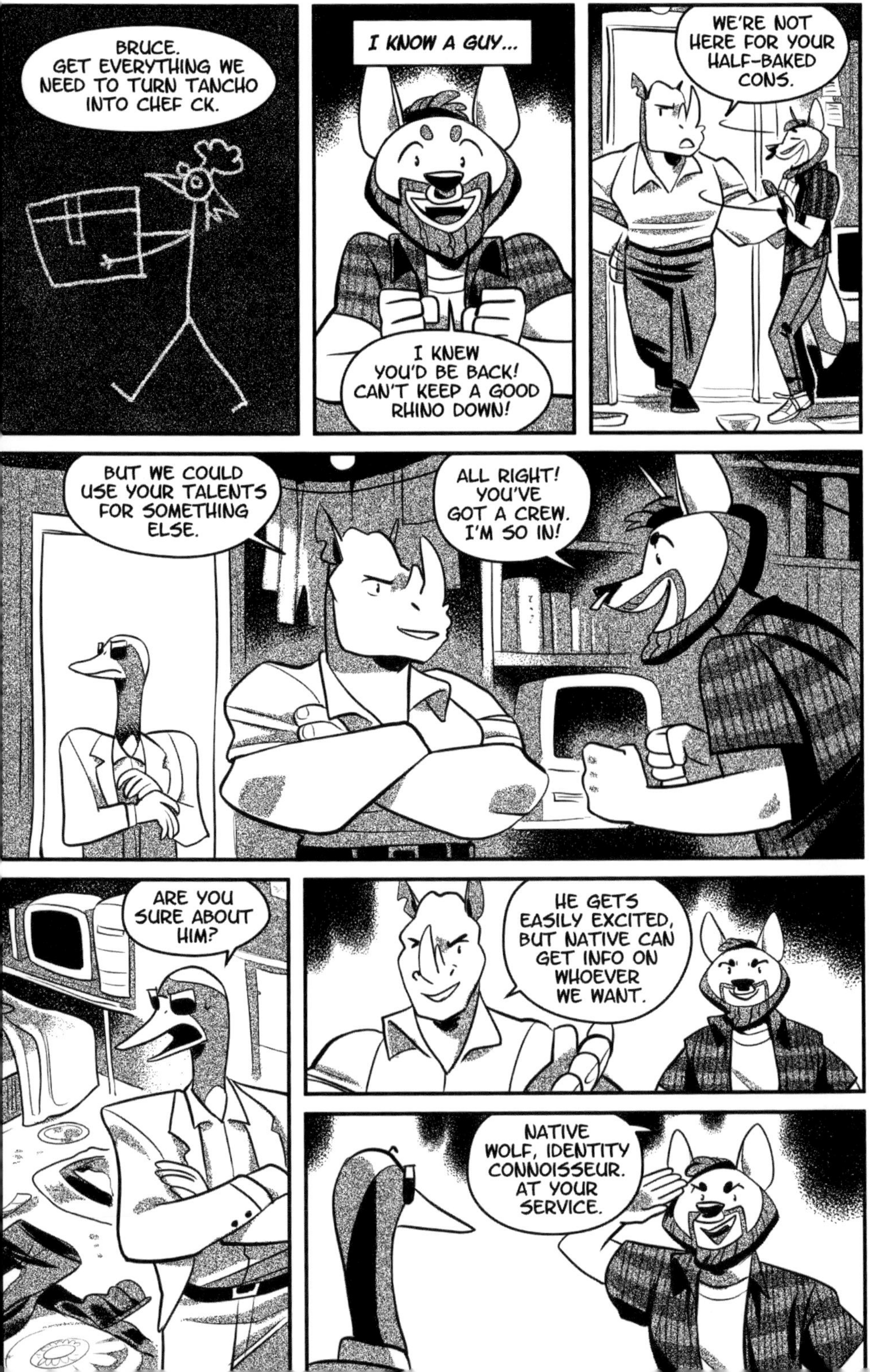
BRUCE. GET EVERYTHING WE NEED TO TURN TANCHO INTO CHEF CK.
I KNOW A GUY...
I KNEW YOU'D BE BACK! CAN'T KEEP A GOOD RHINO DOWN!
WE'RE NOT HERE FOR YOUR HALF-BAKED CONS.
BUT WE COULD USE YOUR TALENTS FOR SOMETHING ELSE.
ALL RIGHT! YOU'VE GOT A CREW. I'M SO IN!
ARE YOU SURE ABOUT HIM?
HE GETS EASILY EXCITED, BUT NATIVE CAN GET INFO ON WHOEVER WE WANT.
NATIVE WOLF, IDENTITY CONNOISSEUR. AT YOUR SERVICE.

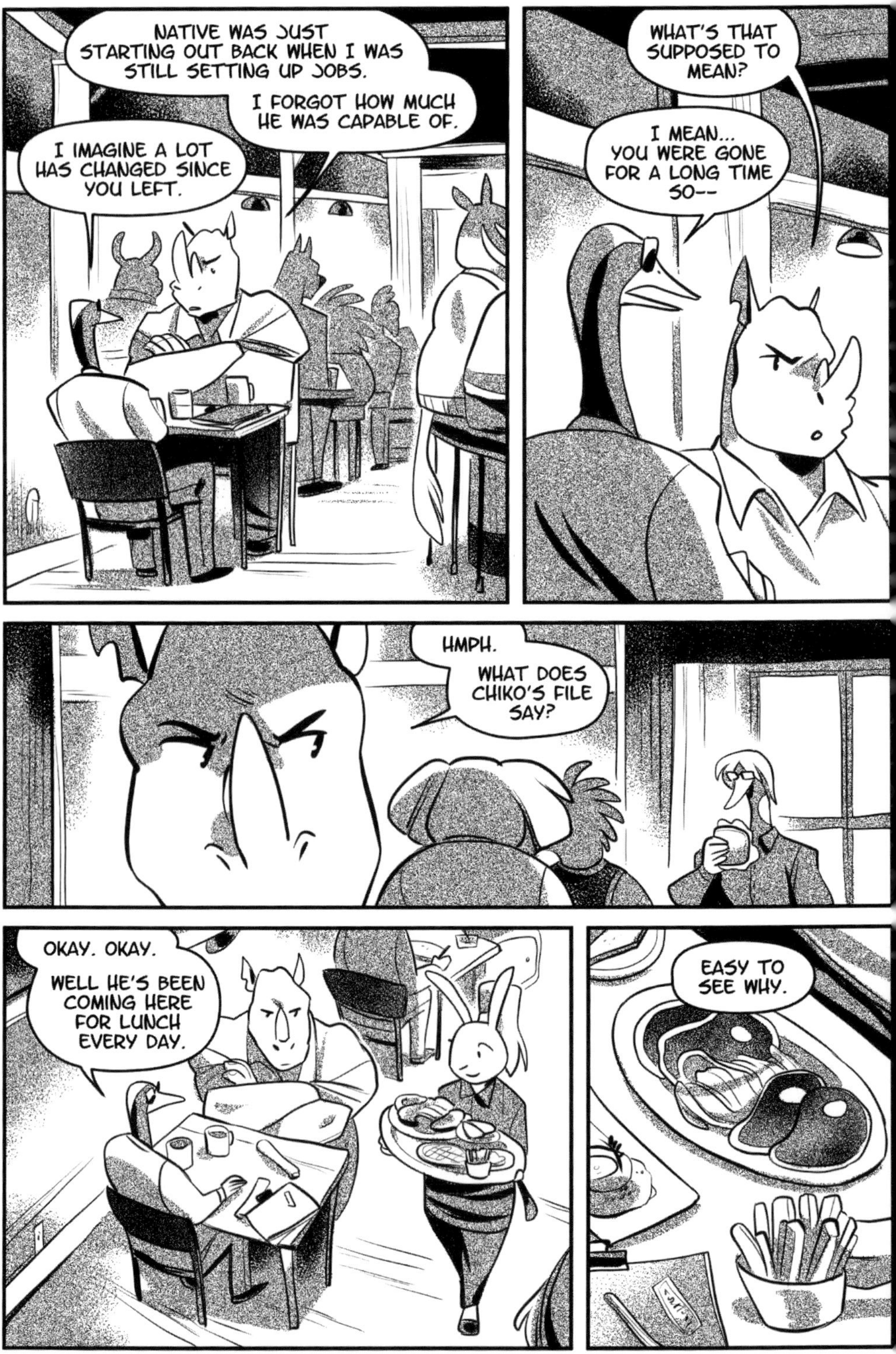
NATIVE WAS JUST STARTING OUT BACK WHEN I WAS STILL SETTING UP JOBS.
I FORGOT HOW MUCH HE WAS CAPABLE OF.
I IMAGINE A LOT HAS CHANGED SINCE YOU LEFT.
WHAT'S THAT SUPPOSED TO MEAN?
I MEAN... YOU WERE GONE FOR A LONG TIME SO--
HMPH.
WHAT DOES CHIKO'S FILE SAY?
OKAY. OKAY.
WELL HE'S BEEN COMING HERE FOR LUNCH EVERY DAY.
EASY TO SEE WHY.

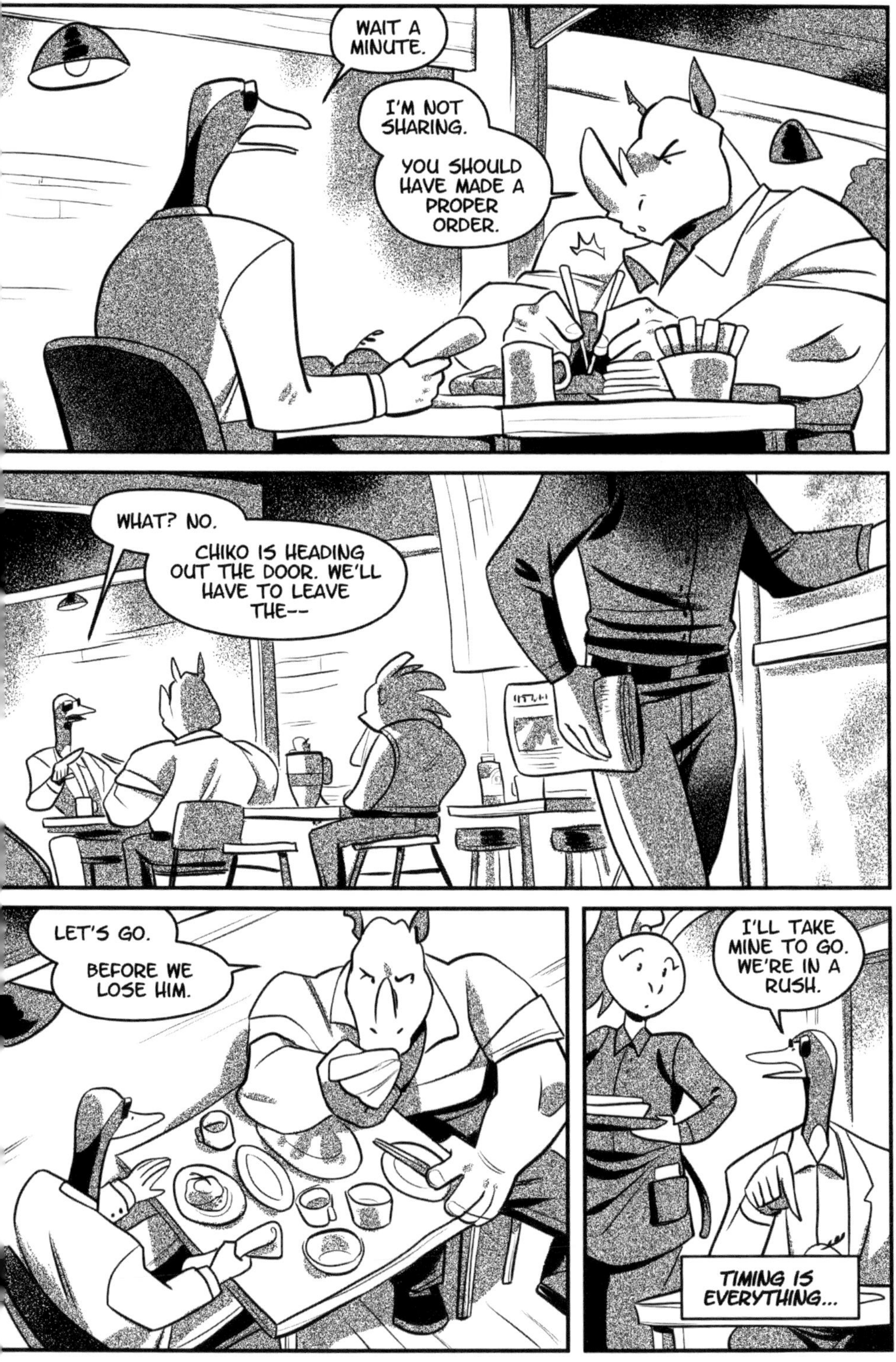
WAIT A MINUTE.
I'M NOT SHARING.
YOU SHOULD HAVE MADE A PROPER ORDER.
WHAT? NO.
CHIKO IS HEADING OUT THE DOOR. WE'LL HAVE TO LEAVE THE--
LET'S GO.
BEFORE WE LOSE HIM.
I'LL TAKE MINE TO GO. WE'RE IN A RUSH.
TIMING IS EVERYTHING...

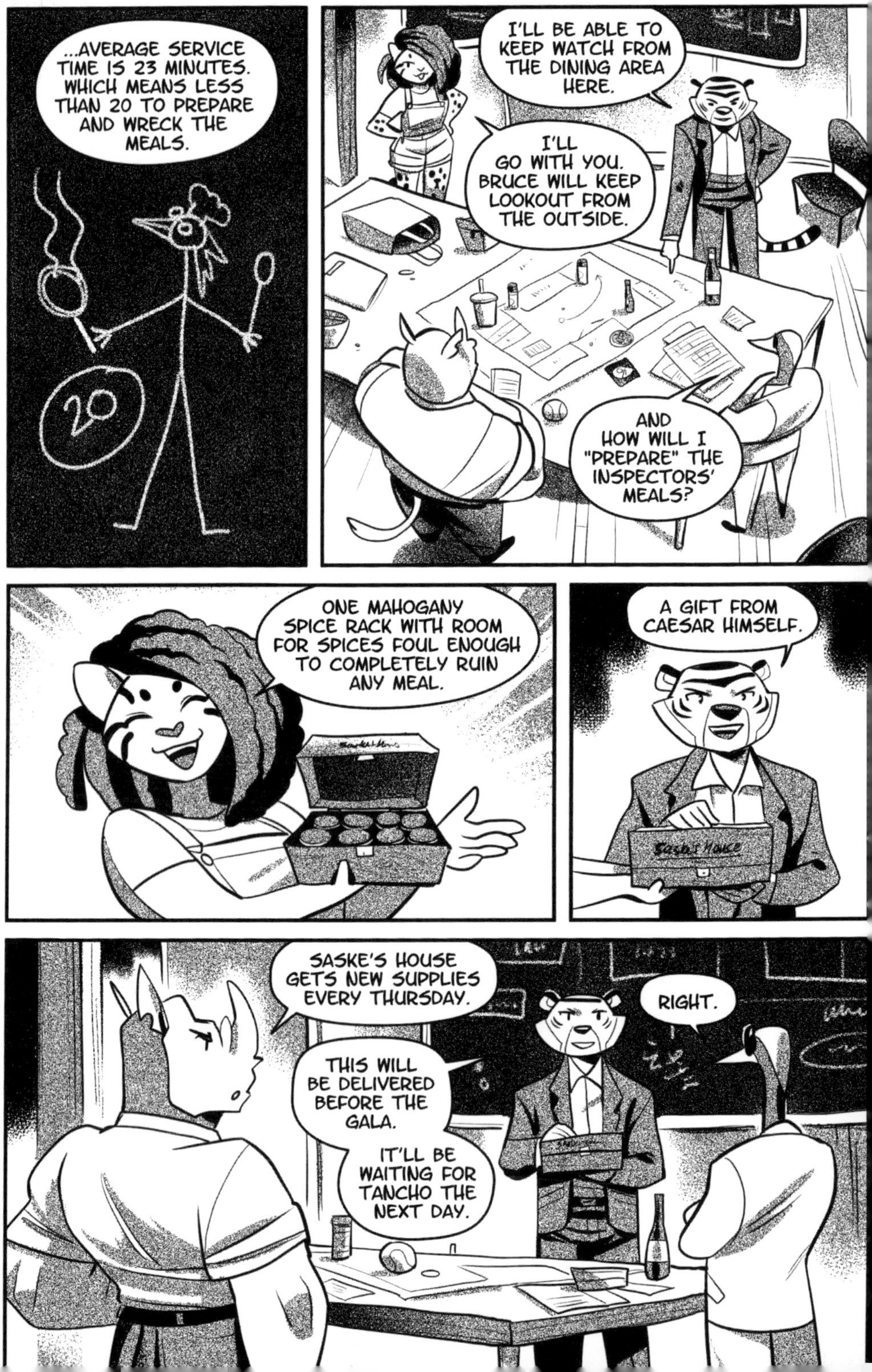
...AVERAGE SERVICE TIME IS 23 MINUTES. WHICH MEANS LESS THAN 20 TO PREPARE AND WRECK THE MEALS.
20
I'LL BE ABLE TO KEEP WATCH FROM THE DINING AREA HERE.
I'LL GO WITH YOU. BRUCE WILL KEEP LOOKOUT FROM THE OUTSIDE.
AND HOW WILL I "PREPARE" THE INSPECTORS' MEALS?
ONE MAHOGANY SPICE RACK WITH ROOM FOR SPICES FOUL ENOUGH TO COMPLETELY RUIN ANY MEAL.
A GIFT FROM CAESAR HIMSELF.
SASKE'S HOUSE GETS NEW SUPPLIES EVERY THURSDAY.
RIGHT.
THIS WILL BE DELIVERED BEFORE THE GALA.
IT'LL BE WAITING FOR TANCHO THE NEXT DAY.

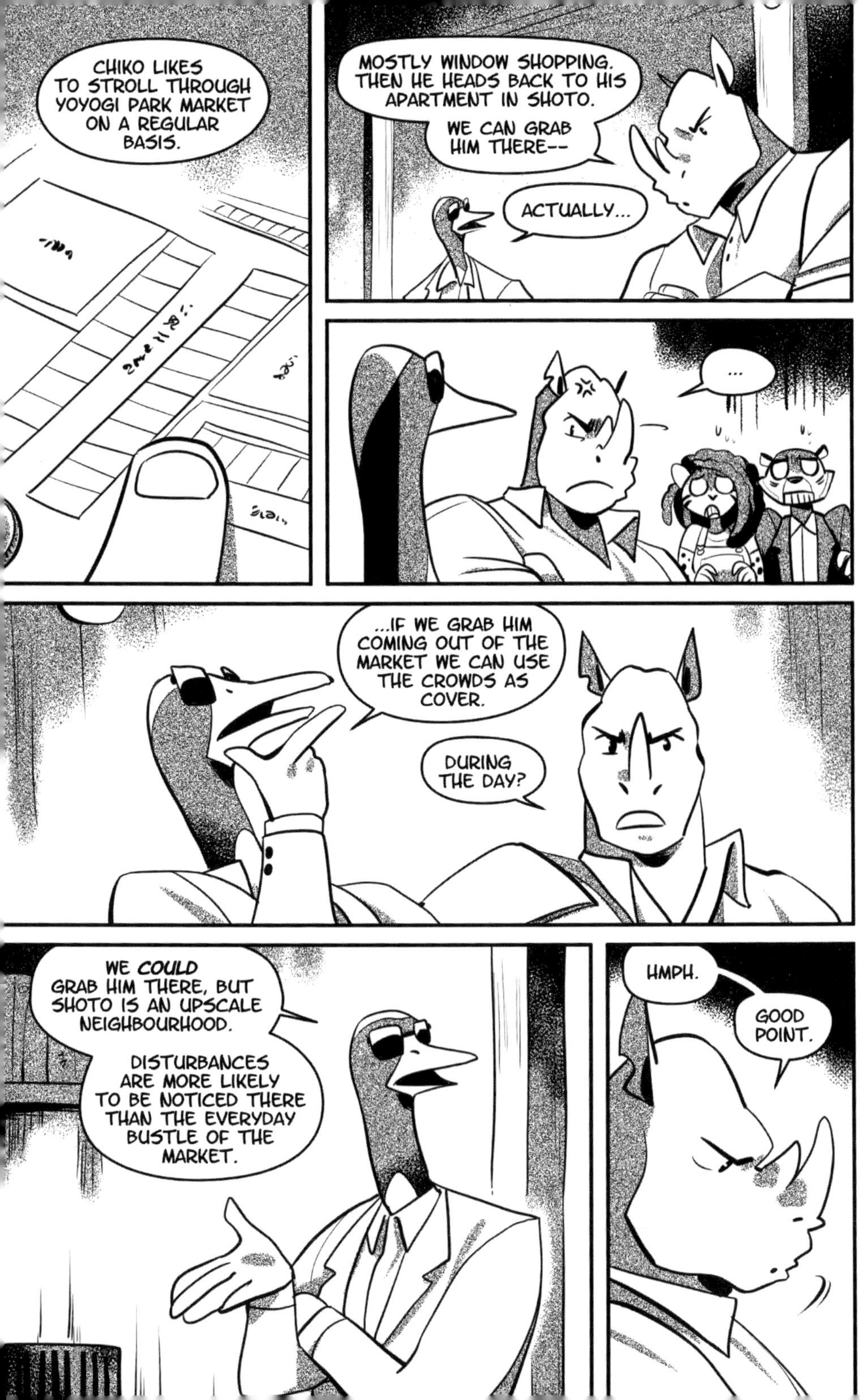
CHIKO LIKES TO STROLL THROUGH YOYOGI PARK MARKET ON A REGULAR BASIS.
MOSTLY WINDOW SHOPPING. THEN HE HEADS BACK TO HIS APARTMENT IN SHOTO.
WE CAN GRAB HIM THERE--
ACTUALLY...
...
...IF WE GRAB HIM COMING OUT OF THE MARKET WE CAN USE THE CROWDS AS COVER.
DURING THE DAY?
WE COULD GRAB HIM THERE, BUT SHOTO IS AN UPSCALE NEIGHBOURHOOD.
DISTURBANCES ARE MORE LIKELY TO BE NOTICED THERE THAN THE EVERYDAY BUSTLE OF THE MARKET.
HMPH.
GOOD POINT.

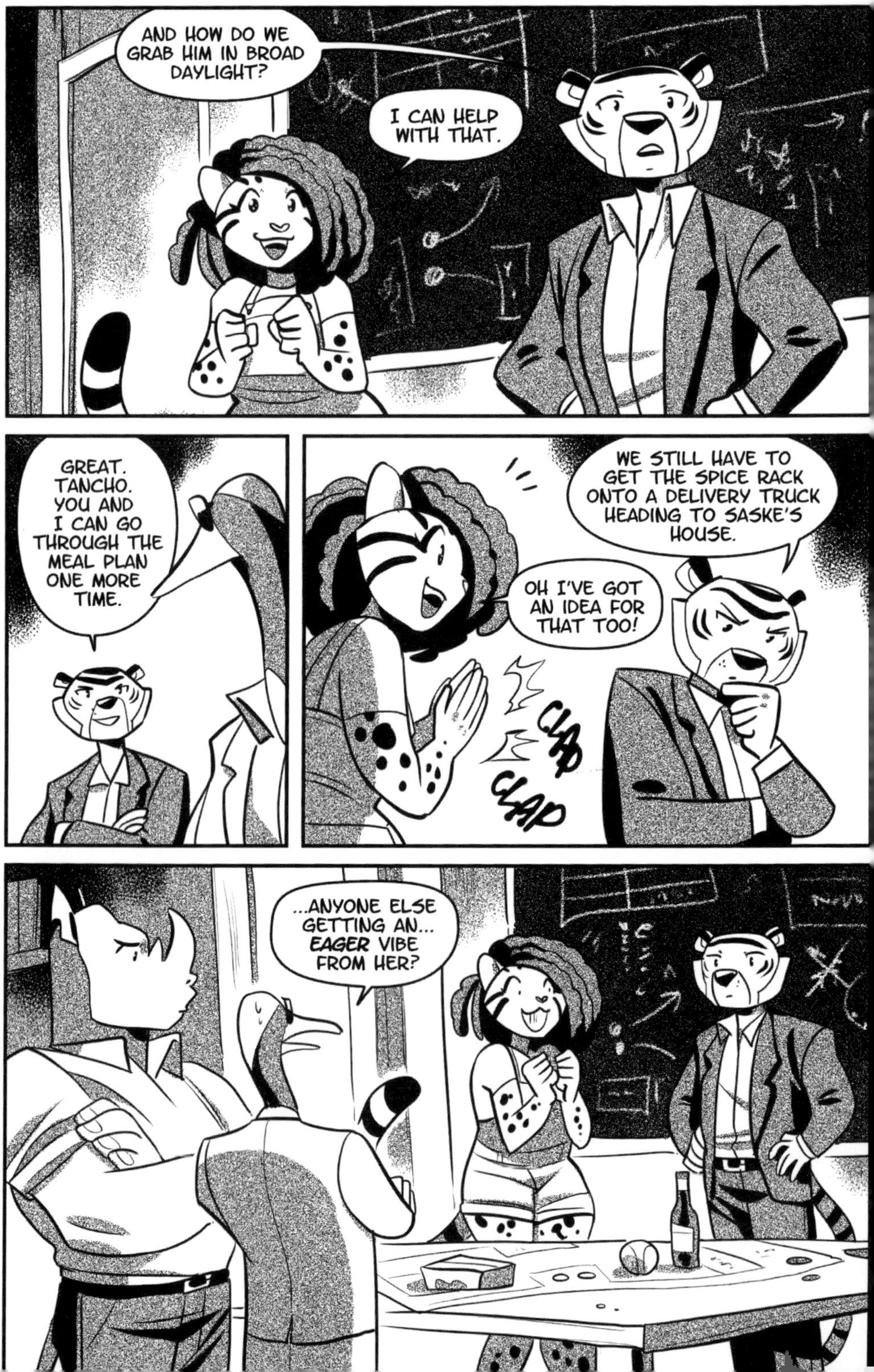
AND HOW DO WE GRAB HIM IN BROAD DAYLIGHT?
I CAN HELP WITH THAT.
GREAT. TANCHO. YOU AND I CAN GO THROUGH THE MEAL PLAN ONE MORE TIME.
WE STILL HAVE TO GET THE SPICE RACK ONTO A DELIVERY TRUCK HEADING TO SASKE'S HOUSE.
OH I'VE GOT AN IDEA FOR THAT TOO!
CLAP
CLAP
...ANYONE ELSE GETTING AN... *EAGER* VIBE FROM HER?

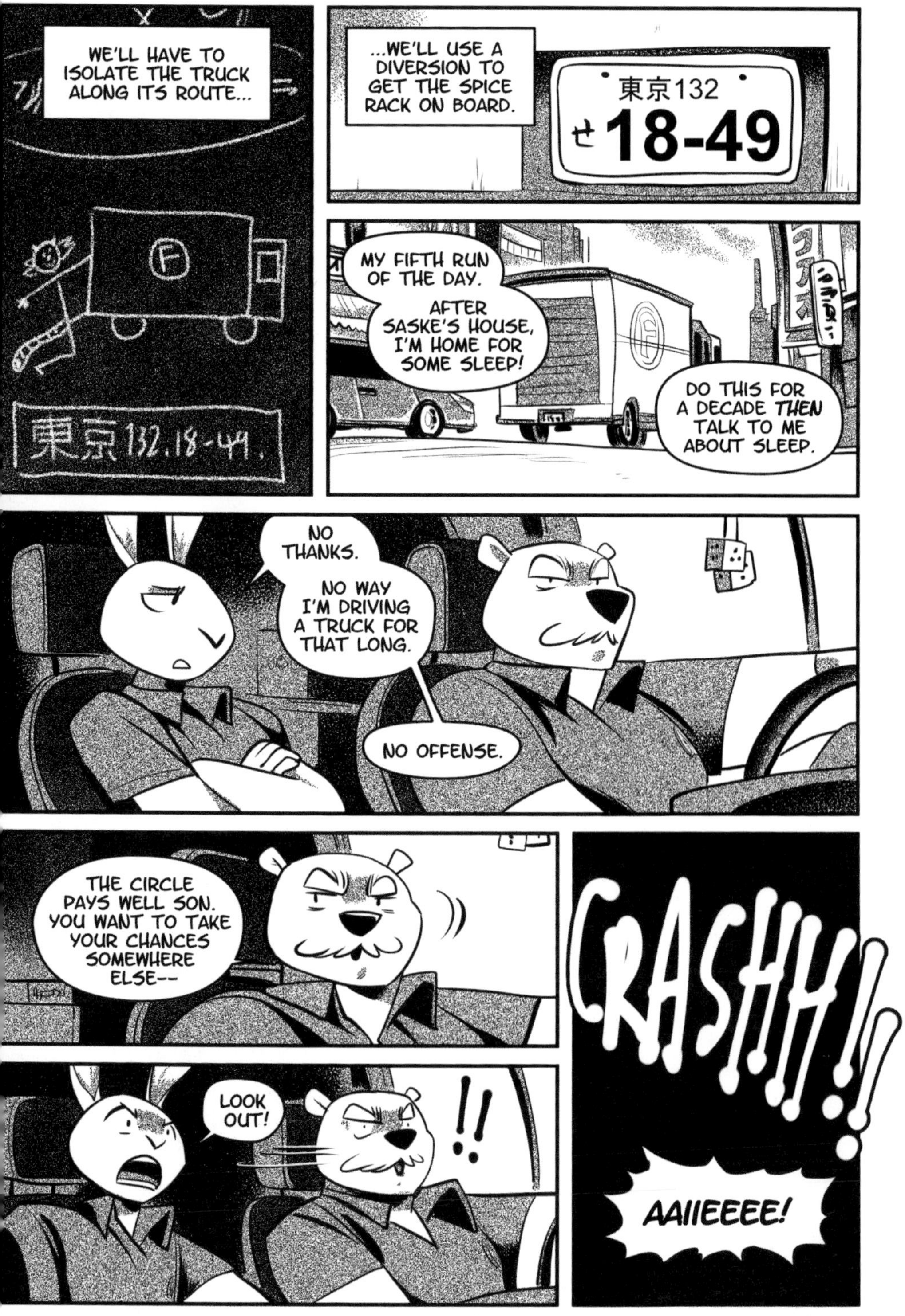
WE'LL HAVE TO ISOLATE THE TRUCK ALONG ITS ROUTE...
東京132.18-49.
...WE'LL USE A DIVERSION TO GET THE SPICE RACK ON BOARD.
東京132
せ 18-49
MY FIFTH RUN OF THE DAY.
AFTER SASKE'S HOUSE, I'M HOME FOR SOME SLEEP!
DO THIS FOR A DECADE *THEN* TALK TO ME ABOUT SLEEP.
NO THANKS.
NO WAY I'M DRIVING A TRUCK FOR THAT LONG.
NO OFFENSE.
THE CIRCLE PAYS WELL SON. YOU WANT TO TAKE YOUR CHANCES SOMEWHERE ELSE--
LOOK OUT!
!!
CRASHH!!
AAIIEEEE!

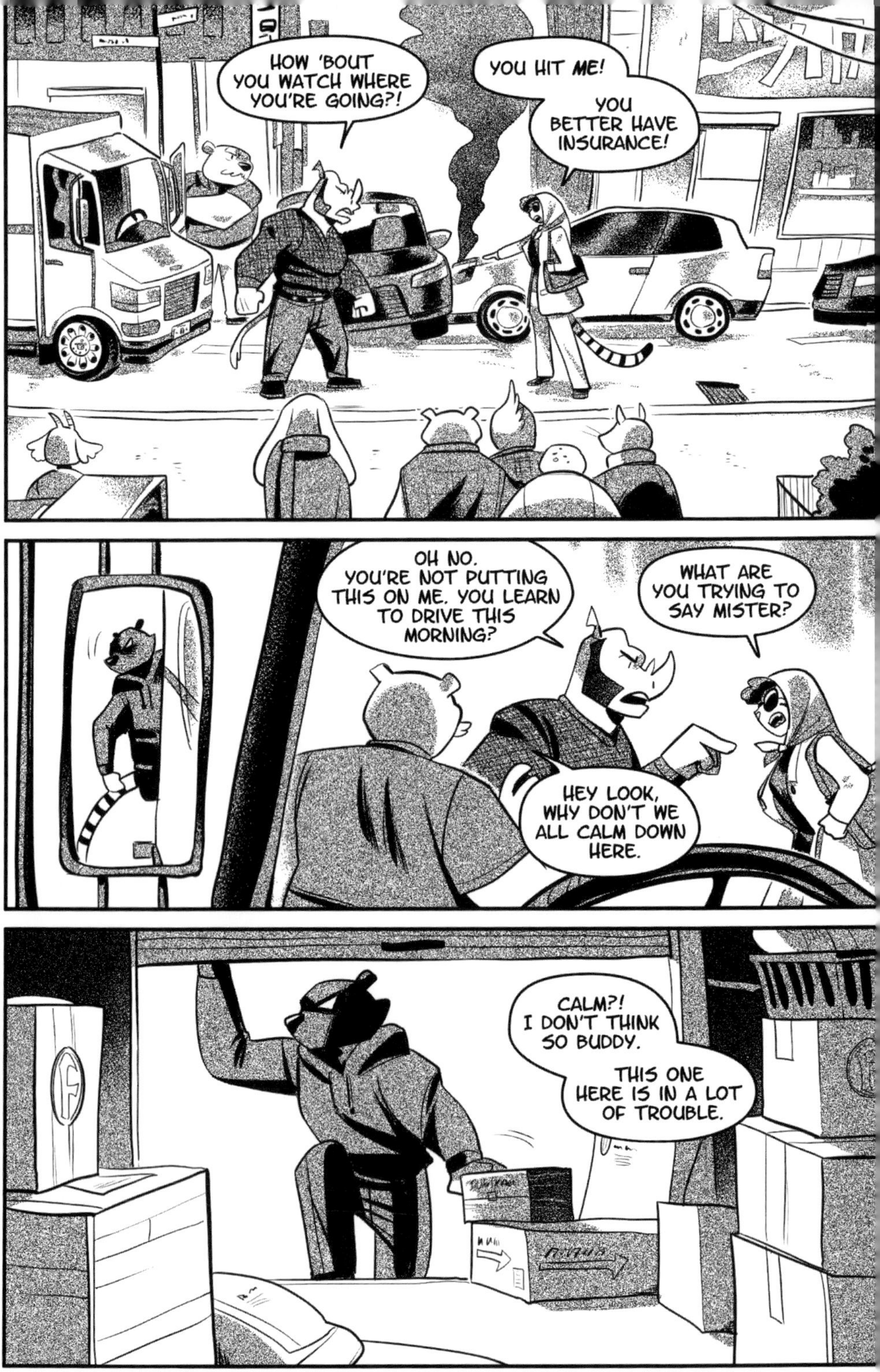

HOW 'BOUT YOU WATCH WHERE YOU'RE GOING?!
YOU HIT ME!
YOU BETTER HAVE INSURANCE!
OH NO. YOU'RE NOT PUTTING THIS ON ME. YOU LEARN TO DRIVE THIS MORNING?
WHAT ARE YOU TRYING TO SAY MISTER?
HEY LOOK, WHY DON'T WE ALL CALM DOWN HERE.
CALM?! I DON'T THINK SO BUDDY.
THIS ONE HERE IS IN A LOT OF TROUBLE.

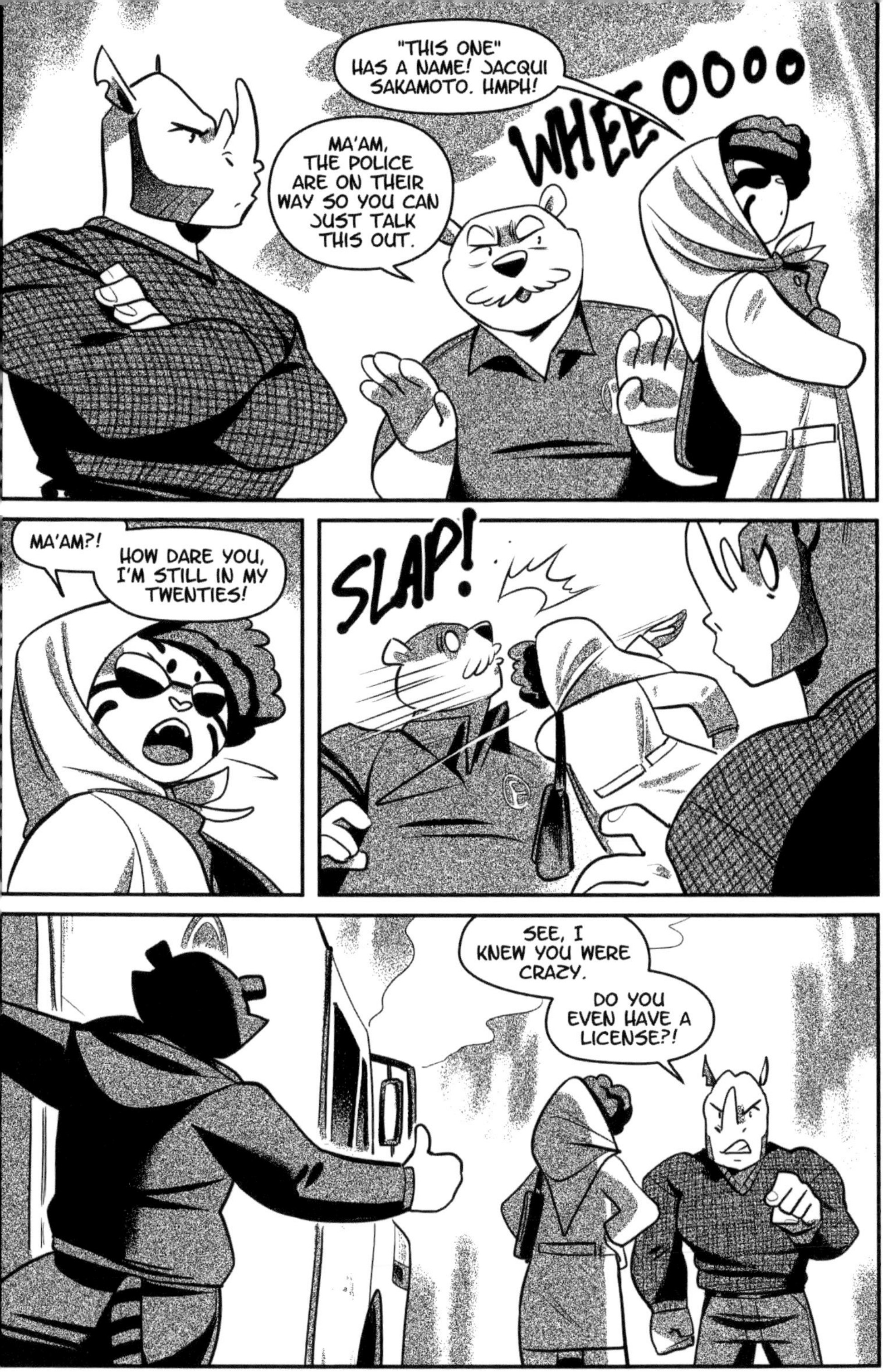
"THIS ONE" HAS A NAME! JACQUI SAKAMOTO. HMPH!
MA'AM, THE POLICE ARE ON THEIR WAY SO YOU CAN JUST TALK THIS OUT.
WHEEOOOO
MA'AM?!
HOW DARE YOU, I'M STILL IN MY TWENTIES!
SLAP!
SEE, I KNEW YOU WERE CRAZY.
DO YOU EVEN HAVE A LICENSE?!

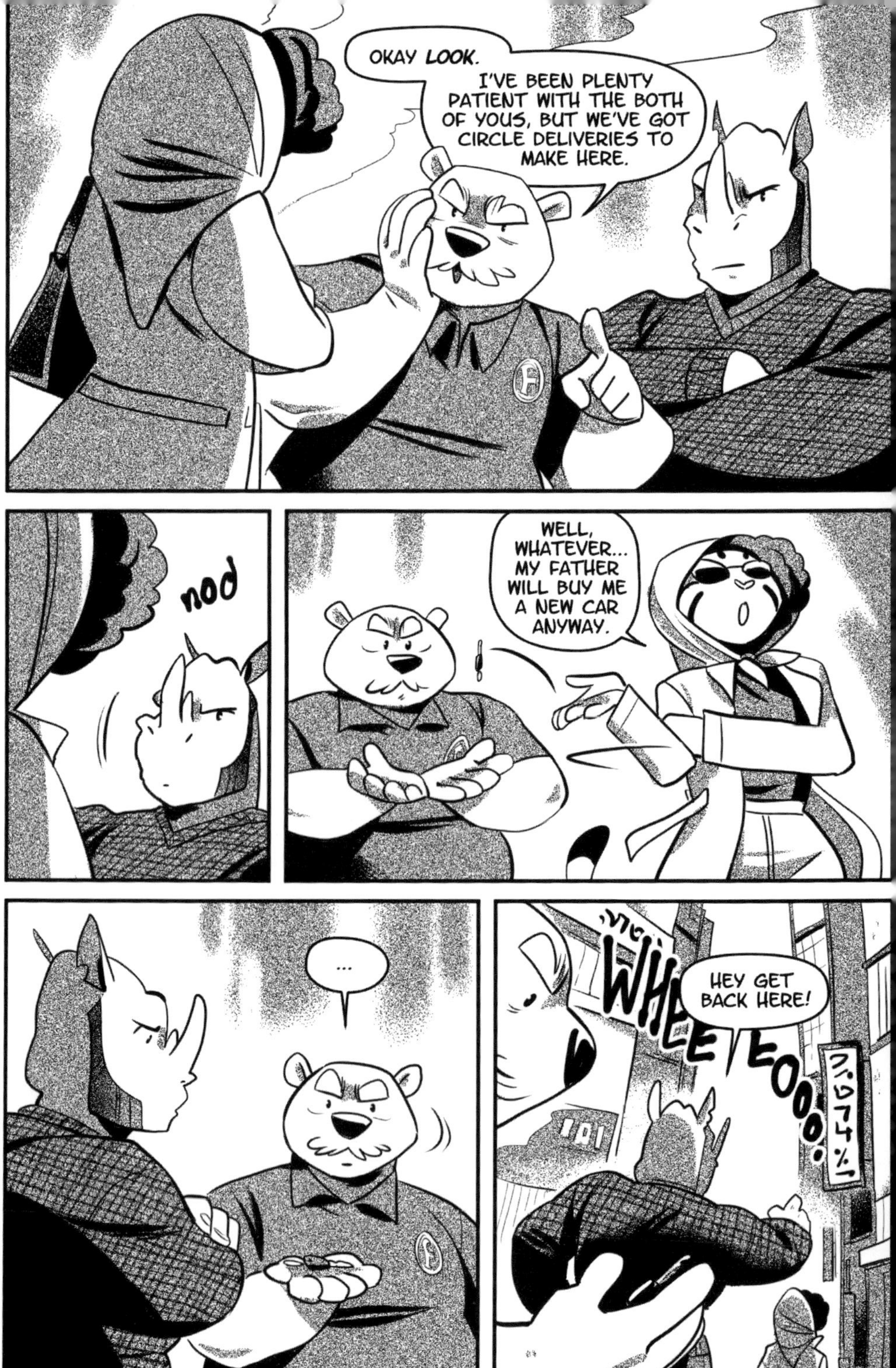
OKAY *LOOK*.
I'VE BEEN PLENTY PATIENT WITH THE BOTH OF YOUS, BUT WE'VE GOT CIRCLE DELIVERIES TO MAKE HERE.
nod
WELL, WHATEVER... MY FATHER WILL BUY ME A NEW CAR ANYWAY.
...
WHEEEOOO.
HEY GET BACK HERE!

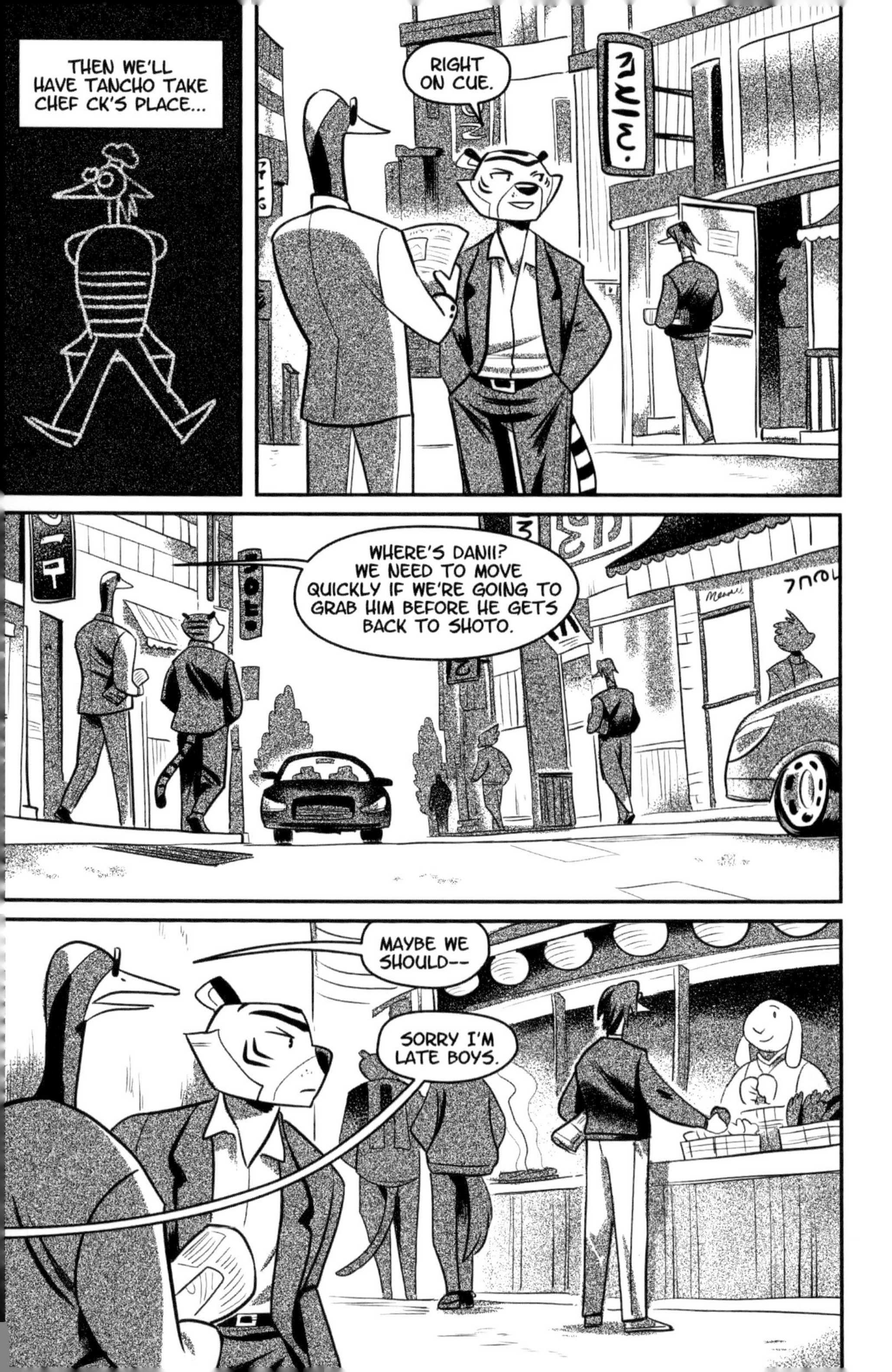
THEN WE'LL HAVE TANCHO TAKE CHEF CK'S PLACE...
RIGHT ON CUE.
WHERE'S DANII? WE NEED TO MOVE QUICKLY IF WE'RE GOING TO GRAB HIM BEFORE HE GETS BACK TO SHOTO.
MAYBE WE SHOULD--
SORRY I'M LATE BOYS.

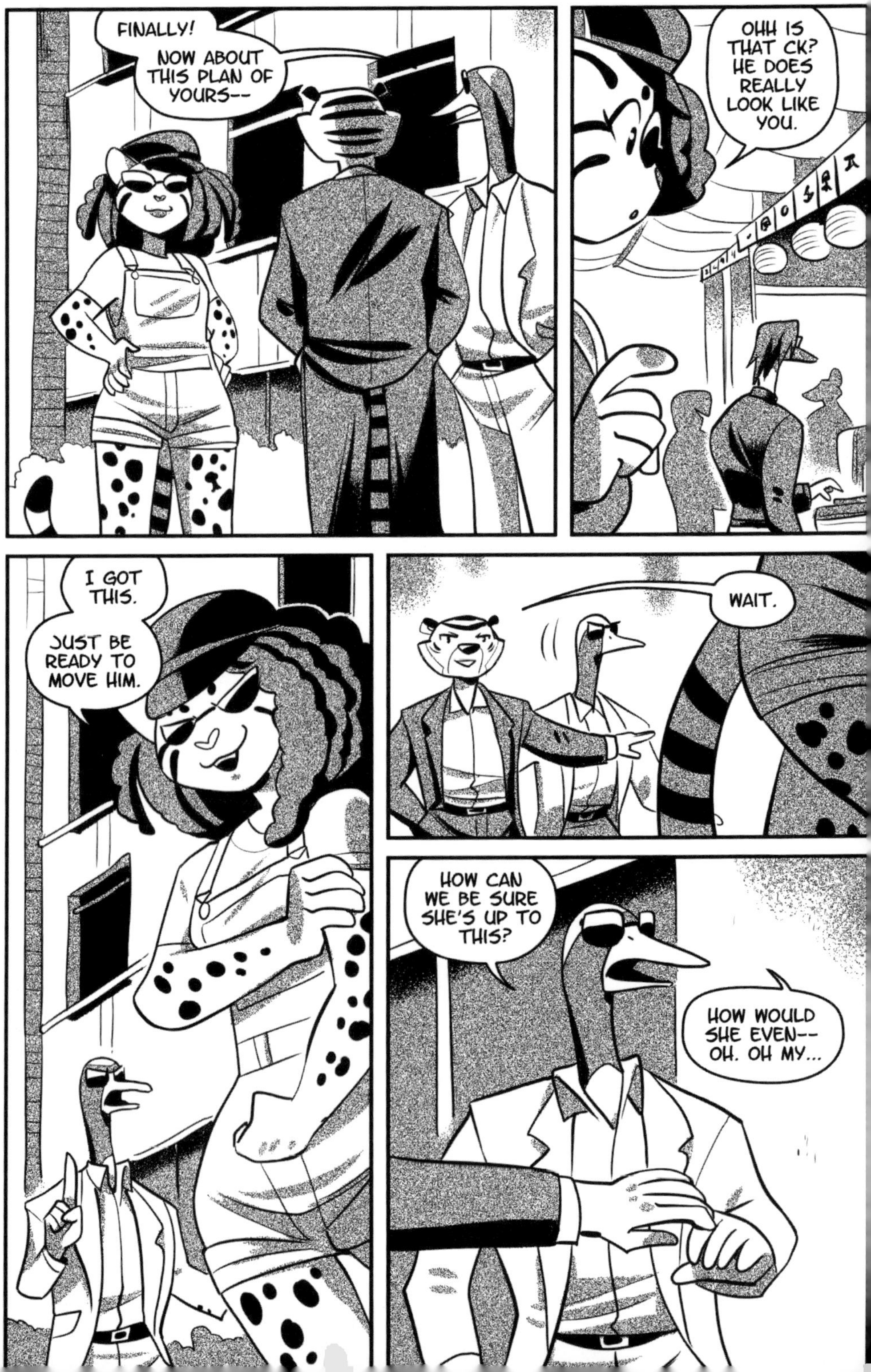
FINALLY!
NOW ABOUT THIS PLAN OF YOURS--
OHH IS THAT CK? HE DOES REALLY LOOK LIKE YOU.
I GOT THIS.
JUST BE READY TO MOVE HIM.
WAIT.
HOW CAN WE BE SURE SHE'S UP TO THIS?
HOW WOULD SHE EVEN-- OH. OH MY...

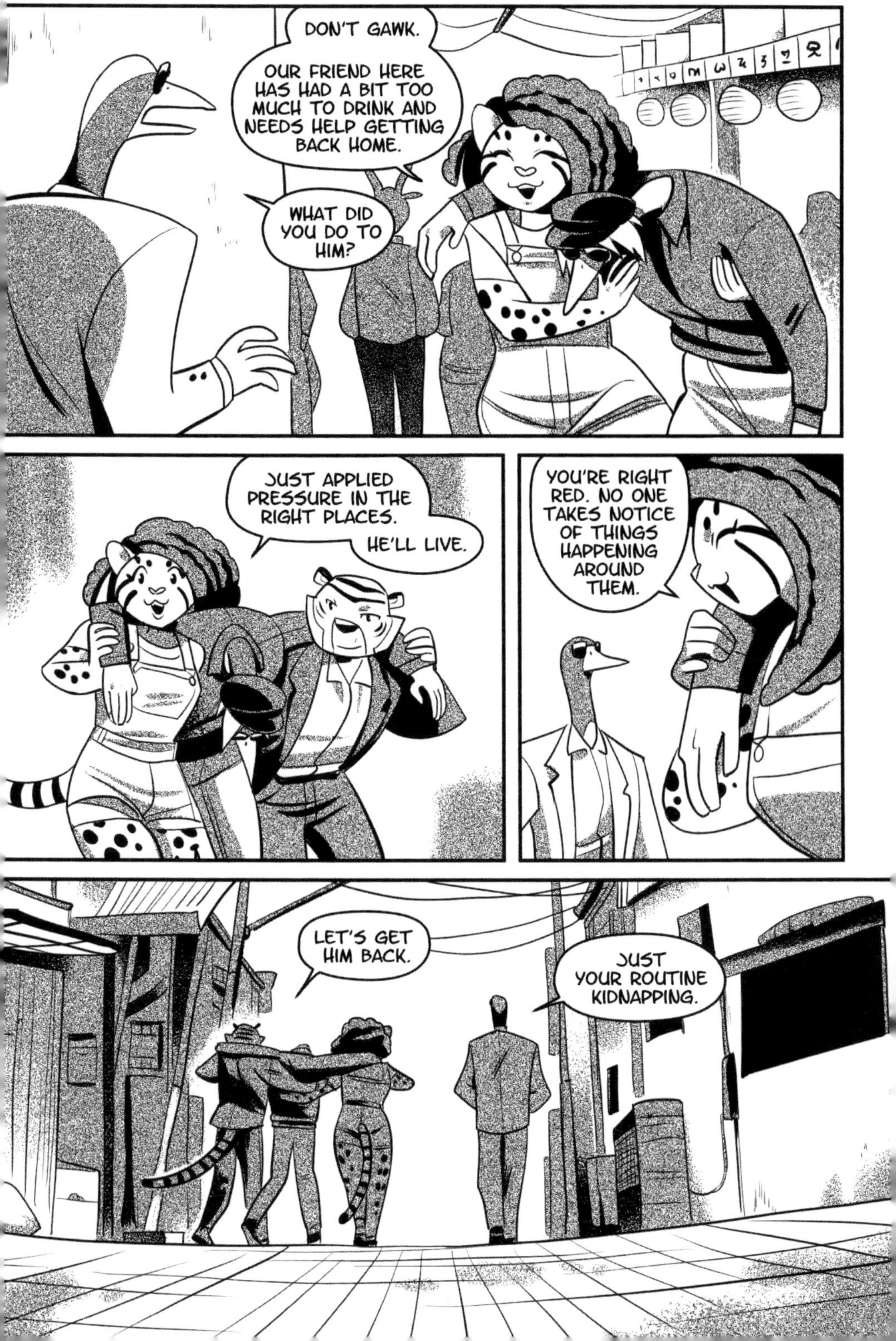
DON'T GAWK.
OUR FRIEND HERE HAS HAD A BIT TOO MUCH TO DRINK AND NEEDS HELP GETTING BACK HOME.
WHAT DID YOU DO TO HIM?
JUST APPLIED PRESSURE IN THE RIGHT PLACES.
HE'LL LIVE.
YOU'RE RIGHT RED. NO ONE TAKES NOTICE OF THINGS HAPPENING AROUND THEM.
LET'S GET HIM BACK.
JUST YOUR ROUTINE KIDNAPPING.

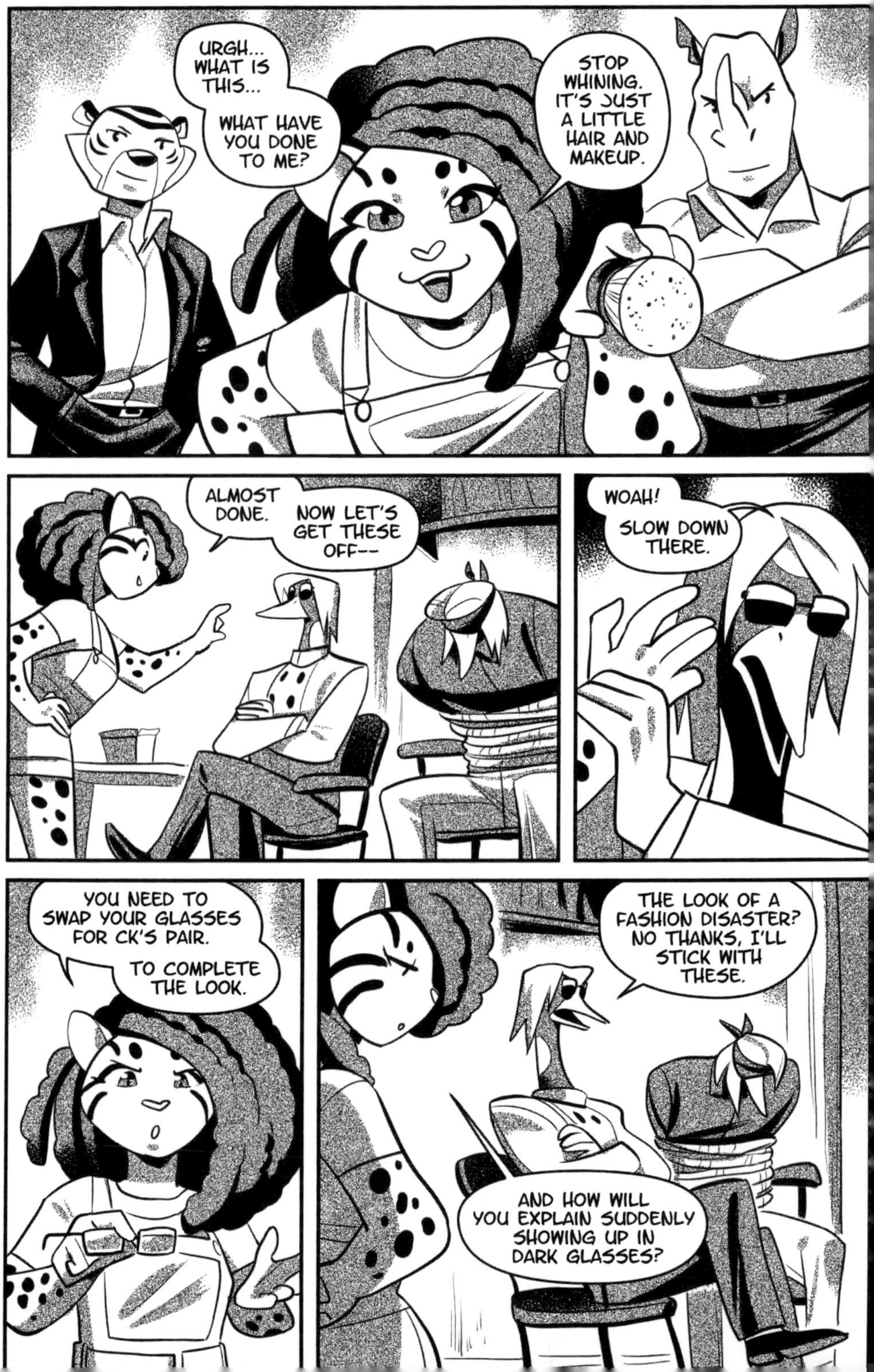
URGH... WHAT IS THIS...
WHAT HAVE YOU DONE TO ME?
STOP WHINING. IT'S JUST A LITTLE HAIR AND MAKEUP.
ALMOST DONE.
NOW LET'S GET THESE OFF--
WOAH!
SLOW DOWN THERE.
YOU NEED TO SWAP YOUR GLASSES FOR CK'S PAIR.
TO COMPLETE THE LOOK.
THE LOOK OF A FASHION DISASTER? NO THANKS, I'LL STICK WITH THESE.
AND HOW WILL YOU EXPLAIN SUDDENLY SHOWING UP IN DARK GLASSES?

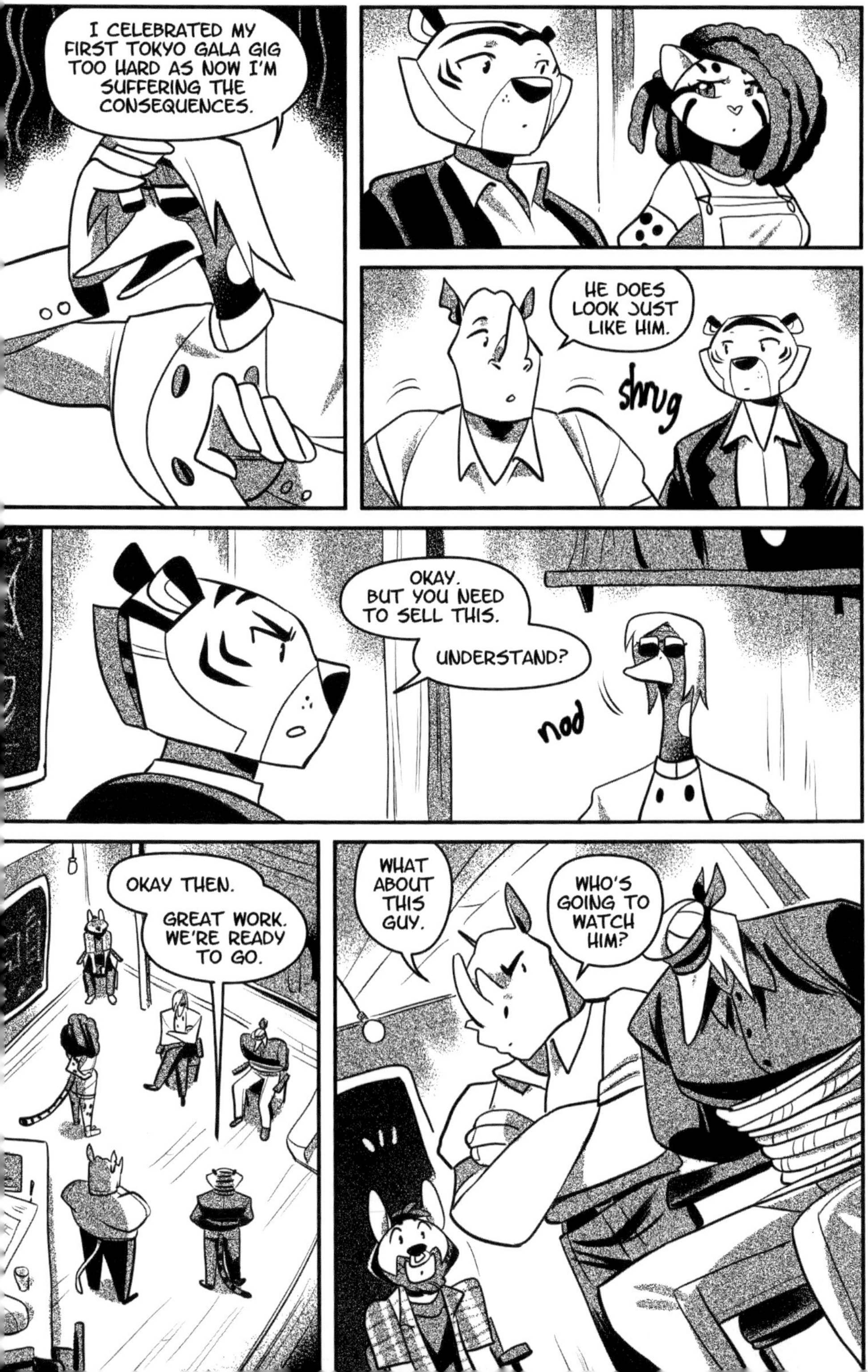
I CELEBRATED MY FIRST TOKYO GALA GIG TOO HARD AS NOW I'M SUFFERING THE CONSEQUENCES.
HE DOES LOOK JUST LIKE HIM.
shrug
OKAY. BUT YOU NEED TO SELL THIS.
UNDERSTAND?
nod
OKAY THEN.
GREAT WORK. WE'RE READY TO GO.
WHAT ABOUT THIS GUY.
WHO'S GOING TO WATCH HIM?

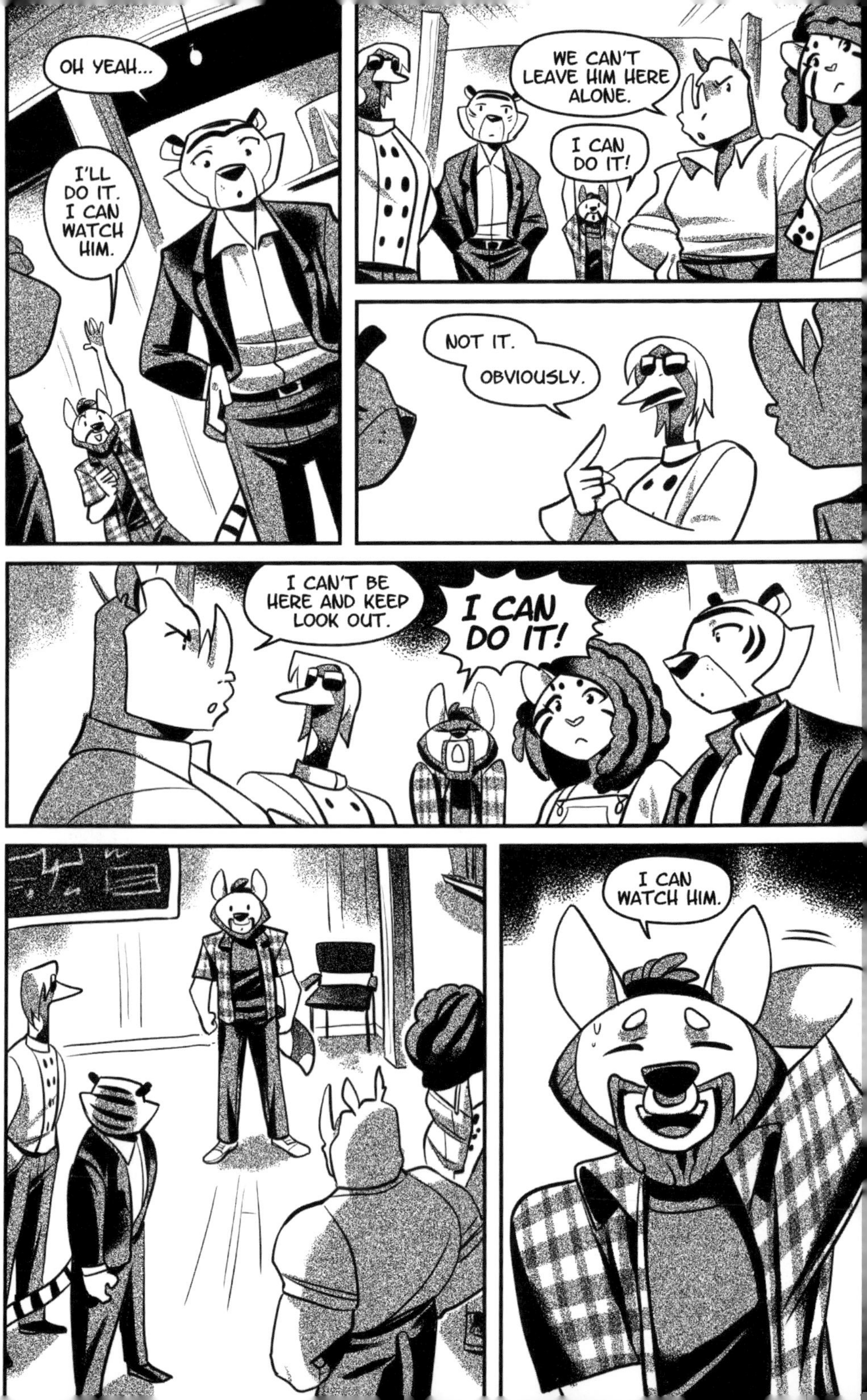
OH YEAH...
I'LL DO IT. I CAN WATCH HIM.
WE CAN'T LEAVE HIM HERE ALONE.
I CAN DO IT!
NOT IT.
OBVIOUSLY.
I CAN'T BE HERE AND KEEP LOOK OUT.
I CAN DO IT!
I CAN WATCH HIM.

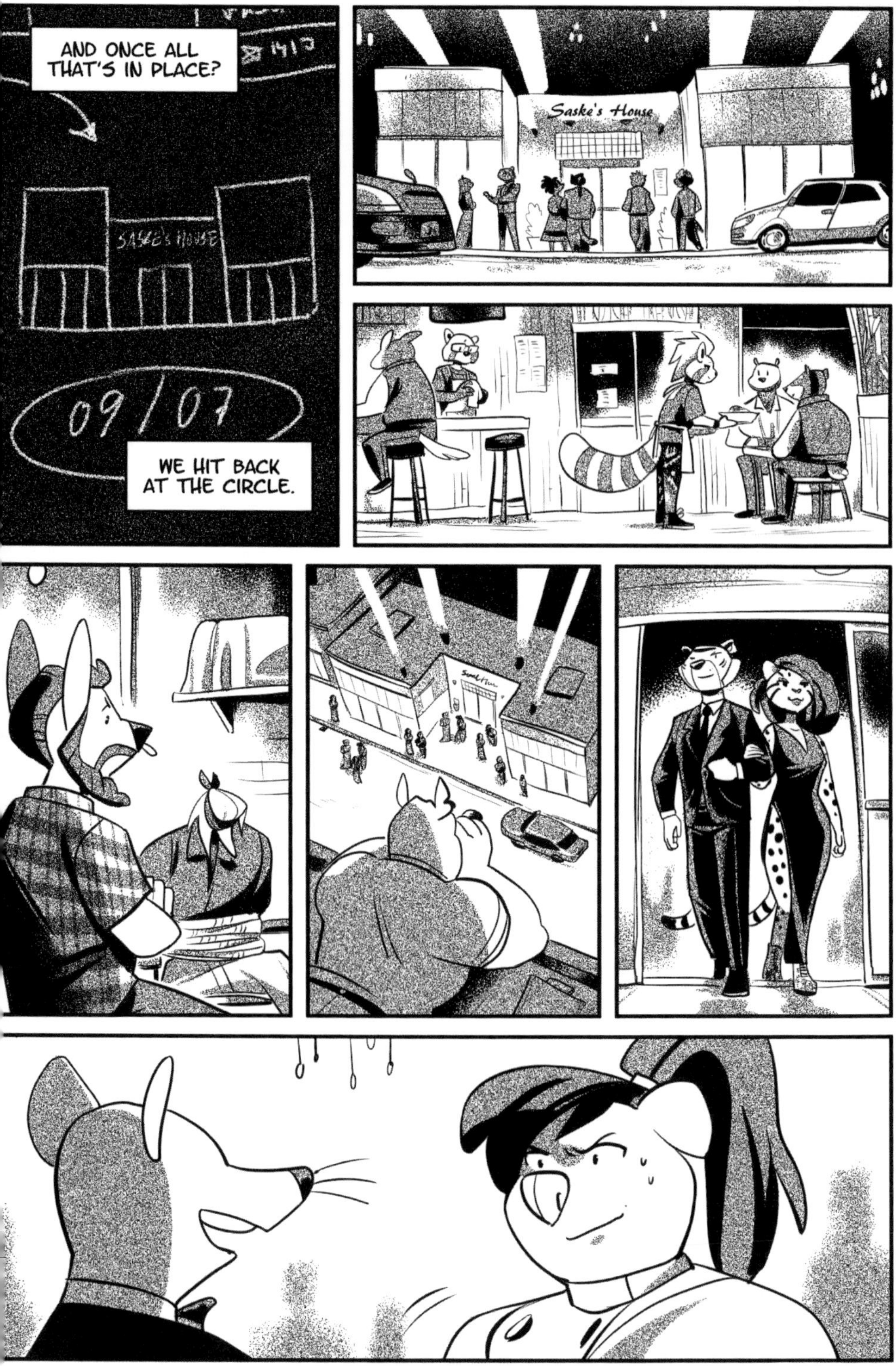
AND ONCE ALL THAT'S IN PLACE?
SASKE'S HOUSE
09/07
WE HIT BACK AT THE CIRCLE.
Saske's House

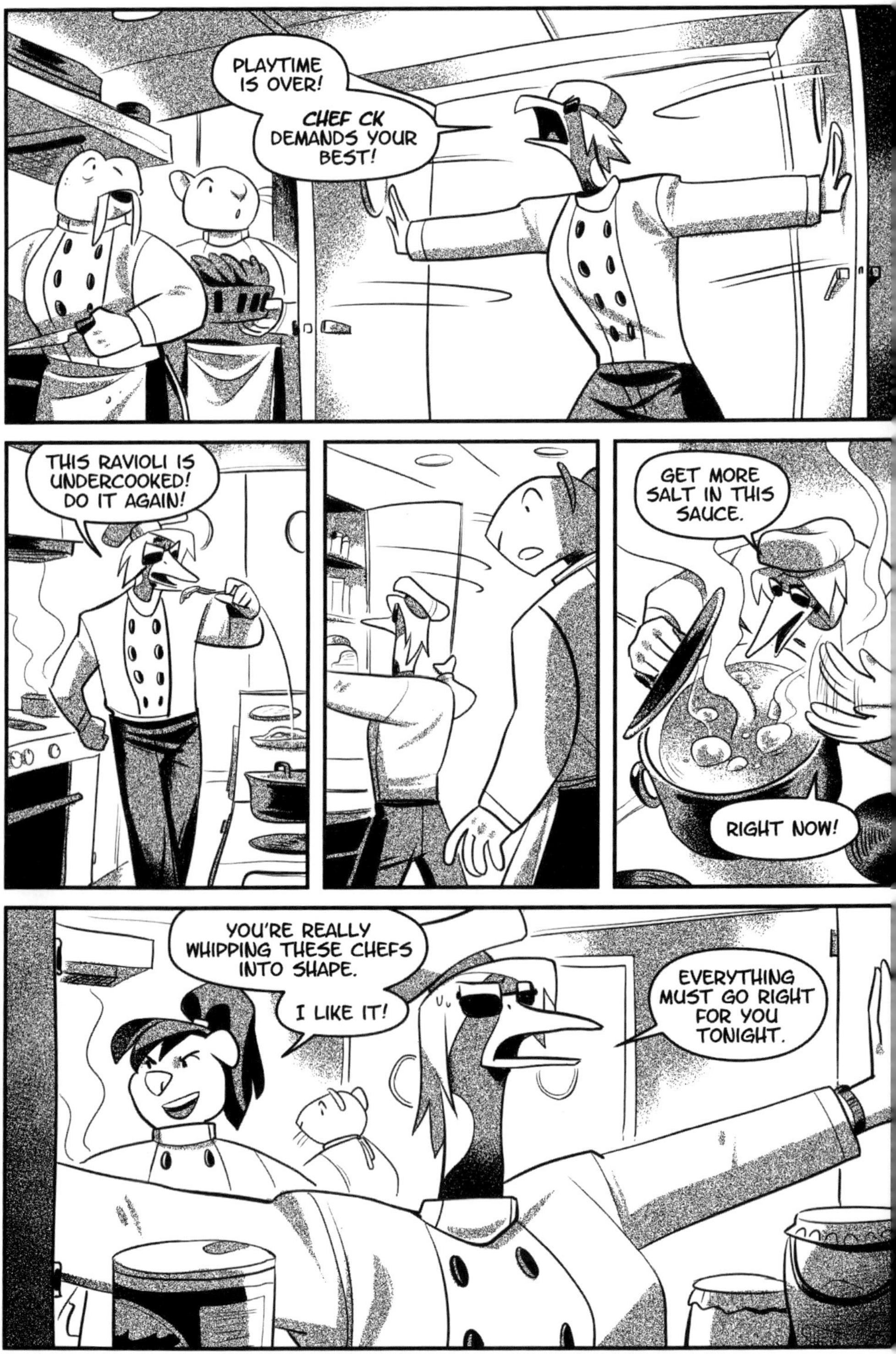
PLAYTIME IS OVER!
CHEF CK DEMANDS YOUR BEST!
THIS RAVIOLI IS UNDERCOOKED! DO IT AGAIN!
GET MORE SALT IN THIS SAUCE.
RIGHT NOW!
YOU'RE REALLY WHIPPING THESE CHEFS INTO SHAPE.
I LIKE IT!
EVERYTHING MUST GO RIGHT FOR YOU TONIGHT.

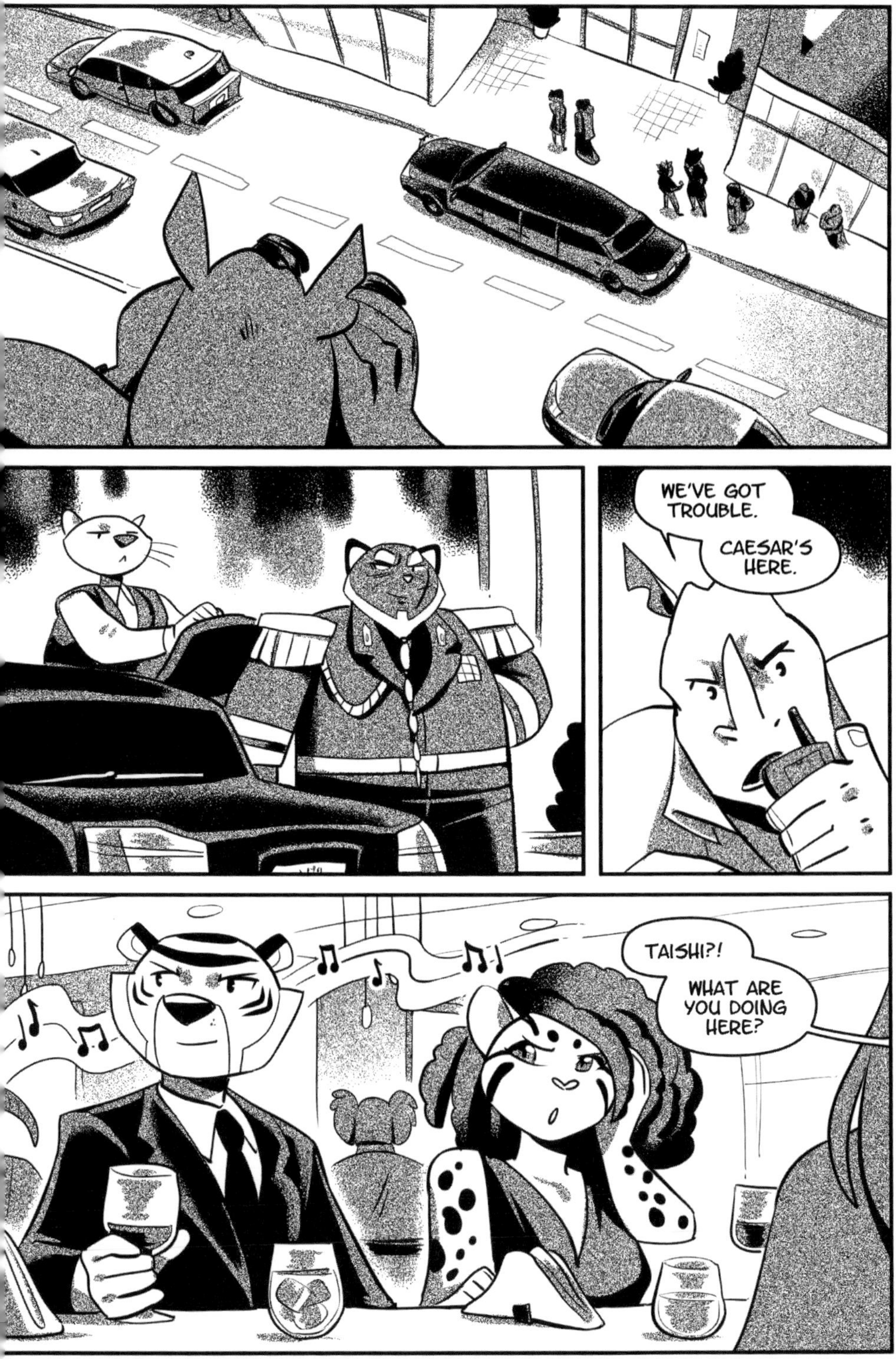
WE'VE GOT TROUBLE.
CAESAR'S HERE.
TAISHI?!
WHAT ARE YOU DOING HERE?

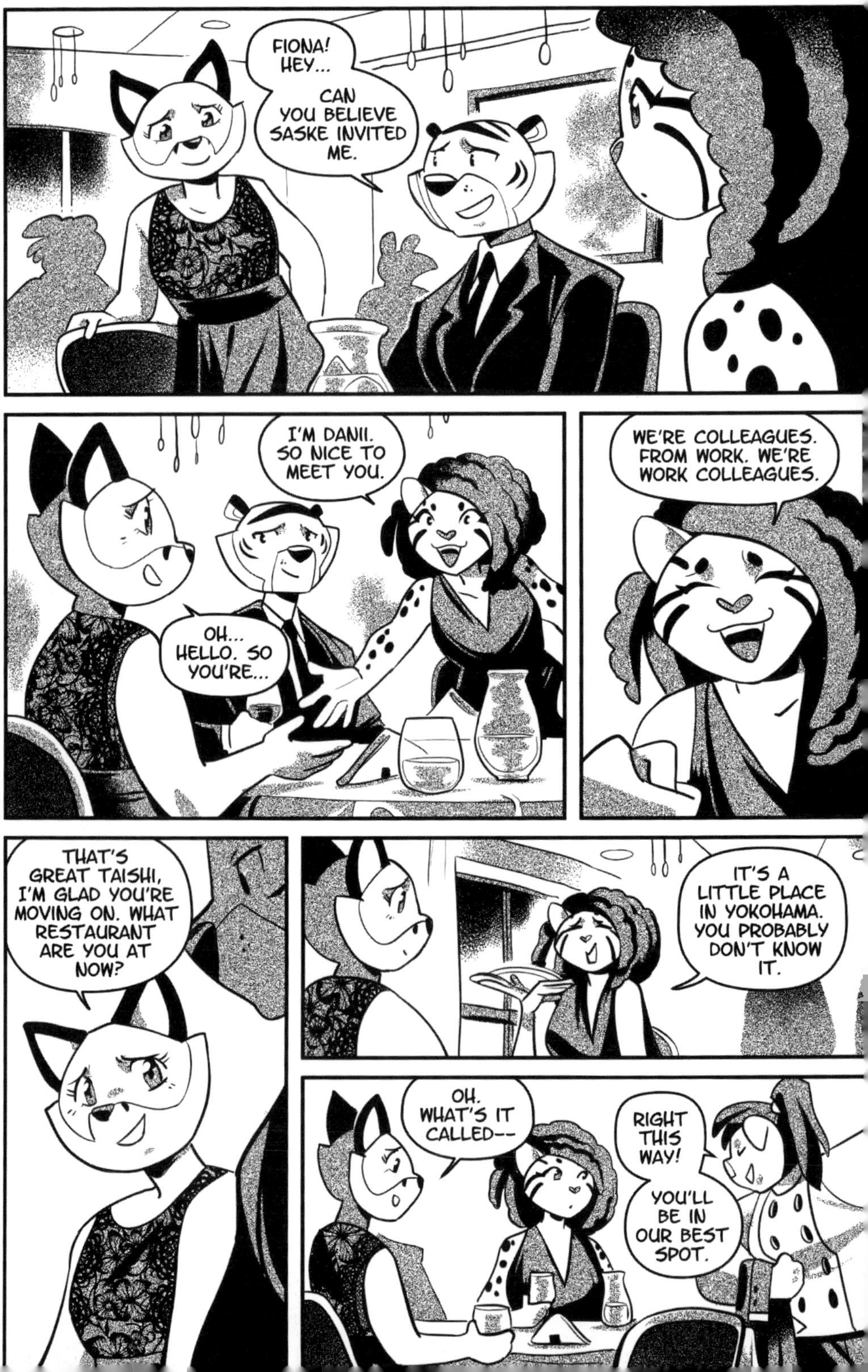
FIONA! HEY... CAN YOU BELIEVE SASKE INVITED ME.
I'M DANII. SO NICE TO MEET YOU.
OH... HELLO. SO YOU'RE...
WE'RE COLLEAGUES. FROM WORK. WE'RE WORK COLLEAGUES.
THAT'S GREAT TAISHI, I'M GLAD YOU'RE MOVING ON. WHAT RESTAURANT ARE YOU AT NOW?
IT'S A LITTLE PLACE IN YOKOHAMA. YOU PROBABLY DON'T KNOW IT.
OH. WHAT'S IT CALLED--
RIGHT THIS WAY!
YOU'LL BE IN OUR BEST SPOT.

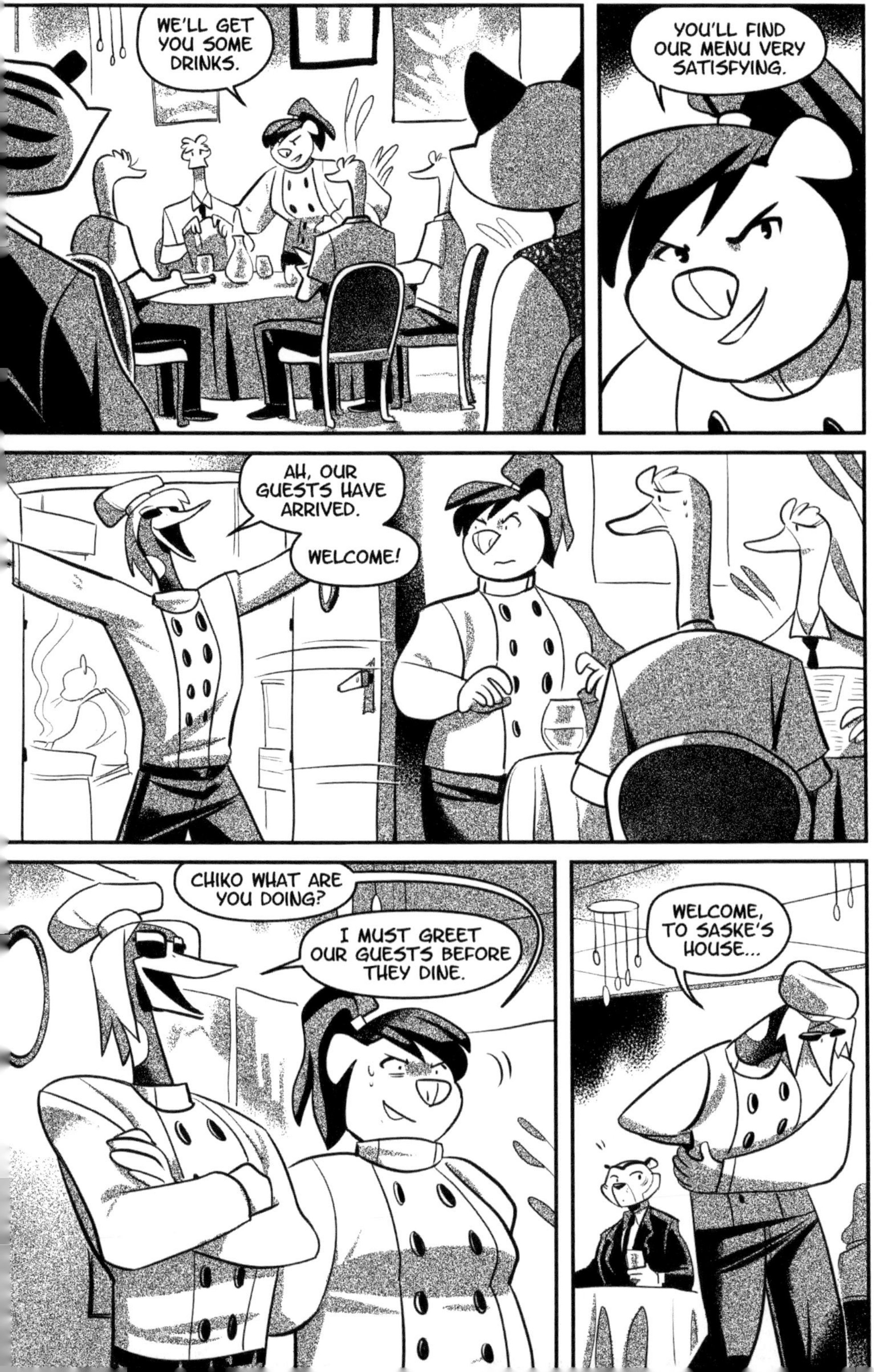
WE'LL GET YOU SOME DRINKS.
YOU'LL FIND OUR MENU VERY SATISFYING.
AH, OUR GUESTS HAVE ARRIVED.
WELCOME!
CHIKO WHAT ARE YOU DOING?
I MUST GREET OUR GUESTS BEFORE THEY DINE.
WELCOME, TO SASKE'S HOUSE...

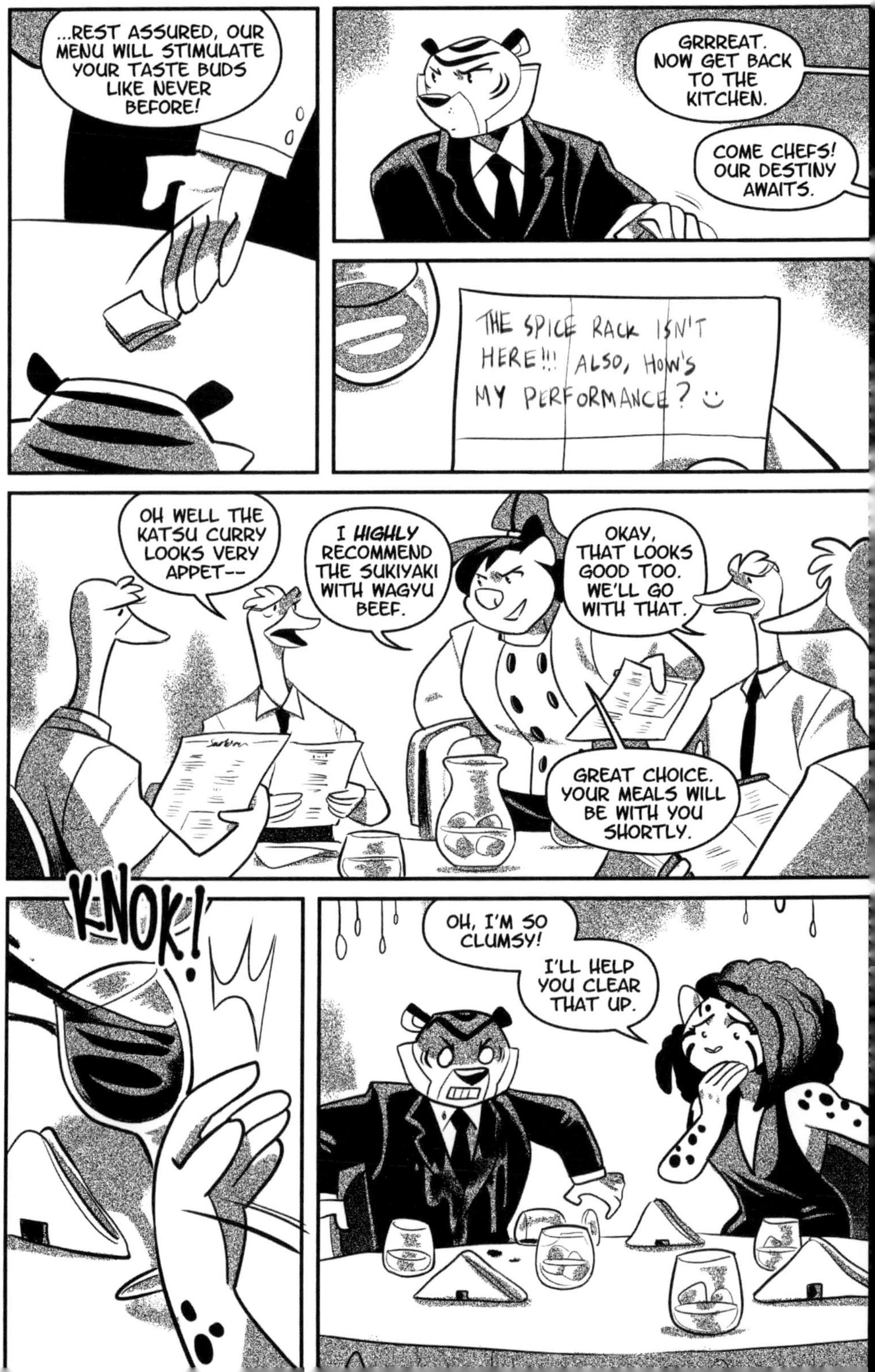
...REST ASSURED, OUR MENU WILL STIMULATE YOUR TASTE BUDS LIKE NEVER BEFORE!
GRRREAT. NOW GET BACK TO THE KITCHEN.
COME CHEFS! OUR DESTINY AWAITS.
THE SPICE RACK ISN'T HERE!!! ALSO, HOW'S MY PERFORMANCE? :)
OH WELL THE KATSU CURRY LOOKS VERY APPET--
I HIGHLY RECOMMEND THE SUKIYAKI WITH WAGYU BEEF.
OKAY, THAT LOOKS GOOD TOO. WE'LL GO WITH THAT.
GREAT CHOICE. YOUR MEALS WILL BE WITH YOU SHORTLY.
K-NOK!
OH, I'M SO CLUMSY!
I'LL HELP YOU CLEAR THAT UP.

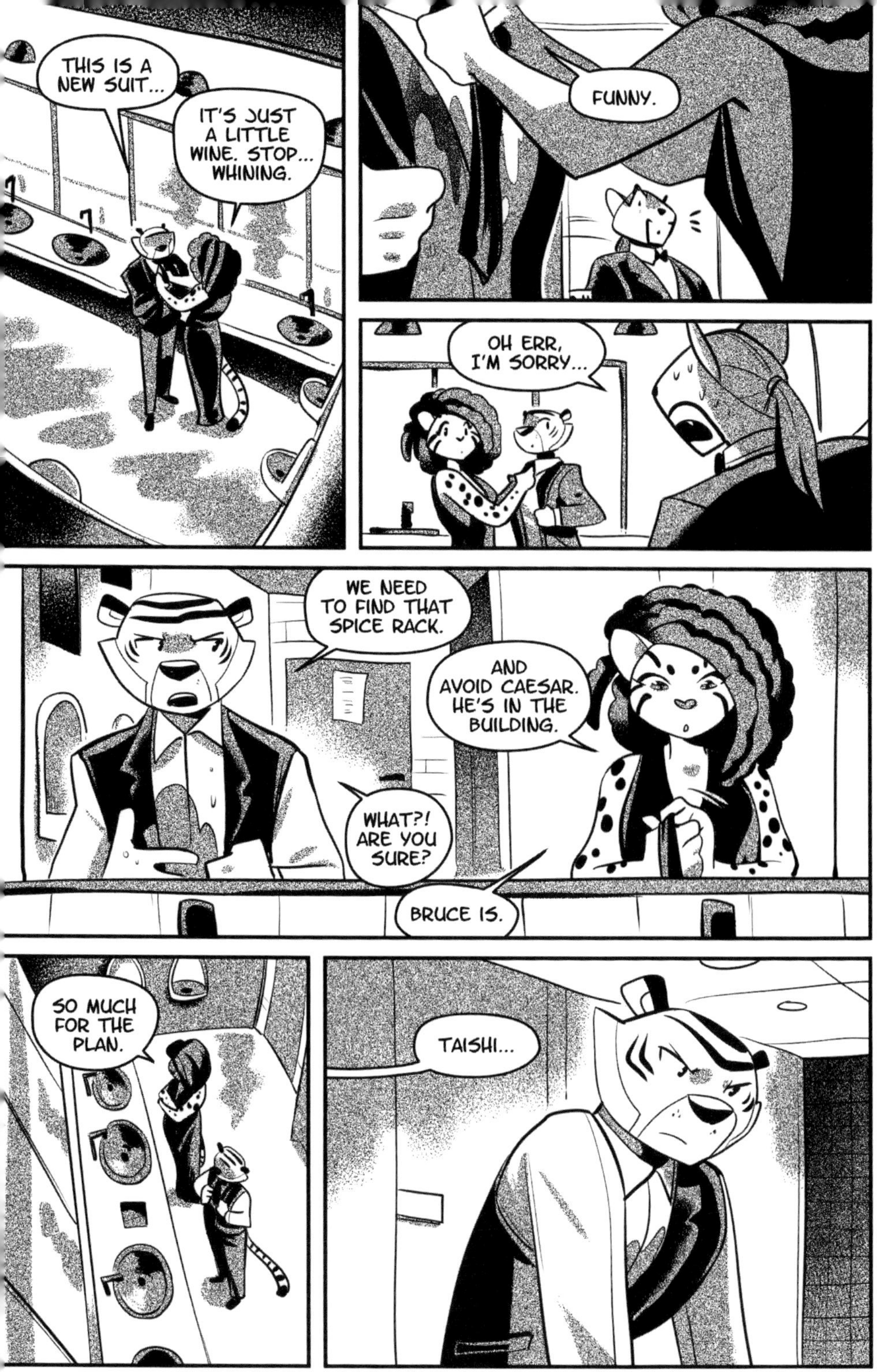
THIS IS A NEW SUIT...
IT'S JUST A LITTLE WINE. STOP... WHINING.
FUNNY.
OH ERR, I'M SORRY...
WE NEED TO FIND THAT SPICE RACK.
AND AVOID CAESAR. HE'S IN THE BUILDING.
WHAT?! ARE YOU SURE?
BRUCE IS.
SO MUCH FOR THE PLAN.
TAISHI...

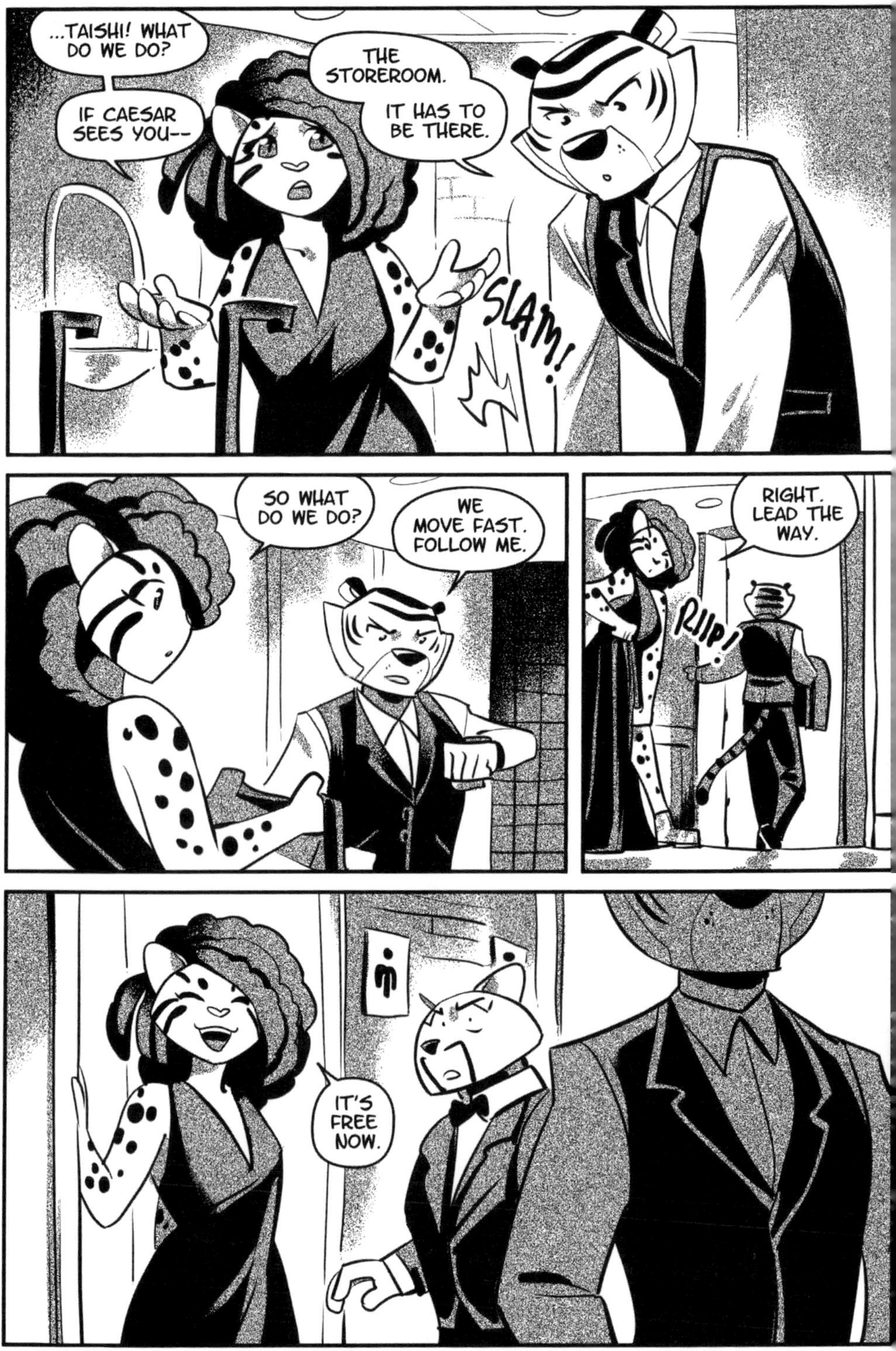
...TAISHI! WHAT DO WE DO?
IF CAESAR SEES YOU--
THE STOREROOM.
IT HAS TO BE THERE.
SLAM!
SO WHAT DO WE DO?
WE MOVE FAST. FOLLOW ME.
RIGHT. LEAD THE WAY.
RIIP!
IT'S FREE NOW.

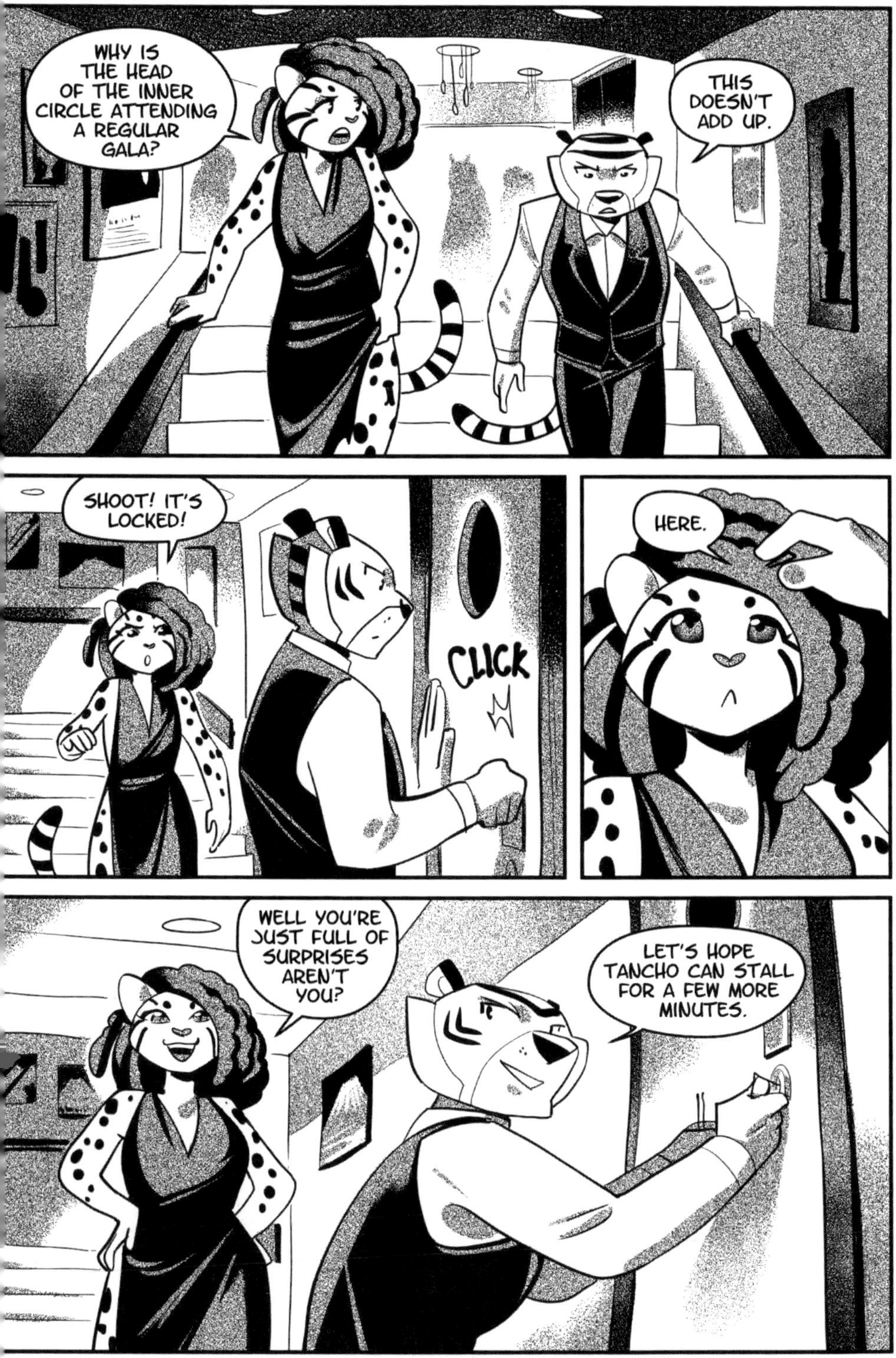
WHY IS THE HEAD OF THE INNER CIRCLE ATTENDING A REGULAR GALA?
THIS DOESN'T ADD UP.
SHOOT! IT'S LOCKED!
CLICK
HERE.
WELL YOU'RE JUST FULL OF SURPRISES AREN'T YOU?
LET'S HOPE TANCHO CAN STALL FOR A FEW MORE MINUTES.

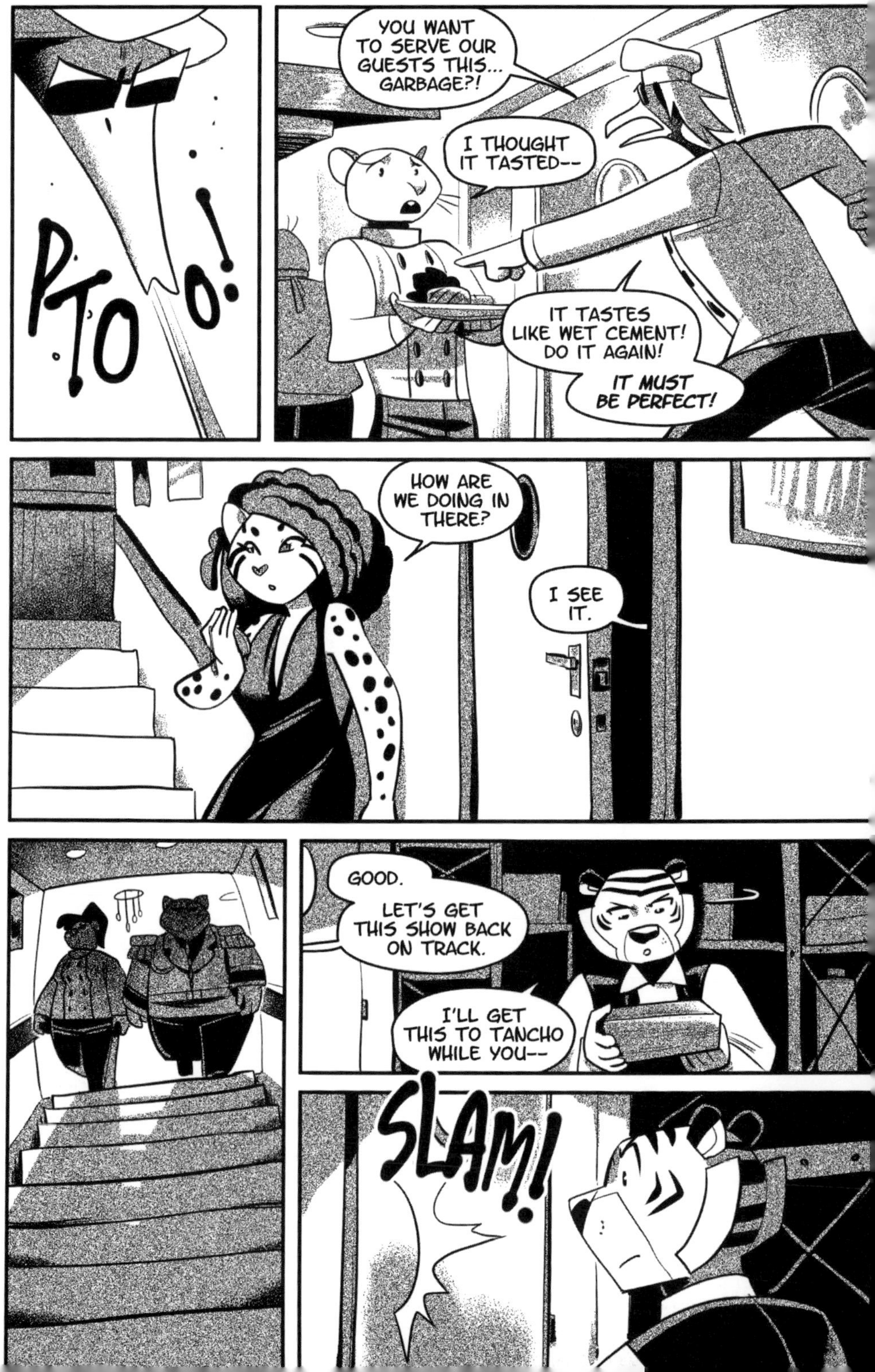
PTOO!
YOU WANT TO SERVE OUR GUESTS THIS... GARBAGE?!
I THOUGHT IT TASTED--
IT TASTES LIKE WET CEMENT! DO IT AGAIN!
IT MUST BE PERFECT!
HOW ARE WE DOING IN THERE?
I SEE IT.
GOOD.
LET'S GET THIS SHOW BACK ON TRACK.
I'LL GET THIS TO TANCHO WHILE YOU--
SLAM!!

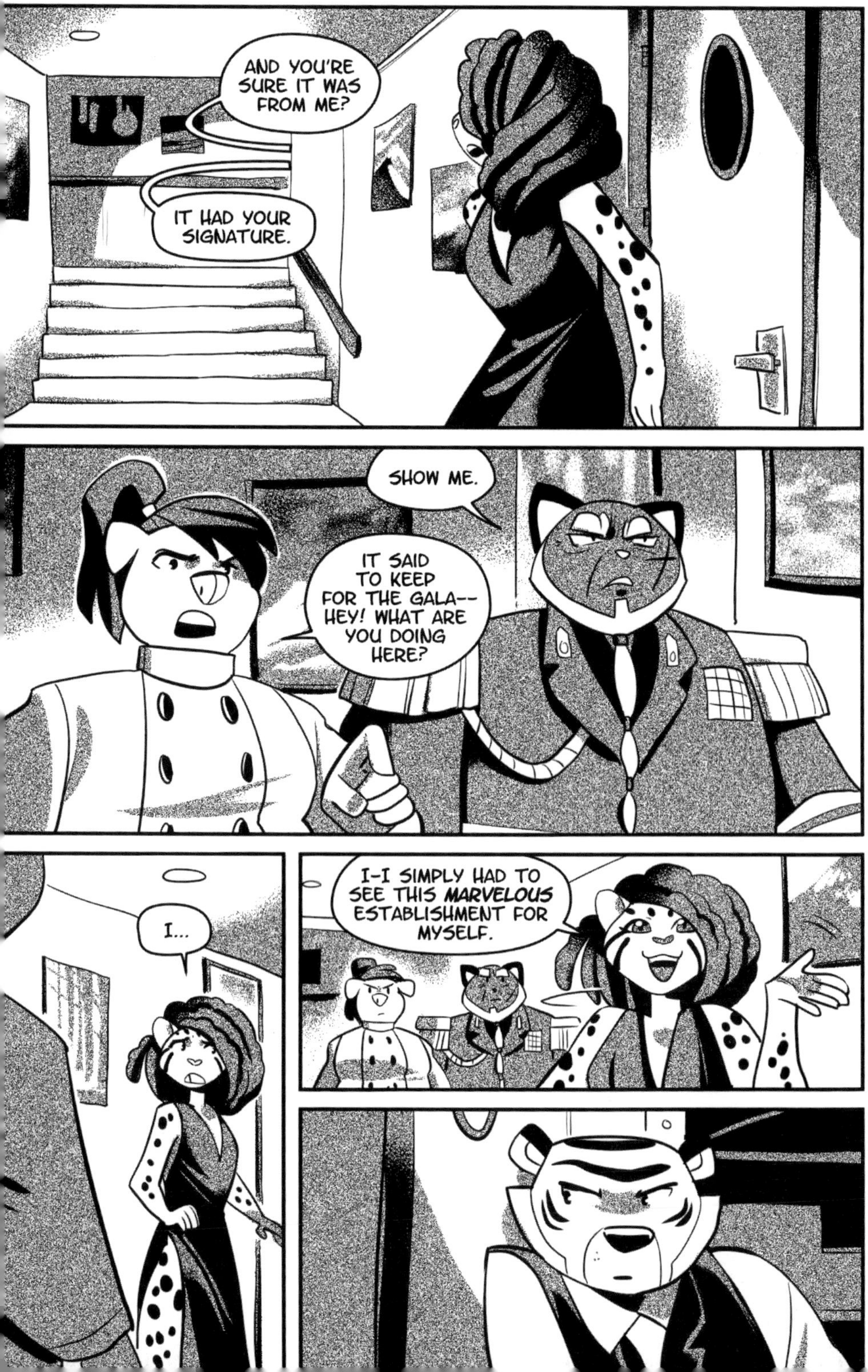
AND YOU'RE SURE IT WAS FROM ME?
IT HAD YOUR SIGNATURE.
SHOW ME.
IT SAID TO KEEP FOR THE GALA-- HEY! WHAT ARE YOU DOING HERE?
I...
I-I SIMPLY HAD TO SEE THIS *MARVELOUS* ESTABLISHMENT FOR MYSELF.

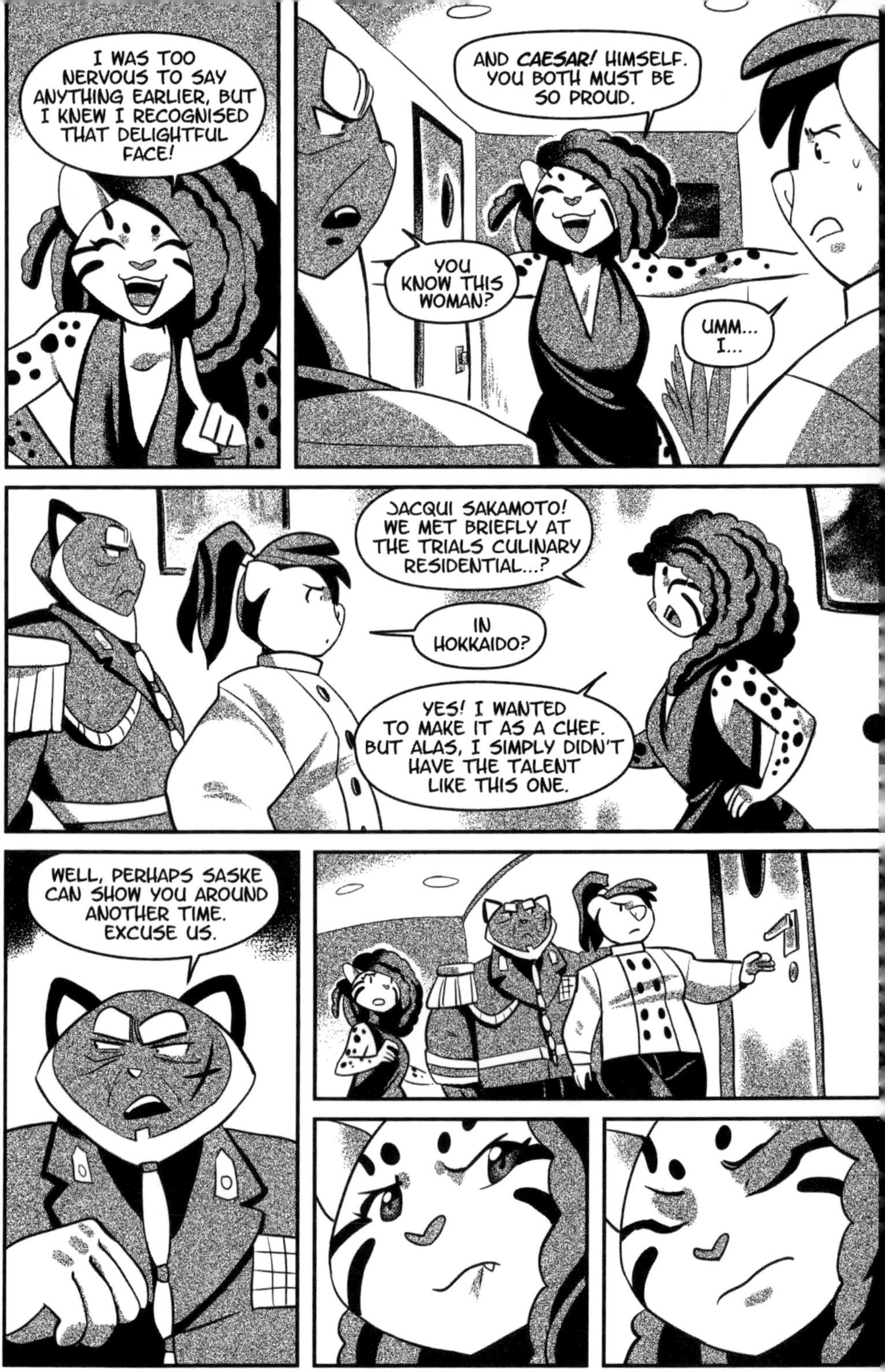

I WAS TOO NERVOUS TO SAY ANYTHING EARLIER, BUT I KNEW I RECOGNISED THAT DELIGHTFUL FACE!
AND CAESAR! HIMSELF. YOU BOTH MUST BE SO PROUD.
YOU KNOW THIS WOMAN?
UMM... I...
JACQUI SAKAMOTO! WE MET BRIEFLY AT THE TRIALS CULINARY RESIDENTIAL...?
IN HOKKAIDO?
YES! I WANTED TO MAKE IT AS A CHEF. BUT ALAS, I SIMPLY DIDN'T HAVE THE TALENT LIKE THIS ONE.
WELL, PERHAPS SASKE CAN SHOW YOU AROUND ANOTHER TIME. EXCUSE US.

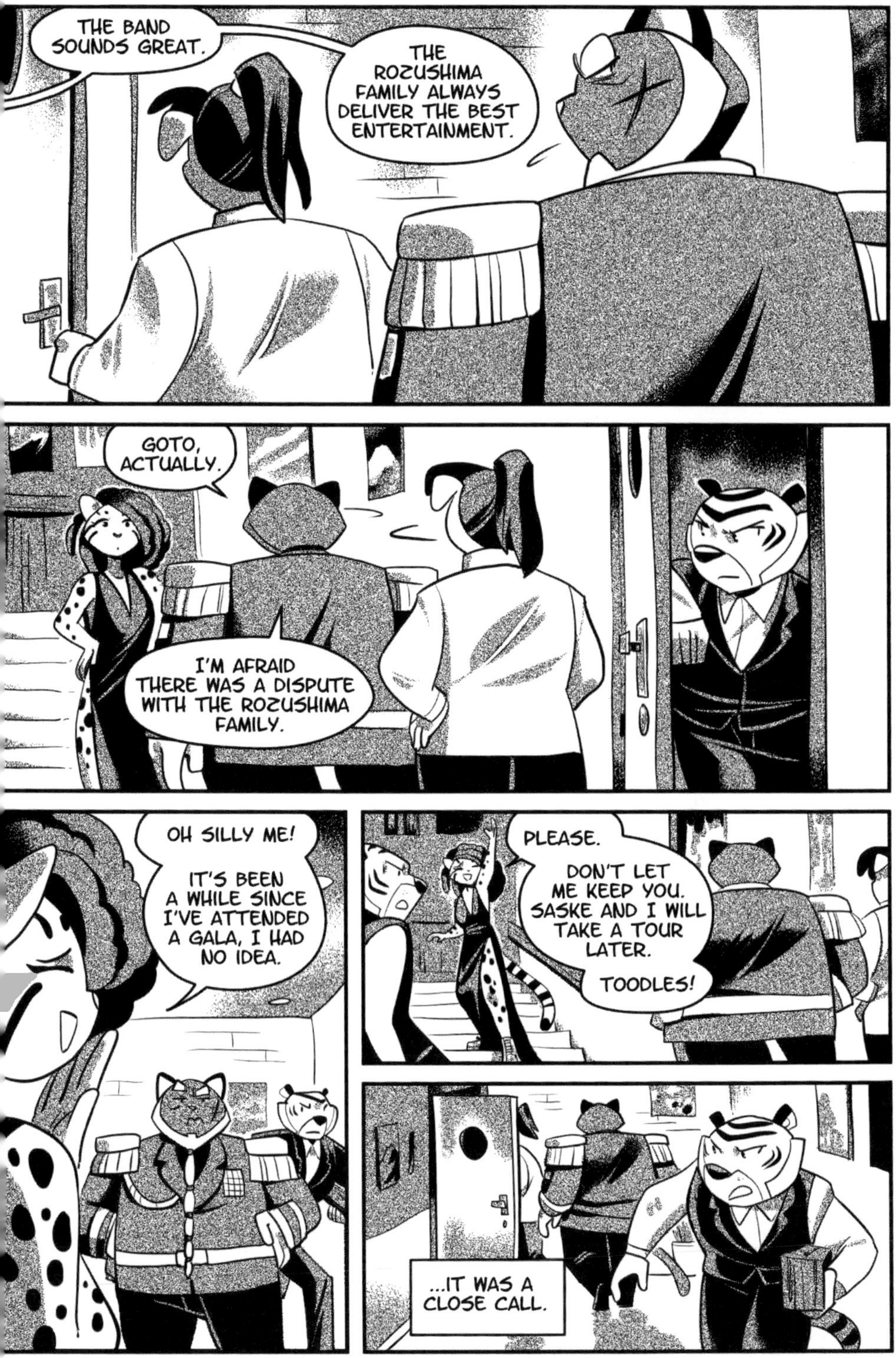
THE BAND SOUNDS GREAT.
THE ROZUSHIMA FAMILY ALWAYS DELIVER THE BEST ENTERTAINMENT.
GOTO, ACTUALLY.
I'M AFRAID THERE WAS A DISPUTE WITH THE ROZUSHIMA FAMILY.
OH SILLY ME!
IT'S BEEN A WHILE SINCE I'VE ATTENDED A GALA, I HAD NO IDEA.
PLEASE.
DON'T LET ME KEEP YOU. SASKE AND I WILL TAKE A TOUR LATER.
TOODLES!
...IT WAS A CLOSE CALL.

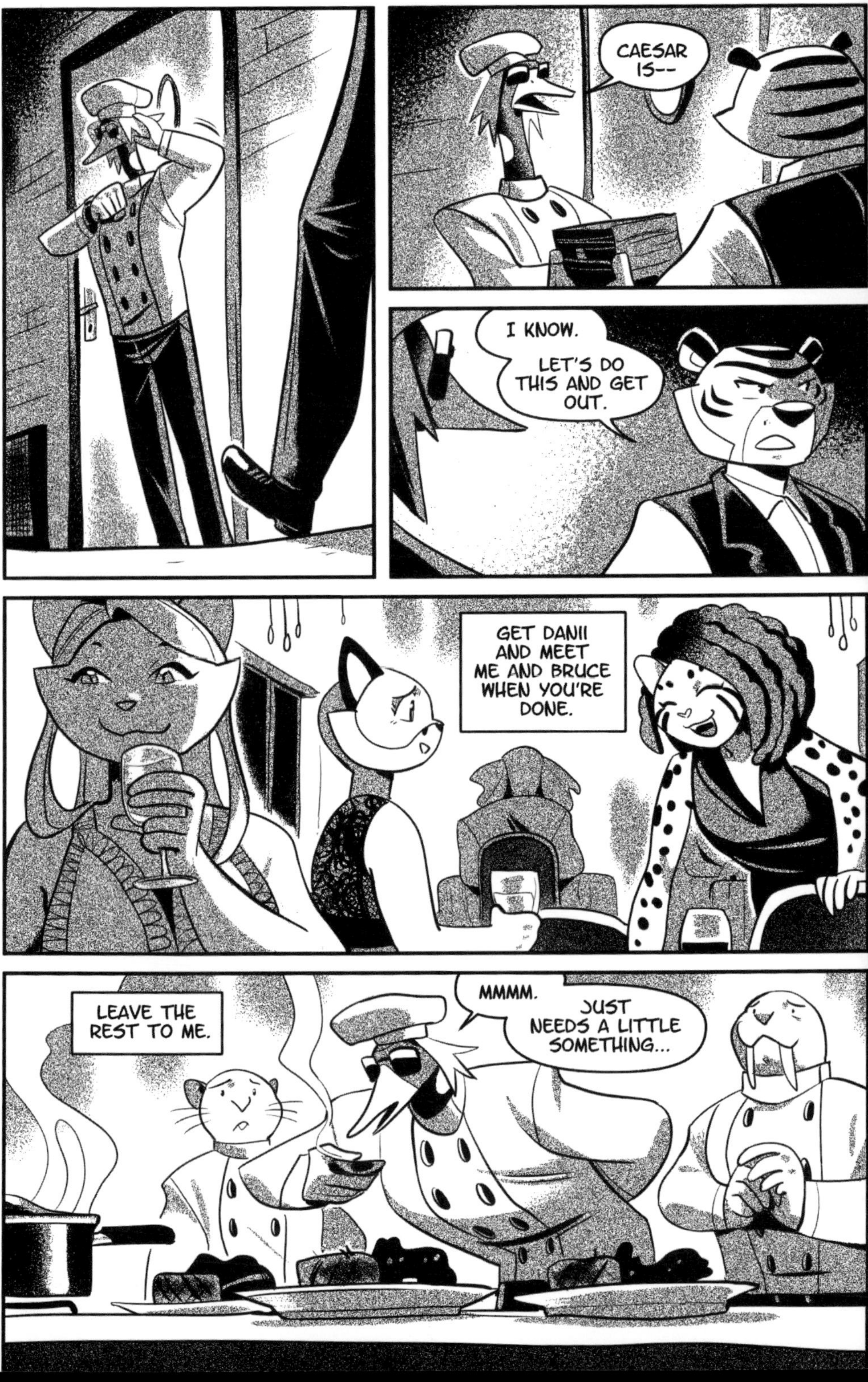

CAESAR IS--
I KNOW.
LET'S DO THIS AND GET OUT.
GET DANII AND MEET ME AND BRUCE WHEN YOU'RE DONE.
LEAVE THE REST TO ME.
MMMM.
JUST NEEDS A LITTLE SOMETHING...

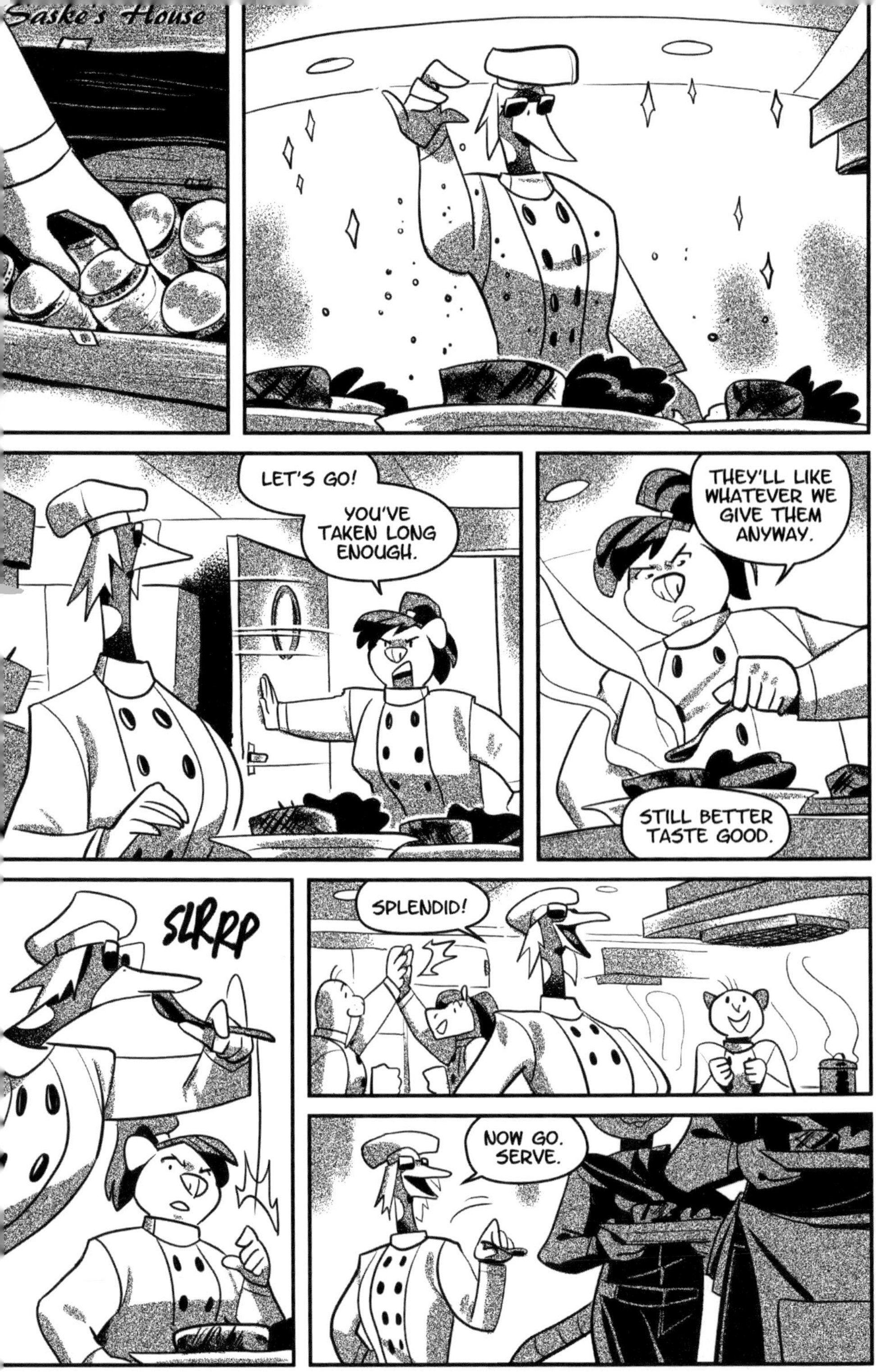
Saske's House
LET'S GO!
YOU'VE TAKEN LONG ENOUGH.
THEY'LL LIKE WHATEVER WE GIVE THEM ANYWAY.
STILL BETTER TASTE GOOD.
SLRRP
SPLENDID!
NOW GO. SERVE.

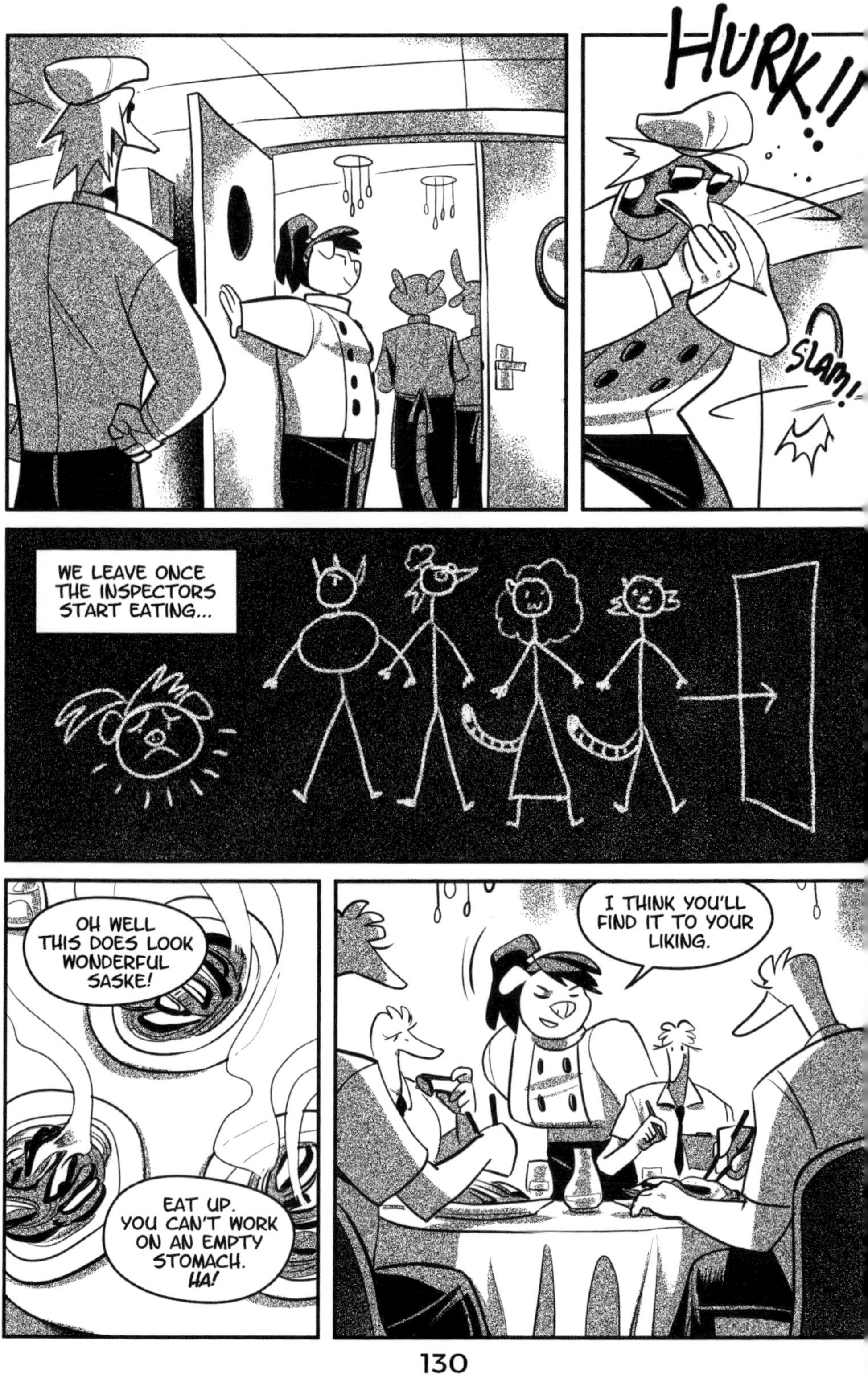
HURK!!
SLAM!
WE LEAVE ONCE THE INSPECTORS START EATING...
OH WELL THIS DOES LOOK WONDERFUL SASKE!
EAT UP. YOU CAN'T WORK ON AN EMPTY STOMACH. HA!
I THINK YOU'LL FIND IT TO YOUR LIKING.

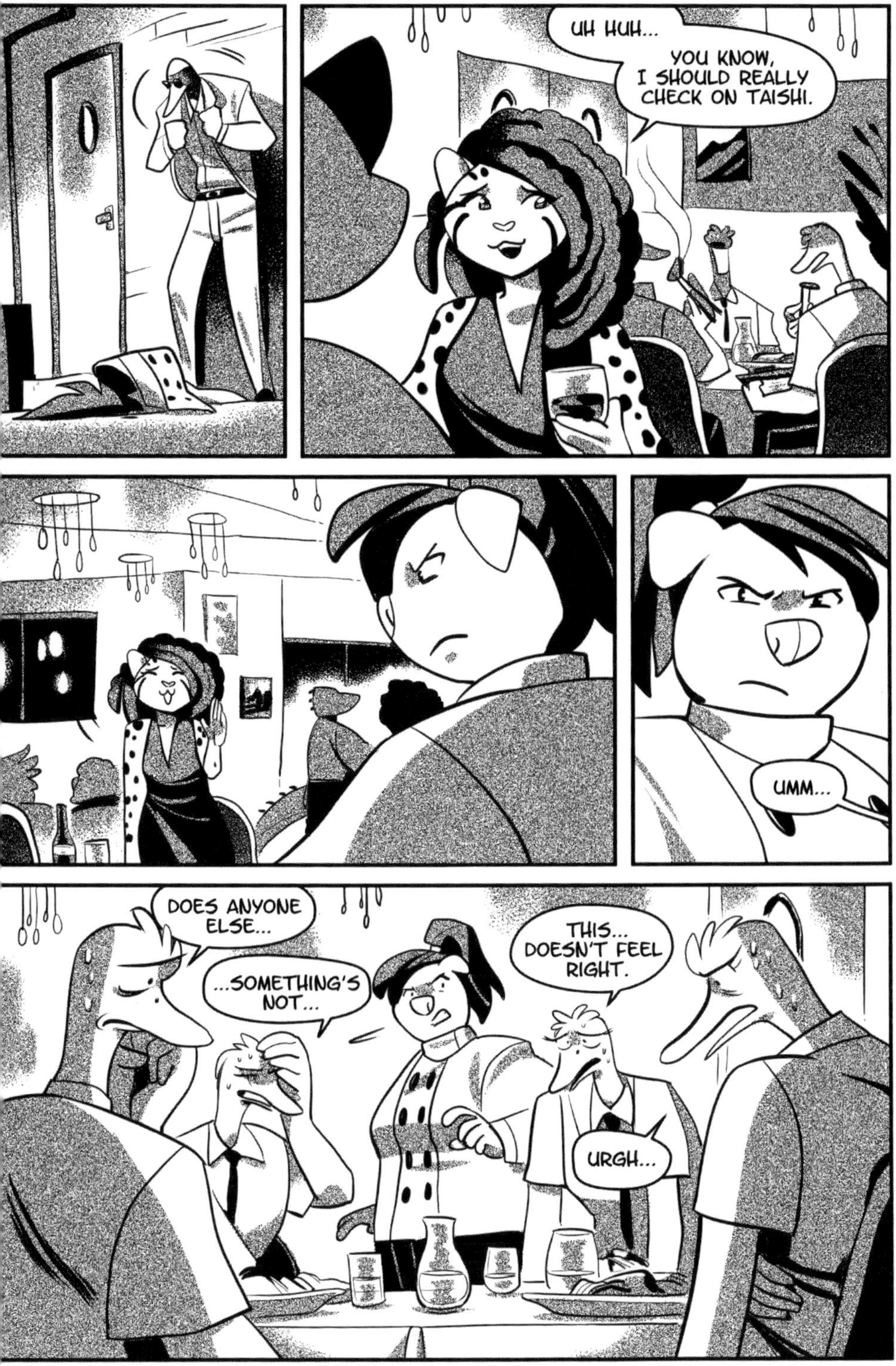
UH HUH...
YOU KNOW, I SHOULD REALLY CHECK ON TAISHI.
UMM...
DOES ANYONE ELSE...
...SOMETHING'S NOT...
THIS... DOESN'T FEEL RIGHT.
URGH...

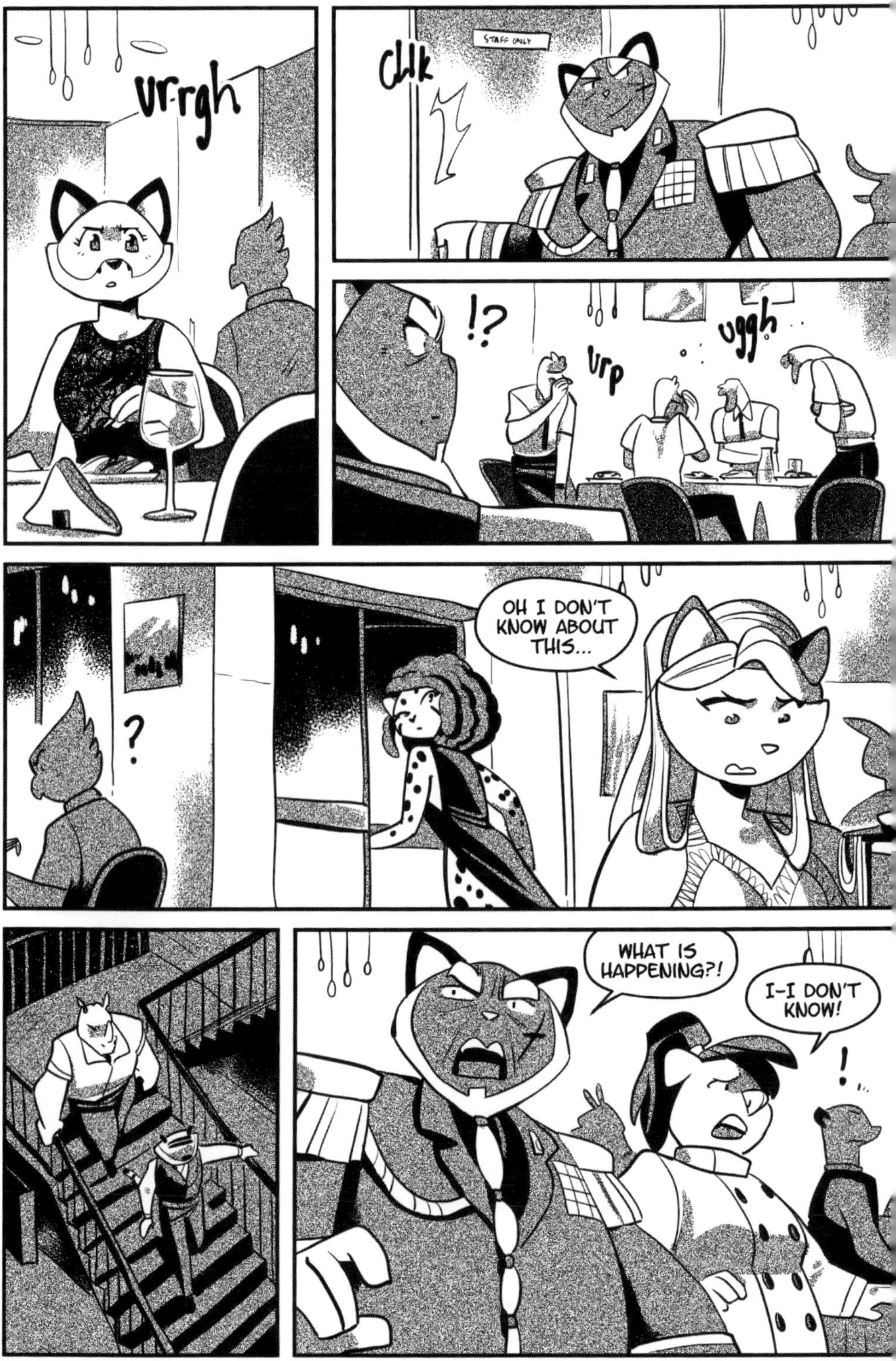
urrgh
Clik
STAFF ONLY
!?
urp
uggh...
?
OH I DON'T KNOW ABOUT THIS...
WHAT IS HAPPENING?!
I-I DON'T KNOW!
!...

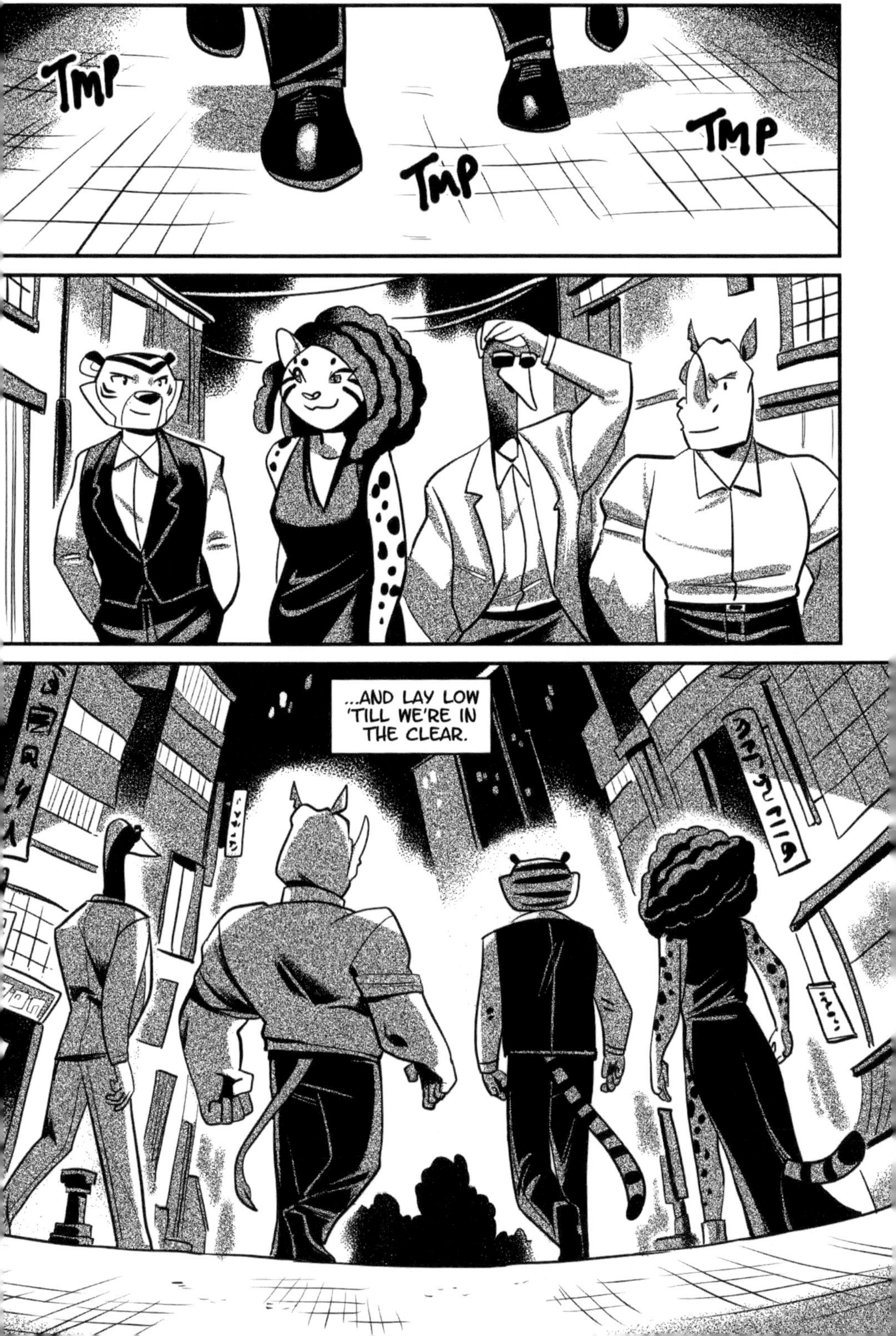
TMP
TMP
TMP
...AND LAY LOW 'TILL WE'RE IN THE CLEAR.

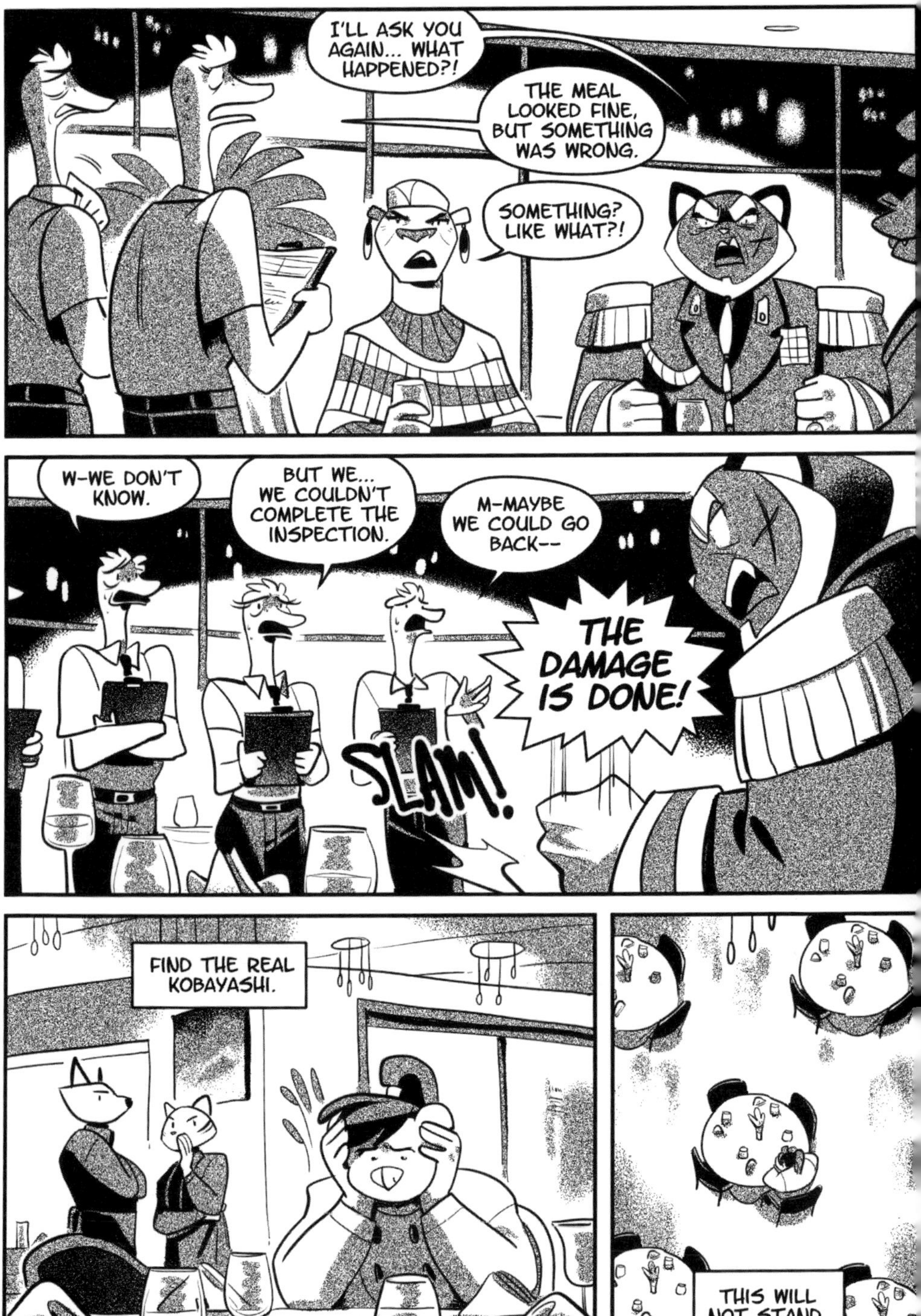
I'LL ASK YOU AGAIN... WHAT HAPPENED?!
THE MEAL LOOKED FINE, BUT SOMETHING WAS WRONG.
SOMETHING? LIKE WHAT?!
W-WE DON'T KNOW.
BUT WE... WE COULDN'T COMPLETE THE INSPECTION.
M-MAYBE WE COULD GO BACK--
THE DAMAGE IS DONE!
SLAM!
FIND THE REAL KOBAYASHI.
THIS WILL NOT STAND.

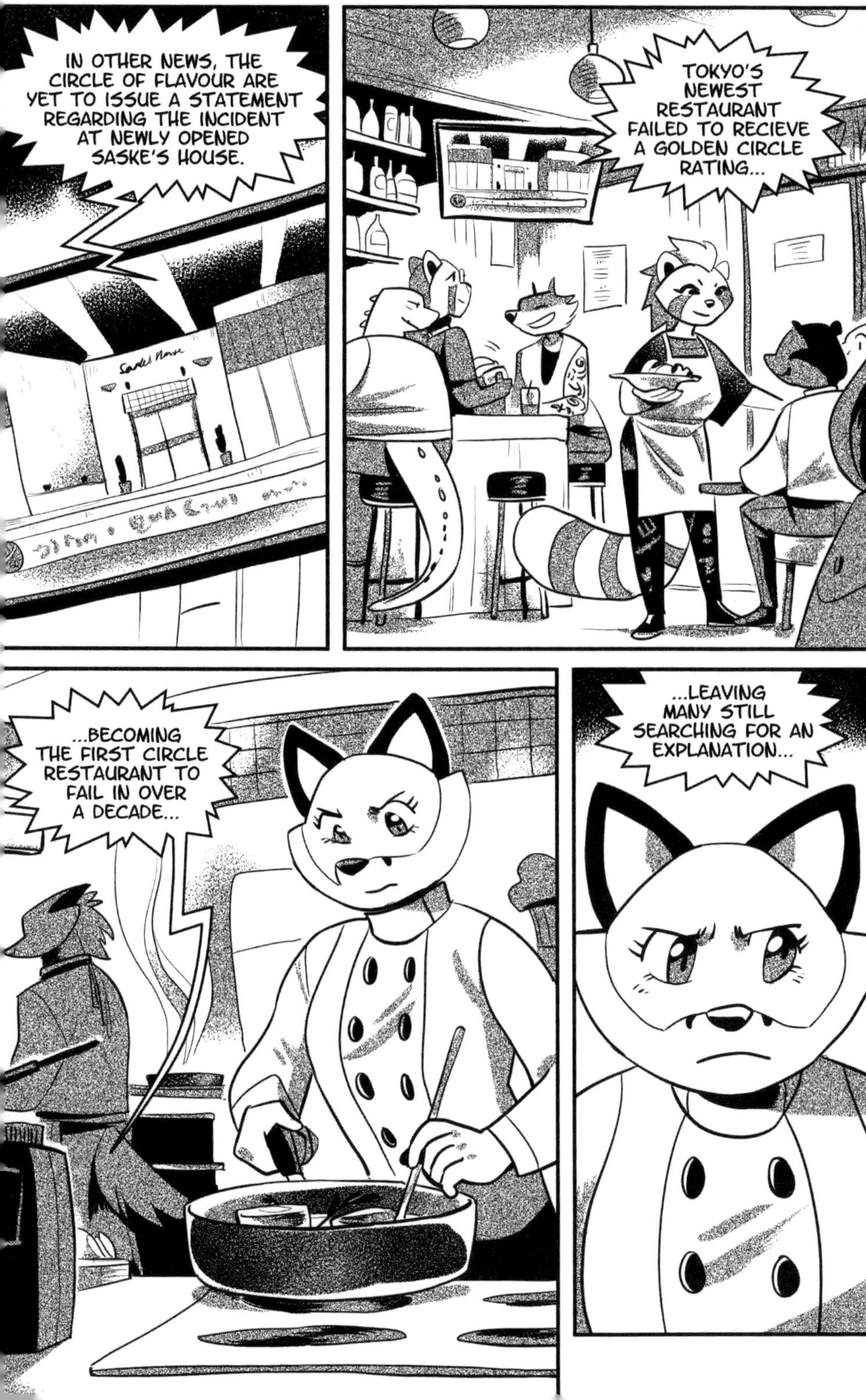
IN OTHER NEWS, THE CIRCLE OF FLAVOUR ARE YET TO ISSUE A STATEMENT REGARDING THE INCIDENT AT NEWLY OPENED SASKE'S HOUSE.
TOKYO'S NEWEST RESTAURANT FAILED TO RECIEVE A GOLDEN CIRCLE RATING...
...BECOMING THE FIRST CIRCLE RESTAURANT TO FAIL IN OVER A DECADE...
...LEAVING MANY STILL SEARCHING FOR AN EXPLANATION...

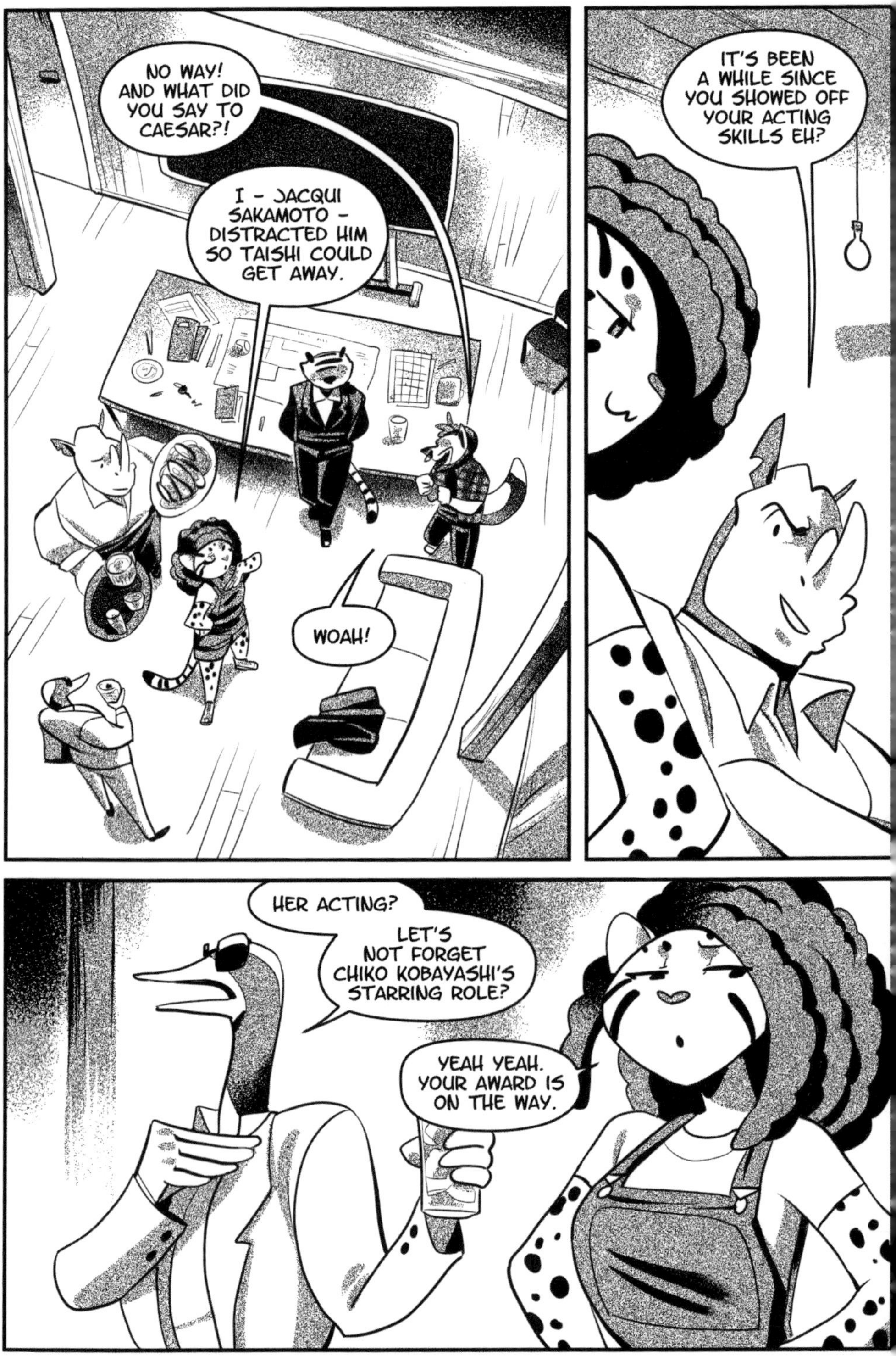
NO WAY! AND WHAT DID YOU SAY TO CAESAR?!
I - JACQUI SAKAMOTO - DISTRACTED HIM SO TAISHI COULD GET AWAY.
WOAH!
IT'S BEEN A WHILE SINCE YOU SHOWED OFF YOUR ACTING SKILLS EH?
HER ACTING?
LET'S NOT FORGET CHIKO KOBAYASHI'S STARRING ROLE?
YEAH YEAH. YOUR AWARD IS ON THE WAY.

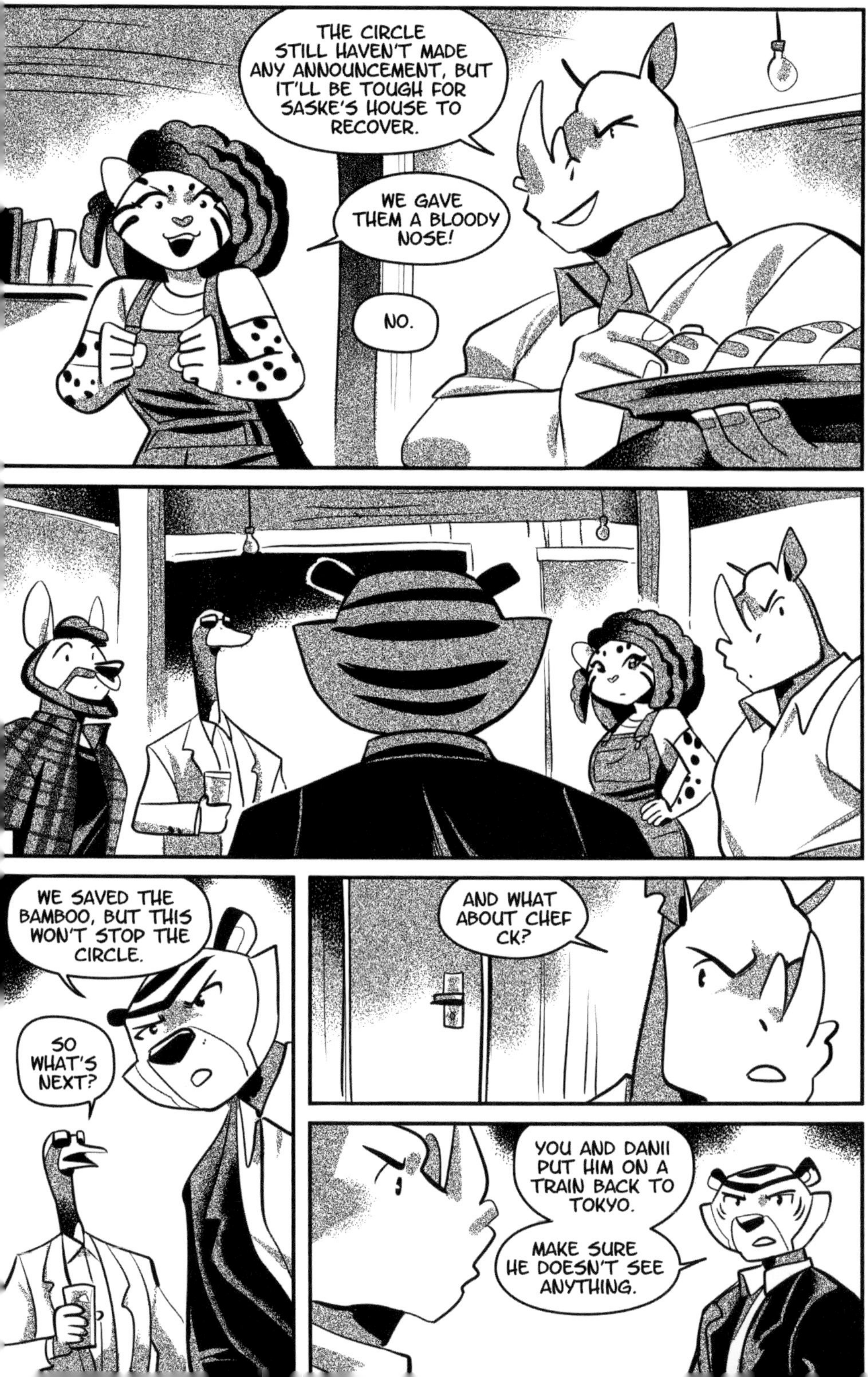
THE CIRCLE STILL HAVEN'T MADE ANY ANNOUNCEMENT, BUT IT'LL BE TOUGH FOR SASKE'S HOUSE TO RECOVER.
WE GAVE THEM A BLOODY NOSE!
NO.
WE SAVED THE BAMBOO, BUT THIS WON'T STOP THE CIRCLE.
SO WHAT'S NEXT?
AND WHAT ABOUT CHEF CK?
YOU AND DANII PUT HIM ON A TRAIN BACK TO TOKYO.
MAKE SURE HE DOESN'T SEE ANYTHING.

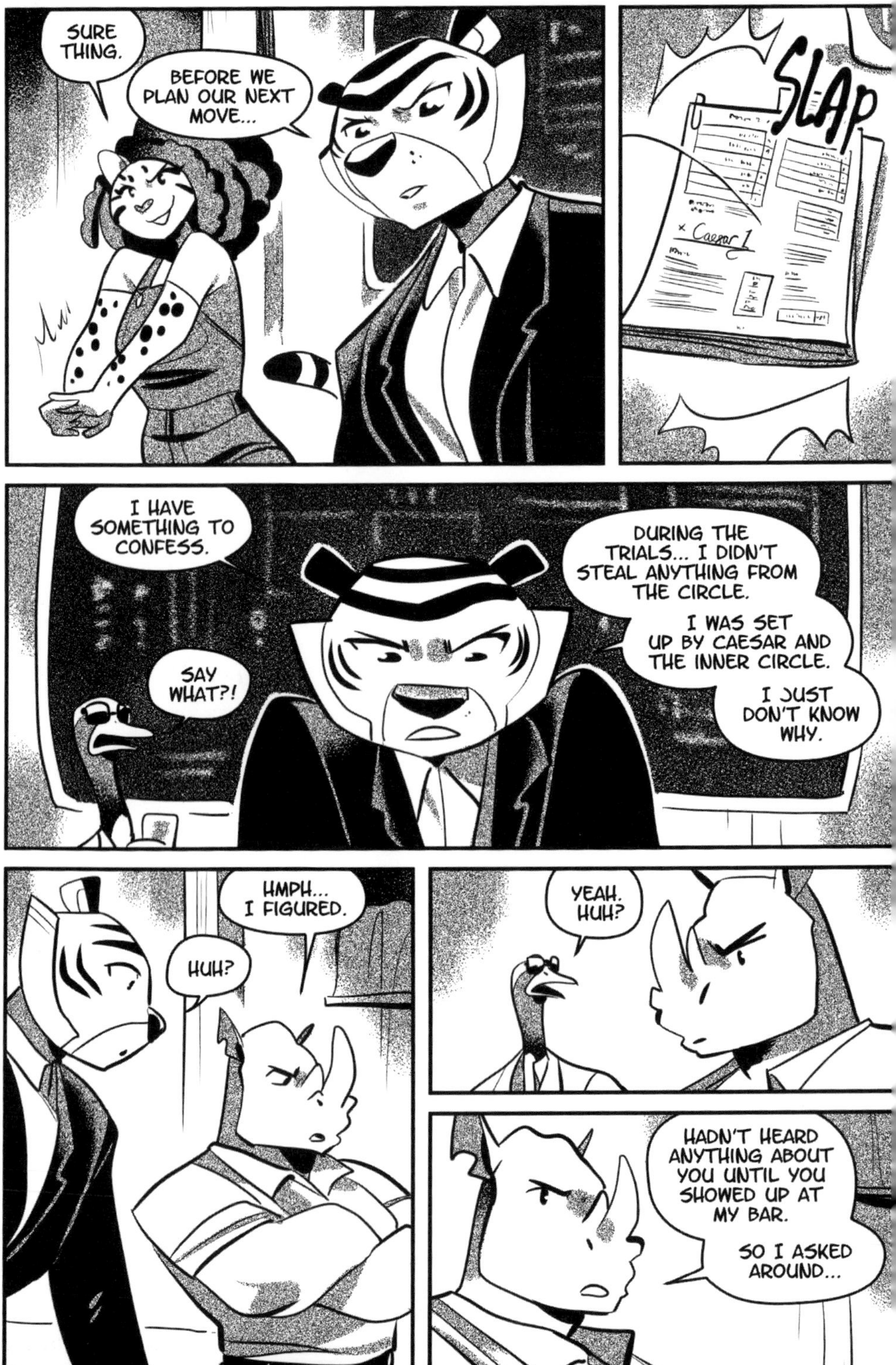

SURE THING.
BEFORE WE PLAN OUR NEXT MOVE...
SLAP
Caesar 1
I HAVE SOMETHING TO CONFESS.
DURING THE TRIALS... I DIDN'T STEAL ANYTHING FROM THE CIRCLE.
I WAS SET UP BY CAESAR AND THE INNER CIRCLE.
I JUST DON'T KNOW WHY.
SAY WHAT?!
HMPH... I FIGURED.
HUH?
YEAH. HUH?
HADN'T HEARD ANYTHING ABOUT YOU UNTIL YOU SHOWED UP AT MY BAR.
SO I ASKED AROUND...

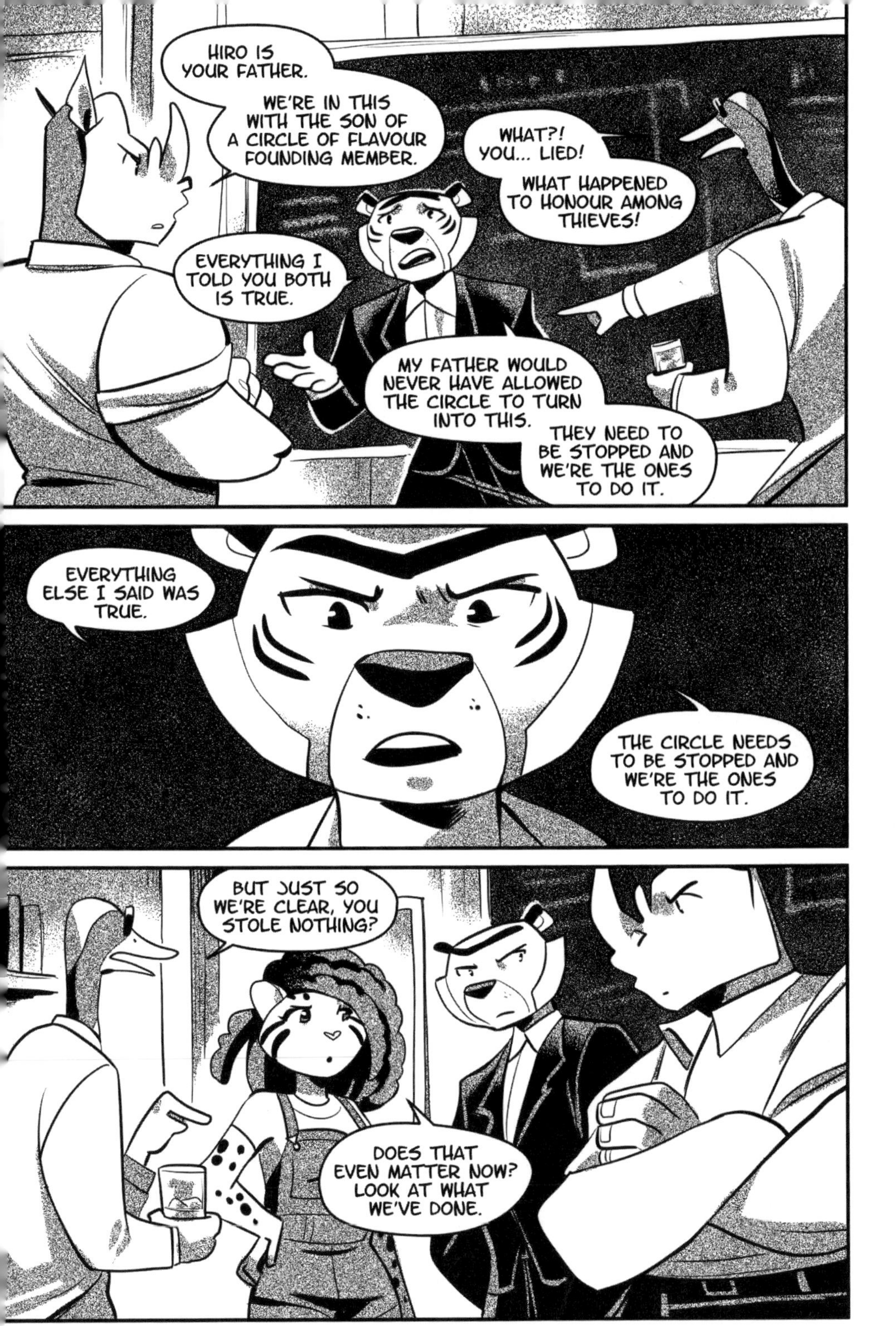
HIRO IS YOUR FATHER.
WE'RE IN THIS WITH THE SON OF A CIRCLE OF FLAVOUR FOUNDING MEMBER.
WHAT?! YOU... LIED!
WHAT HAPPENED TO HONOUR AMONG THIEVES!
EVERYTHING I TOLD YOU BOTH IS TRUE.
MY FATHER WOULD NEVER HAVE ALLOWED THE CIRCLE TO TURN INTO THIS.
THEY NEED TO BE STOPPED AND WE'RE THE ONES TO DO IT.
EVERYTHING ELSE I SAID WAS TRUE.
THE CIRCLE NEEDS TO BE STOPPED AND WE'RE THE ONES TO DO IT.
BUT JUST SO WE'RE CLEAR, YOU STOLE NOTHING?
DOES THAT EVEN MATTER NOW? LOOK AT WHAT WE'VE DONE.

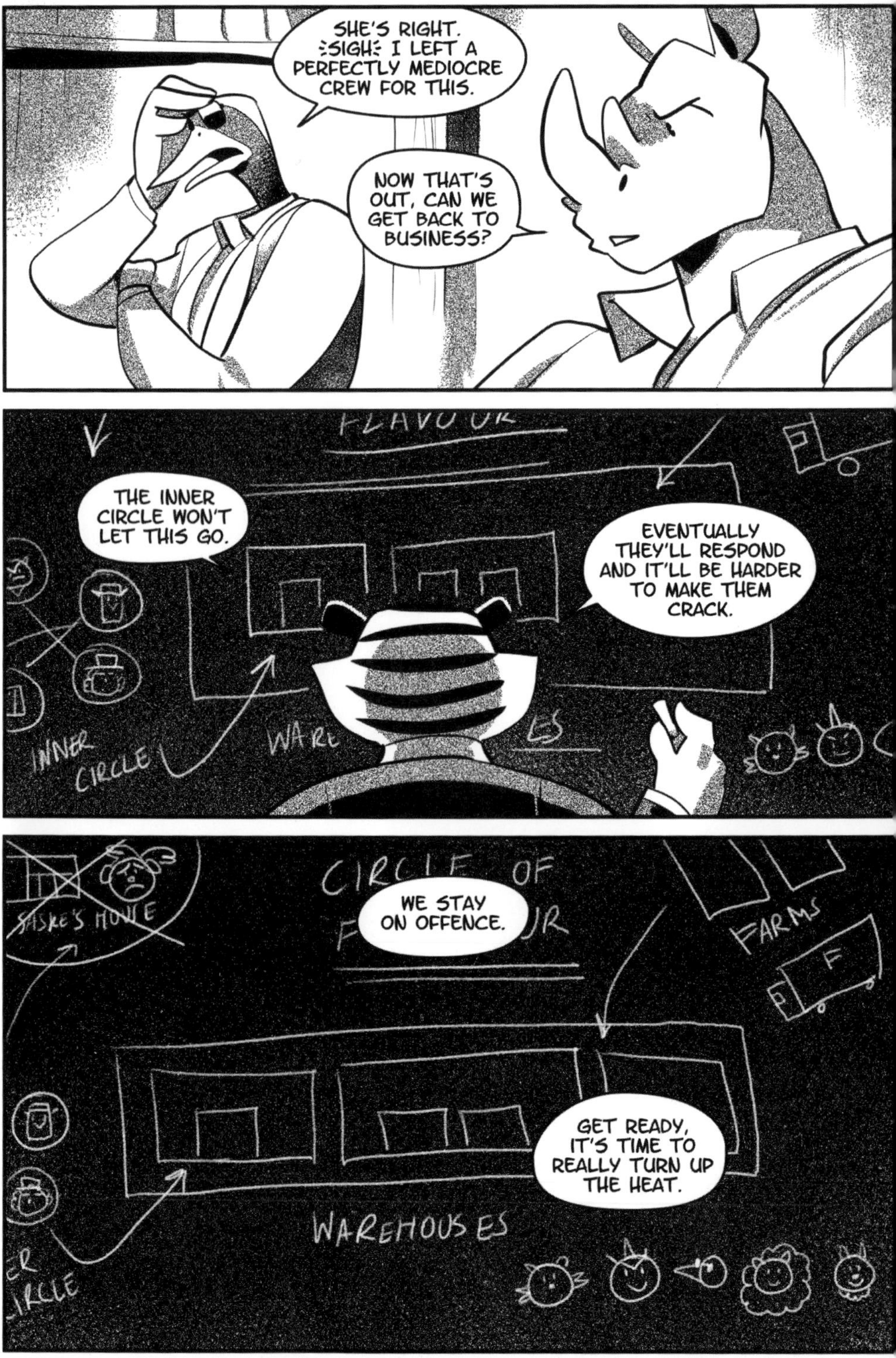
SHE'S RIGHT. :SIGH: I LEFT A PERFECTLY MEDIOCRE CREW FOR THIS.
NOW THAT'S OUT, CAN WE GET BACK TO BUSINESS?
THE INNER CIRCLE WON'T LET THIS GO.
INNER CIRCLE
EVENTUALLY THEY'LL RESPOND AND IT'LL BE HARDER TO MAKE THEM CRACK.
WE STAY ON OFFENCE.
FARMS
GET READY, IT'S TIME TO REALLY TURN UP THE HEAT.
WAREHOUSES

THANK YOU

We're grateful to everyone who has picked up a copy of Hot Lunch Vol.1 and taken the time to read the third story out of our anthropomorphic universe.

This graphic novel wouldn't have been possible without the support of our Kickstarter backers below, who showed great patience through a challenging production process for our team.

We appreciate you and hope you stick with us on the journey to more stories!!

◇ STARTERS ◇

AceArtemis7..............Caitlin Jane Hughes
Captain Anton........Chiedozie Ukachukwu
Ellen Power............................ErBoProxy
Gokcen Yuksek.....................Jay Lofstead
Jeff Smith........................Owen Edmonds
Purple Moon Drama............Will Scotland

◇ HOUSE SPECIALS ◇

David Austin.......................................DL
Jonathan........................Jonathan Boone
Joseph D. Bliska..............Lawrence Evans
Marian Swint.......................Mark Horton
Omeda Elements...........Rebecca Rajendra
Rosanda McGrath..........Sergey Anikushin
Trejaan Cavelion

◇ SET MENU ◇

Aaron Jaunty • Chelsea Eggleton
Cherish York • Daniel Morris

Danny Leigh • Emerson Kasak
Gary S • Henna Yoshi Khokher

Ian Moore • James Locke
Jon • Layla H

Linda Canton • Lisa Stepanovic
Lloyd • Michael Nimmo

Nat-Nat • Paul D Jarman
Raptures Demise • Reece
Simon Jennings

◇ DESSERTS ◇

Akimika.....................................Devilwuff
Gina Polydorou.......................Jabril Muse
Kristina Gmta Brown............Lottie Brown
Mimidoo Ahua...................Rakesh Khimji
Rob Giles.............................Shawn Pryor
Sparkxster +.........................Susanna Lee

◇ SPECIAL THANKS ◇

Special thanks to our friend Ariyo Femi-Sunmaila who lives in Japan and gave us some helpful tips to shape the story along the way.

And a special thank you to Lao who co-founded the mayamada brand and helped build it to where it is now. Having stepped down from the business in 2019, he won't be along for the ride in this next phase but has left his character (figuratively and literally) to keep an eye on things.

THERE'S MORE MANGA TO COME!

STAY TUNED...

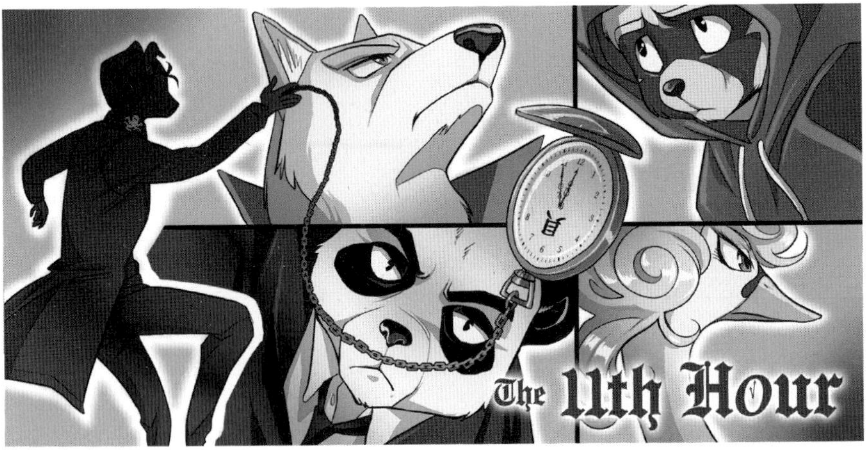
The 11th Hour

LISTEN TO THE "STORY X STORY" PODCAST AS WE DISCUSS COOL STORIES ACROSS POP CULTURE, PLUS GIVE YOU ADVICE FOR CREATING YOUR OWN.

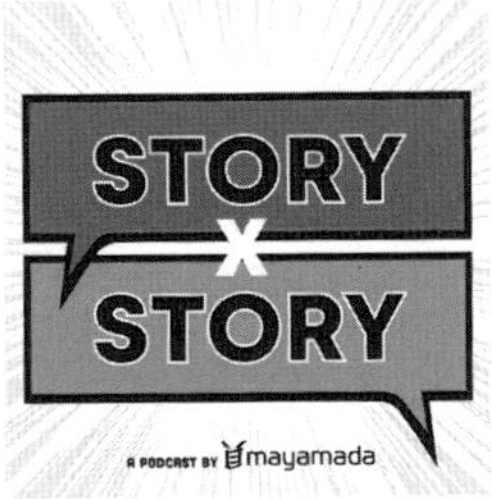
STORY
X
STORY
A PODCAST BY mayamada

AVAILABLE ON SOUNDCLOUD, GOOGLE PODCASTS, SPOTIFY AND APPLE PODCASTS TODAY!

YOU CAN ALSO PICK UP CLOTHING AND OTHER MERCHANDISE FROM THE MAYAMADA UNIVERSE!

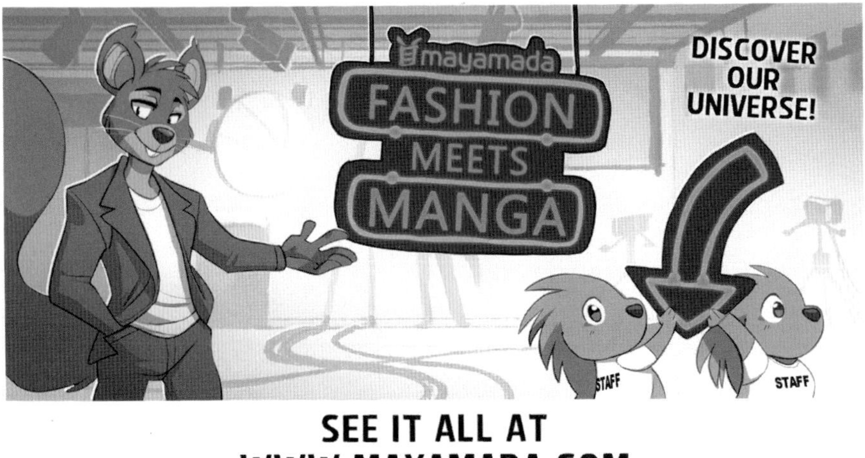
mayamada
FASHION
MEETS
MANGA
DISCOVER
OUR
UNIVERSE!
STAFF
STAFF

SEE IT ALL AT
WWW.MAYAMADA.COM

MAYAMADA MAYAMADATEES